WD

Ultimate

Ultimate
CV

Over 100 winning CVs to help you get the interview and the job

2nd edition

Martin Yate

KOGAN
PAGE

First published in the United States in 1993 as *Knock 'em Dead* by Adams Media Corporation
First published in Great Britain in 2003 as *The Ultimate CV Book* by Kogan Page Limited
Reprinted in 2003, 2004, 2005, 2007
Second edition published in 2008 as *Ultimate CV*

Kogan Page Limited
120 Pentonville Road
London N1 9JN
United Kingdom
www.koganpage.com

© Martin Yate, 1993, 1995, 19[98, 2001, 2003, 2008]

The right of Martin Yate to be [identified as the author of this work has] been asserted by him in accordanc[e with the Copyright, Designs and Patent]s Act 1988.

British Library Cataloguing in Publication Data

A CIP record for this book is available from the British Library

ISBN 978 0 7494 5327 5

Typeset by Jean Cussons Typesetting, Diss, Norfolk
Printed and bound in India by Replika Press Pvt Ltd

Contents

Legal, law enforcement, and security CVs

Sales and marketing CVs

Finance, banking, and insurance CVs

Media and public relations CVs

Operations management and human resources CVs

Introduction

Most books on writing CVs haven't adjusted to accommodate today's changing work environment, or the way that companies now store, access, and review CVs. The goal of this book is to help you accelerate your job search with an understanding of the world in which your CV must compete, and the tactics that will enable it to compete most effectively.

No one wants to write a CV. On the list of things we 'want' to do, it comes just above hitting yourself on the head with a hammer; and in part that is because of the self-analysis involved. Although we know ourselves better than anyone else does, actually taking that knowledge and packaging it for public consumption is always an extremely difficult task.

In *Ultimate CV*, I explain the ins and outs of putting a CV together as painlessly as possible. I'll show you the best ways to look at your background and present it to the public in your CV. You'll understand why certain things should be in your CV and how they should look, and why other things should never appear. Today's world of work is complex, and your circumstances are unique, so there will be situations when what is right for one person's CV is wrong for another's. In these cases I'll always share with you what the experts think on the topic, and whenever industry experts disagree I'll give you both sides of the argument, along with my reasoned solution to the dispute. That way you can make a prudent decision based on the factors that affect your particular situation. In addition, you will see a wide variety of styles and approaches that can be used within these practical guidelines to help you create a truly individual CV.

You'll get to read real CVs from real people. Each of the CVs in this book is based on a 'genuine article' that opened the doors of opportunity for its writer. CVs are included for today's and tomorrow's in-demand jobs, confirmed by the professionals on the front lines: corporate recruiters and other employment industry professionals from across the country. You are quite likely to find a CV that reflects exactly the kind of job you are after; if not, you can still learn lots from the examples, and you can lift and adapt key phrases and use their layouts as templates for your work.

You will also find a number of CVs from people with special challenges. These reflect the pressures and needs of a modern, profession-oriented society struggling into the information age. Like the CV that got a minimum-wage factory worker a £40,000-a-year professional sales job, or the one that helped a recovering alcoholic and drug-abuser get back on his feet again. Included here are winning CVs of people who are recovering from serious emotional challenges, re-entering society after prison time, starting over after a divorce, and sometimes changing careers into the bargain. What's more, these examples have proved themselves effective in every corner of the nation; their writers landed both interviews and jobs.

A powerful, on-target CV, properly distributed, is only one element in a successful job search; for this reason, *Ultimate CV* is part of an integrated series of books crafted to help you land jobs and prosper in them. This book will at times touch on subjects that are handled in greater depth elsewhere in the series. In these instances, I will refer you to the appropriate work. For example, the self-knowledge you develop in preparing your CV will also help you prepare for job interviews.

The wide range of CV examples here, and the nuts-and-bolts advice about CV production and distribution, will give you everything you need to create a distinctive, professional CV – and get it in front of the people who count! You will find something on every single page that you can put to work in your job search right now, today.

The power of a great CV

Who needs a CV? Everyone, unless you are so well-known that your reputation precedes you.

You didn't come to a book like this for a good read; you came because you are facing serious challenges in your professional life, which you realize will impact the quality of your life outside of working hours. Maybe you are a seasoned pro who has discovered that your current CV no longer does the job. You are probably right; after adding job after job since those long-ago college days, your document now probably looks more like a patchwork quilt than a focused CV. Perhaps you are fresh out of school and are wondering how you can create a professional CV that will catapult you into the professional world. Or perhaps you have been struggling along without a CV and simply filling out application forms, but have finally made the commitment to do it right this time.

Whatever your reason for reading this book, the following pages will help you get your act together. By the end of the process you will not only have a knock 'em dead CV, you will also have a much firmer grasp of the job search process along with some crucial lifetime career management skills.

The person who is better organized and more focused will be viewed more favourably than his or her competition – and that is exactly what the development of your CV will do for you. Creating a CV helps you in your job search way beyond opening doors. It will help you understand what employers need and what you have to offer; as a result, it will give you ammunition to handle those tough interview questions. Furthermore, an effective CV is a staunch friend who speaks well of your candidacy long after you leave the interview.

No one ever gets added to the payroll for the love of mankind. Management never gets up and collectively sighs, 'Ah, it's a loverly day in the neighbourhood... let's hire some accountants.' People get added to the payroll to make money, and to save money or save time for the company;

and they all do this at some level by anticipating and preventing problems from arising and solving them in a timely manner when they do arise.

No CV ever gets read, and no one ever gets interviewed or hired unless someone somewhere is trying to solve a problem. That problem may be finding a quicker way to manufacture silicon chips, or it may be getting the telephone calls answered now that the receptionist has suddenly left. As disparate as these examples might seem, both are still concerned with problem solving. And invariably, the problem that needs a solution is the same: productivity. The simple question is, 'How on earth are we going to get things done quicker/cheaper/more efficiently without a _____?' CVs that get acted upon are those that position the writer as someone knowledgeable enough about the job to anticipate, prevent, and solve its problems, thus contributing positively to the bottom line in some way.

Your CV's job is to speak loudly and clearly of your value as a potential on-staff problem solver in a specific functional area. And this value must be clearly expressed in a few brief seconds, because that's all the attention your CV will get in its first perusal. *Initially* your CV just helps get your foot in the door, and because you can't be there to answer questions, it has to stand on its own.

A strong focus leads to positive results

Many people make the mistake of thinking that a CV is a simple recitation of all you have done in your professional life. They're wrong – this will result in a CV that will lack focus, punch, and ultimately results. The most productive CVs start with a clear focus on the target job, looking at the job's responsibilities from the point of view of the hiring team.

Let's start with this exercise for determining what is worth focusing on in your efforts to obtain your target job:

1. Develop your own job description of the target job by looking at job postings and recruitment advertisements.
2. Under each bullet point you enter, ID your skills, achievements, contributions in this area.
3. Think of the best people you have ever seen doing this job and what made them stand out.
4. Think of the worst people you have ever seen doing this job and what made them stand out.

On completion of this simple exercise you will not only have a clear idea of whether or not you can do the job, you'll have:

- the clear focus on the target job that will make your CV truly productive;
- knowledge of what employers want to hear about in your CV, and examples that will do the job;
- a selection of the critical keywords that need to appear within your CV to ensure that it gets selected from the CV databases by headhunters and hiring managers.

So the most productive CVs are focused on what has happened in your business life, as it relates to your ability to shine in the job you have targeted as the next logical step in your career. It speaks of the actions you took to make things happen, and what supportive professional behaviours you brought to the task; and it pictures (you hope) a professional who understands the small yet necessary role that job plays in the overall deliverables of the department and the company.

The long and the short of it

Now given the choice, you'd never be writing a CV (or reading this book, in fact), but as you don't really have a choice in the matter, you might as well learn how to do it right. CVs evolved as a solution to a productivity problem. Can you imagine what would happen to a business if everyone who applied for a job was given even a cursory ten-minute interview? The nation would simply grind to a halt, then topple into bankruptcy, because employers would do nothing but interview. The solution: Find a way to get a glimpse of applicants' potentials before meeting them face-to-face. Thus the CV evolved as a screening and timesaving tool for the company.

Now look at the realities of being on the receiving end of a CV. You may think that *writing* a CV is a tough job, but consider for a moment the plight of the person who has to read them. In the world of enjoyable reading, CVs are pretty far down the list; they offer little competition to murder mysteries, tales of international intrigue, or love stories.

Nevertheless, CVs are a required part of every manager's reading, and, because they are usually deadly dull and appear in such vast numbers, they are avoided like the plague. To combat this deep-seated avoidance, you should follow this general rule that will help your CV get read and acted upon in the quickest possible time: It needs to be both short and long. Short on words, but long on promise and an energy that reflects the real you. It needs to be specifically vague: specific enough to whet the reader's appetite to know more, vague enough that the reader needs to get in communication with you.

Good CV writing focuses attention on your strengths as they relate to the deliverables of a specific target job. At the same time, it draws attention away from those areas that lack definition or vigour. Writing a good CV requires that you first focus on the job you want, and then makes you analyse your work history in support of that goal. The entire process is one where you take the time to look at and then package yourself as a desirable product, and this does an awful lot to help you prepare for job interviews. In a very real sense, putting a CV together is the foundation for succeeding at the job interview. Preparation for one is preparation for the other. With a CV focused on a specific target job and built from the ground up with the employer's likely needs in mind, you will far more likely grab a reader's attention and gain an invitation to interview.

For example, the interviewer's command to 'tell me about yourself' is one of those tough interview questions that almost all of us have difficulty answering without sounding like a snake oil salesman. Were you totally satisfied with your response the last time it came up? I doubt it. You can only answer this question well if you have taken the time to analyze and package all your strengths and weaknesses in an organized fashion. It is the only way you will ever learn to speak fluently about your background and skills in a fashion guaranteed to impress the interviewer. For this reason, *Ultimate CV* will kill two birds with one stone – it will help you prepare a CV that will open all the right doors for you, and it will give you a real understanding of what you have to offer when those tough questions start flying.

Many interviewers base their questions on CV content. This means that, to a certain extent, you can guide the course of your interviews by preparing an appropriately focused CV. Without one you are obliged to deliver your work history on a job application form, which rarely allows a perfect representation of skills, and which gives the interviewer no flattering starting point from which to base the interview questions.

In addition to helping you get your foot in the door and easing the course of the interview, your CV will be your last and most powerful advocate. After interviewing all the candidates, interviewers review all the contenders by going over their notes, and the candidates' CVs. Your CV becomes your spokesperson long after you have left that last interview, and it has the final word on your candidacy. You can begin to see why having a CV focused on a target job makes so much sense.

The preparation of a good CV also has the benefit of personal discovery. You may find that your job experience is deeper than you imagined, that your contributions to previous employers were more important than you thought, or you may discover some areas for professional growth. In any case, you'll gain a realistic awareness of the kind of performance that will allow you to shine at the interview and in your next job – and that's a powerful awareness to possess.

No sane person will tell you that CV writing is fun, but I will show you the tricks of the trade that make the process easier.

What makes this book truly different is, first, the understanding that comes from my thirty years in the career management business and, second, that the CV examples are all real CVs from real people, CVs that landed them jobs within 'in-demand' professions. They were all sent to me by employment specialists, professional CV writers and headhunters from around the nation. These are the pros on the firing line, the ones who know what works and what doesn't in the professional marketplace.

You will find everything you need to make CV writing fast, effective, and painless. Just follow my instructions, and you'll have a knockout CV and never have to read another word about the damn things as long as you live. With that in mind, do it once and do it right – you'll generate a top-flight CV without knocking yourself out!

So now, for your delight and edification, we'll review the marks of a great CV: what type of CV is right for you, what goes in (and why), and what always stays out (and why), and what might go in depending on your special circumstances. This will be followed by countless CV examples and a 'paint-by-numbers' guide that makes CV writing easy for anyone!

Three ways to sum yourself up

'Give me a moment of your busy day! Listen to me, I've got something to say!'

That's what your CV must scream – in a suitably professional manner, of course. Not in the manner of the would-be retail clothing executive who had his CV 'hand-delivered'... attached to the hand and arm of a store window mannequin.

As it happened, that was only the first surprise in store for the personnel director who received the delivery: the envelope was hand-decorated in gothic script; the cover letter inside was equally decorative (and illegible); the CV writer had glued the four-page CV to fabric, and stitched the whole mess together like a child's book. The crowning glory, however, was yet to come: all the punctuation marks – commas, colons, full stops, and the like – were small rhinestone settings. Yes, it got noticed, but its success had to depend entirely on the recipient's sense of humour – which in this case was most noticeable for its absence.

Here's the point: trying to do something out of the ordinary with any aspect of your CV is risky business indeed. For every interview door it opens, at least two more may be slammed shut.

The best (and most businesslike) bet is to present a logically displayed, eye-appealing CV that will get *read*. That means grabbing the reader right away – on that first page. And that's one big reason for short, power-packed CVs.

We all have different backgrounds. Some of us have worked for one company only, some of us have worked for 11 companies in as many years. Some of us have changed careers once or twice, some of us have maintained a predictable career path. For some, diversity broadens our potential, and for some concentration deepens it. We each require different vehicles to put our work history in the most exciting light. The goals, though, are constant:

- to show off achievements, attributes and cumulation of expertise to the best advantage;
- to minimize any possible weaknesses.

CV experts acknowledge just three essential styles for presenting your credentials to a potential employer: Chronological, Functional and Combination (Chrono-Functional). Your particular circumstances will determine the right format for you. Just three styles, you say? You will see CV books with up to 15 varieties of CV style. Such volumes are, alas, merely filling up space; in the final analysis, each additional style such books mention is a tiny variation on the above three.

The chronological CV

This is the most common and readily accepted form of presentation. It's what most of us think of when we think of CVs – a chronological listing of job titles and responsibilities. It starts with the current or most recent employment, then works backward to your first job (or ten years into the past – whichever comes first).

This format is good for demonstrating your growth in a single profession. It is suitable for anyone with practical work experience who hasn't suffered too many job changes or prolonged periods of employment. It is not suitable if you are just out of school or if you are changing careers. The format would then draw attention to your weaknesses (ie your lack of specific experience in a field) rather than your strengths.

The exact content of every CV naturally varies depending on individual circumstances. A chronological CV usually incorporates six basic components.

- contact information;
- a career objective (sometimes);
- a career summary (sometimes);
- a chronological description of work history (always);
- education (almost always).

The work history is the distinguishing characteristic of the chronological CV, because it ties your job responsibilities and achievements to specific employers, job titles and dates.

Chronological

Jane Swift, 123 Anystreet, Anytown, AT1 0BB. Tel: 020 8123 4567. jane@anyaddress.co.uk

SUMMARY:	Ten years of increasing responsibilities in the employment services industry. Concentration in the high-technology markets.

EXPERIENCE: Howard Systems International, Inc.   2004–Present
Management Consulting Firm
Personnel Manager

Responsible for recruiting and managing consulting staff of five. Set up office and organized the recruitment, selection and hiring of consultants. Recruited all levels of MIS staff from financial to manufacturing markets.

Additional responsibilities:

● Coordinated with outside advertising agencies.
● Developed PR with industry periodicals – placement with over 20 magazines and newsletters.
● Developed effective referral programmes – referrals increased 32%.

EXPERIENCE: Technical Aid Corporation   1995–2004
National Consulting Firm. MICRO/TEMPS Division

Division Manager	2000–2004
Area Manager	1997–2000
Branch Manager	1995–1997

As Division Manager, opened additional West of England offices. Staffed and trained all offices with appropriate personnel. Created and implemented all divisional operational policies responsible for P & L. Sales increased to £20 million, from £0 in 1992.

● Achieved and maintained 30% annual growth over 7-year period.
● Maintained sales staff turnover at 14%.

As Area Manager, opened additional offices, hiring staff, setting up office policies, and training sales and recruiting personnel.

Additional responsibilities:

● Supervised offices in two counties.
● Developed business relationships with accounts – 75% of clients were regular customers.
● Client base increased 28% per year.
● Generated over £200,000 worth of free trade-journal publicity.

As Branch Manager, hired to establish the new MICRO/TEMPS operation. Recruited and managed consultants. Hired internal staff. Sold service to clients.

EDUCATION: London University
BA (Hons) Public Relations, 1994.

There are also some optional categories determined by the space available to you and the unique aspect of your background. These will be discussed in chapter 3.

The functional CV

This format focuses on the professional skills you have developed over the years, rather than on when, where or how you acquired them; it also de-emphasizes dates. Job titles and employers can likewise play a minor part with this type of CV. The attention is always focused on the skill rather than the context or time of its acquisition.

In many ways, the content of the functional CV is similar to the chronological type. Only the approach is different. It is a case of not so much of what you say, but of how you say it.

This functional format is suited to a number of different personal circumstances, specifically those of:

● mature professionals with a storehouse of expertise and jobs;
● entry-level types whose track records do not justify a chronological CV;
● career changers who want to focus on skills rather than experience;
● people whose careers have been stagnant or in ebb, who want to give focus to the skills that can get a career under way again, rather than on the history in which it was becalmed in the first place;
● those returning to the workplace after a long absence;
● people closer to retirement than to the onset of their careers.

For any CV to be effective, it must be conceived with a specific target job in mind, and this is especially true for a functional CV. Because it focuses so strongly on skills and ability to contribute in a particular direction, rather than on a directly relevant work history, you must have an employment objective clearly in mind.

Though a functional CV is a bit more free-form than a chronological one, there are certain essentials that make it work.

● *A functional summary*. Different skills are needed for different jobs, so the functional summary is where you make the tough decisions to determine what goes in to strengthen the focus of your CV.
● *Accomplishments/skills/professional behaviours*. Based on your target job, this is where you identify relevant accomplishments along with the skills and behaviours that made them possible.

- *Dates*. Strictly speaking, a functional CV needn't give dates, but a CV without dates waves a big red flag. So if your employment history lacks stability, a functional CV allows you to de-emphasize dates by their placement.
- *Education*. This is always included.

Inclusion of other optimal categories is determined by the space available and the unique aspects of your background.

Functional

Jane Swift
123 Anystreet
Anytown, AT1 0BB
Tel: 020 8123 4567
jane@anyaddress.co.uk

OBJECTIVE: A position in Employment Services where my management, sales and recruiting talents can be used effectively to improve operations and contribute to company profits.

SUMMARY: Over ten years of Human Resources experience. Extensive responsibility for multiple branch offices and an internal staff of 40+ employees and 250 consultants.

SALES: Sold high-technology consulting services with consistently profitable margins throughout the United Kingdom. Grew sales from £0 to over £20 million a year.

Created training programmes and trained salespeople in six metropolitan markets.

RECRUITING: Developed recruiting sourcing methods for multiple branch offices.

Recruited over 25,000 internal and external consultants in the high-technology professions.

MANAGEMENT: Managed up to 40 people in sales, customer service, recruiting and administration. Turnover maintained below 14% in a 'turnover business'.

FINANCIAL: Prepared quarterly and yearly forecasts. Presented, reviewed and defended these forecasts to the Board of Directors. Responsible for P & L of £20 million sales operation.

PRODUCTION: Responsible for opening multiple offices and accountable for growth and profitability, 100% success and maintained 30% growth over seven-year period in 10 offices.

WORK EXPERIENCE:

2004 to Present   Howard Systems International, London
National Consulting Firm
Personnel Manager

1995–2004   Technical Aid Corporation, London
National Consulting & Search Firm
Division Manager

EDUCATION: BA (Hons) 1994, London University

REFERENCES: Available upon request.

The combination chrono-functional CV

For the upwardly mobile professional with a track record, this is becoming the CV of choice. It has all the flexibility and strength that come from combining both the chronological and functional formats, and it allows you to clearly demonstrate your thorough grasp of the job and its deliverables.

- *A career summary.* The combination CV, more often than not, has some kind of career summary, where you spotlight yourself as a professional with a clear sense of self and a history of solid contributions. It might include a power-packed description of skills, achievements and personal traits that fairly scream 'Success!'

Alternatively, it might contain a 'job objective' that doesn't so much announce what you want in a job, but rather showcases your thorough understanding of the target job and its contribution to the target endeavour. Ideally, whichever focus you choose, your copy will embrace both these concepts, as the CV is not a document that you use to outline your demands, but one that positions you as a desirable solution to an employer's challenges.

- *A description of functional skills.* This is where the combination of styles comes into play. Following the summary, the combination starts out like a functional CV and highlights achievements in different categories relevant to the job/career goals, without any reference to employers.
- *A chronological history.* Then it switches to the chronological approach and names companies, dates, titles, duties and responsibilities. This section can also include further evidence of achievements or special contributions.
- *Education.* Then come the optional categories determined by the space available to you and the *unique* aspects of your background.

In the next chapter we are going to take a look at the component parts that, depending on your unique experiences, might have a place in your CV. As you read this chapter, continue to think which format is best suited to your primary CV. As a practical matter, you may well develop CVs in several different formats just as the professional in this chapter did. If you are not sure what is best, start by creating a chronological CV.

Combination

Jane Swift
123 Anystreet
Anytown, AT1 0BB
Tel: 020 8123 4567
jane@anyaddress.co.uk

OBJECTIVE:

Employment Services Management

SUMMARY: Ten years of increasing responsibilities in the employment services marketplace. Concentration in the high-technology markets.

SALES: Sold high technology consulting services with consistently profitable margins throughout the United Kingdom. Grew sales from £0 to over £20 million a year.

PRODUCTION: Responsible for opening multiple offices and accountable for growth and profitability. 100% success and maintained 30% growth over seven-year period in 10 offices.

MANAGEMENT: Managed up to 40 people in sales, customer services, recruiting and administration. Turnover maintained below 14% in a 'turnover business'. Hired branch managers and sales and recruiting staff throughout the United Kingdom.

FINANCIAL: Prepared quarterly and yearly forecasts. Presented, reviewed and defended these forecasts to the Board of Directors. Responsible for P & L of £20 million sales operation.

MARKETING: Performed numerous market studies for multiple branch opening. Resolved feasibility of combining two different sales offices. Study resulted in savings of over £5,000 per month in operating expenses.

EXPERIENCE: Howard Systems International, Inc.   2004–Present
Management Consulting Firm
Personnel Manager

Responsible for recruiting and managing consulting staff of five. Set up office and organized the recruitment, selection and hiring of consultants. Recruited all levels of MIS staff from financial to manufacturing markets.

Additional responsibilities:

- developed PR with industry periodicals – placement with over 20 magazines and newsletters;
- developed effective referral programmes – referrals increased 320%.

Technical Aid Corporation
1995–2004
National Consulting Firm, MICRO/TEMPS Division

Division Manager	2000–2004
Area Manager	1997–2000
Branch Manager	1995–1997

As Division Manager, opened additional West of England offices. Staffed and trained all offices with appropriate personnel. Created and implemented all division operational policies. Responsibilities for P & L. Sales increased to £20 million, from £0 in 1984.

- Achieved and maintained 30% annual growth over seven-year period.
- Maintained sales staff turnover at 14%.

As Area Manager, opened additional offices, hiring staff, setting up office policies, and training sales and recruiting personnel.

Additional responsibilities:

- Supervised offices in two countries.
- Developed business relationships with accounts – 75% of clients were regular customers.
- Client base increased 28% per year.
- Generated over £200,000 worth of free trade journal publicity.

As Branch Manager, hired to establish the new MICRO/TEMPS operation. Recruited and managed consultants. Hired internal staff. Sold service to clients.

EDUCATION: BA (Hons) 1994, London University

The basic ingredients

Technology continues to create new professions overnight, and with them new career opportunities. The content of these new professions and careers has made the employment world dramatically different from that of just a few years ago. What used to be strictly off-limits in all CVs is now acceptable in many and required in some. One example that comes to mind: the increasing need for technical jargon to explain skills. Elements that were often included, like a photograph, are now frowned upon in most instances; exceptions would be models and actors whose appearance is deemed relevant to the job. So what are the rules?

Writing a CV is a bit like baking a cake. In most instances, the ingredients are essentially the same; what determines the flavour is the order and quantity in which those ingredients are blended. There are certain ingredients that go into almost every CV. There are others that rarely or never go in, and there are those that are added as special touches (a pinch of this, a dash of that), depending on your personal tastes and requirements.

Sound complicated? It really isn't. If a certain ingredient must always go in, you will soon understand why. In circumstances where the business world holds conflicting views, I will explain the divergence so that a reasoned judgement can be made.

First, let's look at the ingredients that are part of every successful CV.

What must always go in

You should create a template for your CV, so that as you proceed and read that an item must go in, go right ahead and add it as you read, making any changes necessary for your particular circumstances. Don't worry about the whole thing looking like a bit of a mess; the biggest challenge in any creative process, especially writing, is capturing the initial idea in some concrete form. Once you have something on paper, the editing process is relatively simple.

Name

We start with the obvious, but there are other considerations about your name besides remembering to put it on your CV. Give your first and last name only. It isn't necessary to include your middle name(s). My name is Martin John Yate – but my CV says simply Martin Yate, because that is the way I would introduce myself in person. Notice also that it isn't M. J. Yate, because that would force the reader to play Twenty Questions about the meaning of my initials. Even if you are known by your initials, don't put them on your CV. If you use quotation marks or parentheses, those on the receiving end might think it a little strange. Better that it comes out at the interview when the interviewer asks you what you like to be called. At the very least you'll have some small talk to break the ice.

It is not required to place Mr, Ms, Miss or Mrs before your name, unless yours is a unisex name like Alex, Leslie, or any of the other names that are used for members of either sex. In such instances it is acceptable to put Mr Alex Jones, or Ms Leslie Jackson.

Finally, if you are the Junior or Senior holder of your name: if you always add 'Jr' or 'Sr' when you sign your name or if that is the way you are addressed to avoid confusion, go ahead and use it. Otherwise, it is extraneous information on the CV, and therefore not needed.

Address

Always give your complete address. Do not abbreviate unless space restrictions make it absolutely mandatory. If you do abbreviate – such as with *St* or *Apt* – be consistent. The county of your residence, however, may be abbreviated according to post office standards. Always include the correct postcode. The accepted format for laying out your address looks like this:

John Smith
123 Anystreet
Anytown
AN1 0BB

If space is an issue you can put your contact information on a single line. Use your judgement.

Telephone number

Always include your telephone number: Few businesses will send you an invitation for an interview in the mail. Including your area code is important even if you have no intention of leaving the area. In this era of decentralization, your CV might end up being screened in another part of the country altogether!

Unless your current employer knows of your job search and approves, leave your work number off the CV, but, if your circumstances dictate, put it in your cover letter. Good cover letters do this with a short sentence that conveys the information and demonstrates you as a responsible employee. For example, something like this can work very well:

> 'I prefer not to use my employer's time by taking personal calls at work, but with discretion you can reach me at 020 8123 4567, extension 555, to initiate contact.'

If you are employed, it is entirely acceptable to replace the name of your current employer with something more generic; I will show you how best to do this in a few pages.

E-mail

Your e-mail address is an integral part of your contact information. If you have an e-mail address, use it. If you don't, get one – because without it you are stating that you are disconnected from the communications technology that affects every job on the planet.

Never use your work e-mail address. It increases the odds of your boss learning that you are looking at broader horizons, because e-mails leave a trail that employers can and do follow. Nowadays, it is common for a member of the IT department to be assigned to monitor appropriate use of company computers, and that always includes tracking internet and e-mail usage. Using company e-mail outside regular working hours won't work either; the trail is still there for prying eyes to see. Please stay away from company telephone and e-mail usage for your job search. It can be and often is regarded as theft of company time and services; as such, it's not only cause for dismissal from your current job, but it also sends the wrong message to potential employers.

Job objective

This section can appear on CVs with any of these headings:

Job Objective
Employment Objective
Career Objective

All are acceptable. Regardless of the heading, your objective is not so much about what you want in a job, as it is a definition of what employers want when hiring this type of person and how your skills and background will allow you to contribute to the company in such a position. A job objective paragraph with an easily visible target job title and a couple of sentences summarizing your value proposition (skills, achievements, credentials and behaviours) can be a powerful way to open your CV: It gives the reader a clear focus and summary of who you are and what you bring to the table. Remember that the functional CV in particular almost demands such an objective.

Even so, feelings run strong about whether or not to include a job objective in the CV. Let's review the cases for and against, and then reach a considered conclusion.

The case for inclusion: Without a job objective, a CV can have no focus, no sense of direction. The CV revolves around your objective like the earth around the sun. And if you don't know where you are going, you can't write a CV, because the body copy has nothing to support. Additionally overworked CV screeners are given a ready focus for their evaluation.

The case for exclusion: A job objective is too constricting and can exclude you from consideration from countless jobs you might have been interested in, and for which you are qualified. And after creating a CV with the intent of opening as many doors as possible, you wouldn't want to have half of them slammed shut. Besides, employers are not generally believed to be overly concerned about what you want from them until they have a damn good idea about what they can get out of you.

The solution: It's a personal judgement call, but objectives that give the reader focus and which demonstrate what you bring to the table rarely do harm and often do good.

Traditionally, these objectives appear at the top of a CV, as a headline and attention grabber. They focus on skills, achievements, and relevant personal behaviours that support the argument.

Including job objectives and the like has as much to do with storage and retrieval systems and computers as it does with people. On the one hand, the CV reader is looking for a problem solver. By seeing that you fit into a general area, he or she will want to rush on to the rest of the CV (where there are more specifics). Then what happens? In the best-case scenario, you will get a call asking you to interview right away. But what happens when there isn't a need for your particular talents that day? Your CV gets filed or logged onto the company's database. They will file your CV according to what you include in it. And unless you give it the right help, it may never see the light of day again. The more your objective describes the target job and uses the right keywords to describe such work, the greater frequency with which it will be retrieved and reviewed in the future.

The same argument holds true for CVs sent to employment agencies and executive recruiters. Such considerations are encouraging many job seekers to include brief and non-specific job objectives in their CVs.

Employment dates

CV readers are often leery of CVs without employment dates. If you expect a response, you can increase your odds dramatically by including them – in one form or another.

With a steady work history and no employment gaps you can be very specific (space allowing) and write:

January 11, 2002 to July 4, 2004 or 1/11/02 to 4/7/07

or, to be a little less specific:

January 2002 – July 2004

But if there are short employment gaps, or the occasional job with short duration, you can improve the look of things:

2001–2002

instead of

December 12, 2001–January 23, 2002

There is no suggestion here that you should lie about your work history, but it is surprising just how many interviewers will be quite satisfied with such dates. There seems to be a myth that everything written on 100g paper needs no further inquiry.

While this technique can effectively hide embarrassing employment gaps, and it may get you in for an interview, you should of course be prepared with an adequate answer to questions about your work history. Even if such questions are posed, you will have the opportunity to explain yourself in person, and that is a distinct improvement over being peremptorily ruled out by some faceless nonentity before you get a chance to speak your piece. The end justifies the means, in this case.

If you abbreviate employment dates, be sure to do so consistently. It is acceptable to list annual dates, rather than month and year, but be aware of the potential penalties if you intend to do more. When references get checked, the very first things verified are dates of employment, and leaving salary. Untruths in either of these areas are grounds for dismissal with cause, and that can dog your footsteps into the future.

Keywords

Just as computers have helped streamline your job-search activities, they have done the same for the recruitment work of many human resource departments. One of the changes gaining ground in corporate America is the use of CV screening and tracking systems. Understanding how this technology affects the way your CV is stored and retrieved will dramatically affect your chances for success in your job hunt.

While electronic CV distribution makes your life easier, it's created an avalanche of electronic paper on the other side of the desk. If a company once had to deal with 100 CVs a day, it now probably sees 1,000 or more. With the high cost of human handling, the wholesale adoption of CV screening and tracking systems by businesses is a given. When computer screening replaces human judgement, the whole game changes. The computer program can't use human logic (although it is already getting pretty close); instead, the computer searches for keywords that describe the position and the professional skills needed to execute the duties effectively.

It works like this: the company representative sits down at the keyboard and opens the storage and retrieval program and keys in a job title into a dialogue box, the program then offers an extensive selection of words that can be used to describe that job. The user scrolls through the list clicking on the keywords that best describe the current needs. At the end of the sequence the user hits a 'search' button and the program goes to work. It searches the CV bank for any CVs that mention any of the keywords; then when this is done it weights the list of CVs with the CVs with the greatest frequency of the selected keywords ranked first.

Your CV – and thousands like it – can be scanned for the necessary keywords in seconds. The user receives a weighted list of the CVs that contain the appropriate keywords. The greater the number of relevant keywords in your CV, the higher your ranking. The higher your ranking, the greater the likelihood that your CV will be rescued from the avalanche and passed along to human eyes for further screening. This has led directly to the denser CVs that we are seeing today and the increasing prevalence of keyword sections.

In some of the CV examples you'll see later in the book you'll see a section that lumps a string of keywords together. This is often referred to as Core Competencies, Special Knowledge, Keyword Preface, Keyword Section, or Areas of Expertise. Here's what the keyword section of a taxation specialist's CV looks like:

AREAS OF EXPERTISE

VAT, Corporation Tax • Income Tax Returns • Vehicle Use Tax Returns • Income Tax Budgeting and Accrual • Property Tax Returns • Local Exemption Certificates • Local Sales, Use and Excise Tax Management • Tax Audit Management • Tax Licence and Bonding Maintenance • Certificates of Authority and Annual Report Filing Maintenance • State Sales and Use Tax Assessment • Excise Tax Collection and Deposits • National Insurance • Tax Amnesty Programmes

---

A keyword section not only dramatically increases your chances of getting the computer's attention, but HR people appreciate them as a brief synopsis of the whole CV. A keyword/core competencies section also allows you to succinctly identify skill sets that might not otherwise make it into your CV, and demonstrate that you obviously have more to offer than that discussed in detail within the body of the CV.

One last point. This approach also allows you to repeat highly important keywords that appear in the body of your CV. This repetition of keywords that speak to especially relevant competencies can improve the ranking of your CV in the weighted list, because the search programs count the frequency with which keywords are used as part of the weighting process.

Job titles

The purpose of a job title on your CV is not to reflect exactly what you were called by a particular employer, but rather to provide a generic identification that will be understood by as many employers as possible. So if your current title is 'Junior Accountant, Level Three,' realize that such internal titling may well bear no relation to the titling of any other company on earth.

To avoid painting yourself into a career corner, you can be 'specifically vague' with job titles like:

Administrative Assistant

instead of

Secretary

Accountant

instead of

Junior Accountant Level II

It is imperative that you examine your current role at work, rather than rely on your starting or current title. Job titles within companies change much more slowly than the jobs themselves, so a job change can be the opportunity for some to escape stereotyping and the career stagnation that accompanies it. This approach is important because of the way titles and responsibilities vary.

This obviously doesn't apply when you apply for a job in certain specific professions, such as health care: a cardiologist wouldn't want to be specifically vague by tagging herself as a Health Assistant.

Company name

The names of your employers should be included. There is no need to include the street address or telephone number of past or present employers, although it can be useful to include the city and county.

When working for a multiple-division corporation you may want to list the divisional employer: 'ABC Industries' might not be enough, so you would perhaps add 'Computer Memory Division.' By the way, it is quite all right to abbreviate words like Corporation (Corp.), Company (Co.), Limited (Ltd.), or Division (Div.), but remember to be consistent in your editing process.

Here is how you might combine a job title, company name, and address:

Design Engineer.
ABC Industries, Inc., Computer Memory Div., Reading, Berkshire

The information you are supplying is relevant to the reader, but you don't want it to detract from space usable to sell yourself. If, for instance, you live in a nationally known city, such as Oxford, you need not add the county if space is at a premium.

There is a possible exception to these guidelines. Employed professionals are justified in omitting current employers when their industry has been reduced to a small community of professionals who know, or know of, each other, and where a confidentiality breach is likely to have damaging repercussions. This usually happens to professionals on the higher rungs of the ladder. Of course, if you don't quite fit into this elite category but are still worried about identifying your firm, you are not obliged to list the name of your current employer.

One approach is simply to label a current company in a fashion that has become perfectly acceptable in today's business climate.

A National Retail Chain
A Leading Software Developer
A Major Commercial Bank

A company name can be followed by a brief description of the business line:

A National Retail Chain: Women and junior fashions and accessories.
Established Electronics Manufacturer producing monolithic memories.

This further description is unnecessary when the writer can get the company's function into the heading.

Being succinct in your CV can save precious space for more valuable information and keywords.

Responsibilities

The area where you address your responsibilities and achievements is the meat, or *body copy*, of the CV; it's the area where not only are your responsibilities listed, but your special achievements and other contributions are also highlighted. This is a crucial part of the CV, and it will be dealt with in detail in Chapters 4 and 5.

Endorsements

Remember when you got that difficult job finished so quickly, and all the good things the boss said about your work? Well, in a CV you can very effectively quote him, even if the praise wasn't in writing (though of course it is best to quote directly). A line such as 'Praised as "most innovative and determined manager in the company" ' is a nice plus to be able to add.

These third-party endorsements are not necessary, and they most certainly shouldn't be used to excess. But, used sparingly, an endorsement or two can be very impressive.

Such endorsements become especially effective when the endorsements support your quantified achievements.

Accreditation and licences

Many fields of work require professional licensing or accreditation. If this is the case in your line of work, be sure to list everything necessary. If you are close to a particular accreditation or licence (a C.P.A., for example), you would want to list it with information about the status:

> Passed all parts of C.P.A. exam, September '06
> (expected certification March '07).

Professional affiliations

Your affiliation with associations and societies related to a profession demonstrates a commitment to your career. Membership is also important for networking, so if you are not currently a member of one of your industry's professional associations, give serious consideration to joining. Note the emphasis on 'professional' in the heading. An employer is almost exclusively interested in your professional associations and societies. Omit references to any religious, political, or otherwise potentially controversial affiliations, unless your certain knowledge of that specific company assures that such affiliations will be positively received.

An exception to this rule is in those jobs where a wide circle of acquaintances is regarded as an asset. Some examples would include jobs in public relations, sales, marketing and insurance. In which case, include your membership/involvement with community organizations, charities, and the like, as such involvement demonstrates a professional involved in the community, a fact that speaks to having a wide circle of contacts.

By the same token, a seat on the town council, charitable cause involvement, or fundraising work are all activities that show a willingness to involve oneself and can often demonstrate organizational abilities through titles held in those endeavours. Space permitting, these are all activities worthy of inclusion because they show you as a force for good in your community.

These activities become more important as one climbs the corporate ladder as companies who take their community responsibilities seriously look for staff who feel and act the same way.

As for method of inclusion, brevity is the rule.

> British Heart Association: Area Fundraising Chair

Civil service grade

If you have a civil service job in your background, you will have been awarded a civil service grade. So, in looking for a job with the government, be sure to list it. In transferring from the government to the private sector, you are best advised to translate it into generic terms and ignore the grade altogether, unless you are applying for jobs with government contractors, subcontractors, or other specialized employers familiar with the intricacies of civil service ranking.

Publications and patents

Such achievements are usually found at the end of the CV. While their importance varies from profession to profession, they make a powerful statement about creativity, organization, determination, and follow-through on any CV. They tell the reader that you invest considerable personal time and effort in your career and are therefore a cut above the competition. Publication carries more weight in some industries and professions (where you hear phrases like 'publish or perish'), while patents are a definite plus in the technology and manufacturing fields. You will notice in the CV examples in this book how the writers list dates and names of publications, but do not include copyright information.

> 'Radical Treatments for Chronic Pain.' 2002. *British Medical Journal.*
> 'Pain: Is It Imagined or Real?' 2000. *Science & Health Magazine.*

Languages

Technology allows all companies the opportunity to become global in their activities and many companies have a vibrant international presence. A linguistic talent might give you just the edge you need. If you are fluent in a foreign language, don't hide your light under a bushel. If you understand a foreign language, but perhaps are not fluent, still mention it.

> Fluent in French
> Read German
> Read and write Serbo-Croatian
> Understand Spanish

Education

Educational history is normally listed wherever it helps your case the most, although the exact positioning of the information can vary according to the length of your professional experience, the relative strength of your academic achievements, and your profession.

If you are recently out of school with little practical experience, your educational credentials, which probably constitute your primary asset, will appear near the beginning of the CV.

As you gain experience, your academic credentials become less important in most professions, and gradually slip toward the end of your CV. The exception to this is found primarily in certain professions where academic qualifications dominate a person's career – medicine, for instance. This does not mean that your educational efforts are unimportant in any way; on the contrary, the educational section of your CV can show a commitment to ongoing professional education. This makes a powerful statement about both your competency and commitment, finishing your CV on a high note.

You will notice that all examples for education are in chronological order: The highest level of attainment always comes first, followed by the lesser levels. In this way, a doctorate will be followed by a master's degree, then a bachelor's. For degreed professionals, there is no need to go back further into educational history; it is optional to list your prestigious prep school.

Those who did not achieve the higher levels of educational recognition will list their own highest level of attainment. A word on attainment is in order here. If you attended university, but didn't graduate, you may be tempted to list your school qualifications first, followed by the name of the university you attended. That would give the wrong emphasis: it says you are a dropout. In this instance you would in fact list your university and omit any reference to earlier educational history.

While abbreviations are frowned on in most circumstances, it is normal to abbreviate degrees (Ph.D., M.A., B.A., B.Sc., etc.).

Those with scholarships and awards should list them, and recent graduates will usually also list subjects studied (space and relevancy permitting). The case is a little more confused for the seasoned professional. Many human resources professionals say it makes life easier for them if subjects are listed, so they can further sift and grade the applicants. That's good for them, but it might not be good for you. All you want the CV to do is get you in the door, not slam it in your face. So, as omitting these minutiae will never stop you from getting an interview, I urge you to err on the side of safety and leave 'em out, unless they speak directly to the target job.

If you are a recent entrant into the workplace, both your scholastic achievements and your contributions have increased importance. List your position on the school newspaper or the student council, memberships in clubs, and recognition for scholastic achievement – in short, anything that demonstrates your potential as a productive employee. As your career progresses, however, prospective employers care less about your school life and more about your work life.

Technology is rapidly changing the nature of all work, so if you aren't learning new skills every year, you are being paid for an increasingly obsolescent skill set. At some point this will affect your employability. Employers really appreciate people who invest in their future, and here's some proof from the U.S. Department of Education:

Of postsecondary students who enrolled in any AA degree program but didn't graduate, 48% got better job responsibilities and 29% got pay rises! If they actually graduated, it gets even better: 71% gained improved job responsibilities and 63% got raises. Clearly being enrolled in ongoing education looks good on a CV; you have nothing to lose and everything to gain by committing to your career.

Avoid exaggerations of your skills, accomplishments, and educational qualifications. Research has now proven that three out of every ten CVs feature inflated educational qualifications. Consequently, verification, especially of educational claims, is on the increase. If, after you had been hired, you were discovered to have exaggerated your educational accomplishments, it could cost you your job.

Military

If you have a good military record, include it with your highest rank, especially if you are applying for jobs in the defence sector. A military experience speaks to your determination, and your understanding of teamwork, policies, and procedures. Always list your military experience – it's a plus.

Professional training

Under the educational heading on smart CVs, you will often see a section for continuing professional education, focusing on special courses and seminars attended. For example, if you are computer literate, list the programs you are familiar with.

Summer and part-time employment

This should only be included when the CV writer is either just entering the work force or re-entering it after a substantial absence. The entry-level person can feel comfortable listing dates and places and times. The returnee should include the skills gained from part-time employment in a fashion that minimizes the 'part-time' aspect of the experience – probably by using a functional CV format.

What can never go in

Some information just doesn't belong in CVs. Make the mistake of including it, and at best your CV loses a little power, while at worst, you fail to land the interview.

Titles: CV, fact sheet, curriculum vitae, etc.

It should not be necessary to use any of these variations on a theme as a heading. Their appearance on a properly structured CV is redundant: If it isn't completely obvious from the very look of your document that it is a CV, it needs further work. Such titles take up a whole line, one which could be used more productively. You can either use the space for information with greater impact, or buy yourself an extra line of white space to help you with more accessible formatting.

Availability

All jobs exist because there are problems that need solutions, and interviewers rarely have time for interviews that don't potentially help them solve the problem at hand. Statements about your availability for employment on a CV are redundant. If you are not available, then why are you wasting everyone's time? The only justification for including this item is if you expect to be finishing a project and moving on at such-and-such a time, and not before. In such a case, your enlightened self-interest demands that you always have your eyes and ears open for better career opportunities. You aren't forced to act on those opportunities, but you are best advised to at least know about them. If leaving before the end of a project could affect your integrity and/or references, okay. There's a lot to be said for not burning your bridges, and as careers progress, it's surprising how many of the same people you bump into again and again.

As a rule of thumb, let the subject of availability come up at the face-to-face meeting. After meeting you, an employer is more likely to be prepared to wait until you are available. He or she will probably appreciate your integrity, but will usually pass on an interview if you are not available now.

Reason for leaving

There is no real point to stating your reasons for leaving a job on a CV, yet time and again they are included – to the detriment of the writer. The topic is always covered during an interview anyway; if the employer isn't interested, why should you raise an issue that could turn into a negative? You can usually use the space more productively; however, if you have been caught in a couple of downsizings, there is an argument for listing the reason to countermand any perception of wilful job-hopping.

Salary

Leave out all references to salary, past and present – it is far too rIsky. Too high or too low a salary can knock you out of the running even before you hear the starting gun. Even in responding to a help-wanted advertisement that specifically requests salary requirements, don't give them. A good CV will still get you the interview, and in the course of the discussions with the company, you'll certainly talk about salary anyway. If you somehow feel obliged to give salary requirements, simply write 'competitive' or 'negotiable', and then only in your cover letter – never put salary on a CV.

Charts and graphs

Even if charts and graphs are part of your job, they make poor use of the space available on a CV – and they don't help the reader. The same goes for other examples of your work. If you are a copywriter or graphic artist, for example, it is all right to say that samples are available, but only if you have plenty of CV space to spare; in such instances it is a given that you will bring a portfolio to the interview.

Mention of age, race, religion, sex, national origin

A raft of government legislation has been enacted over recent years forbidding employment discrimination in these areas. It is wisest to avoid reference to these unless they are deemed relevant to the job.

Photographs

In days of old when men were bold and all our cars had fins, it was the done thing to have a photograph in the top right-hand corner of the CV. Today, the fashion is against photographs; including them is a waste of space that says nothing about your ability to do a job. Obviously, careers in modelling, acting, and certain aspects of the media require photos. In these instances, your face is your fortune.

Health/physical description

You are trying to get a job, not a date. Unless your physical health and/or appearance are immediately relevant to the job (for example fitness instruction, modelling or acting), leave these issues alone.

Early background

I often see CVs that tell about early childhood and upbringing. To date, the most generous excuse I can come up with for such anecdotes is that the CVs were prepared by the subject's mother.

Weaknesses

Any weakness, lack of qualifications, or information likely to be detrimental to your cause should always be avoided. Never tell CV readers what you don't have or what you can't or haven't had the opportunity to do yet, they might never ask.

Demands

You will never see demands on a good CV. Don't outline what you feel an employer is expected to give or to provide. The time for making demands is when the employer extends a job offer with a salary and job description attached. That is when the employer will be interested and prepared to listen to what you want. Until then, concentrate on bringing events to that happy circumstance by emphasizing what you can bring to the employer. In your CV you should, to paraphrase John F. Kennedy, ask not what your employer can do for you, but rather what you can do for your employer.

Judgement calls

Here are some areas that fall into neither the *do* nor the *don't* camp. Whether to include them will depend on your personal circumstances.

Career summary

A Career Summary, when it is included in a CV, comes immediately after an Objective. Or it can replace the Objective. The goal is to encapsulate your experience and perhaps highlight one or two of your skills and/or contributions. You hope, in two or three short sentences, to grab the reader's attention with a power pack of the skills and attributes you have developed throughout your career. Good summaries are short; you don't want to show all your aces in the first few lines! (You can see examples of CVs with strong summaries in the sample CV section of this book.)

On the other hand, many experts feel that the content of the summary must be demonstrated by the body of the CV, and that therefore summaries are pointless duplication and a waste of space. The choice is yours. Used wisely and well, they can help give the reader a ready focus.

Personal flexibility, relocation

If you are open to relocation for the right opportunity, make it clear. It will never in and of itself get you an interview, but it won't hurt. On the other hand, never state that you aren't open to relocation. After all, that factor usually comes into play only when you have a job offer to consider. Let nothing stand in the way of a nice collection of job offers! You can always turn a job offer you don't want into an offer you do.

Career objectives

These are okay to include at the very start of your career, before your general direction has been confirmed by experience and track record. Inclusion is also acceptable if you have very clearly defined objectives and are prepared to sacrifice all other opportunities. If that is the case, state your goals clearly and succinctly, remembering not to confuse the nature of long-term career objectives with short-term job objectives.

Beware, though, of the drawbacks. First of all, CV readers aren't famous for paying much attention to objectives; that's why in talking about Job Objectives I emphasized the desirability of reflecting real world job descriptions. Second, I have seen these used on many occasions to make a hiring decision between two candidates. The CVs are compared: A has no objective, B has an objective that doesn't match the initial expectations. Result? A gets the job. Another consideration is that your CV may be on file for years, during which time your objectives are bound to change.

References

It is inappropriate and unprofessional to list the names of references on a CV. You will never see it on a top example. Why? Interviewers are not interested in checking them before they meet and develop a strong interest in you – it's too time-consuming.

Employers assume that references are available, and if they aren't available, you're in trouble! For that reason, there's an argument to be made for leaving that famous line – References Available Upon Request – at the end of your CV, but only if space allows; if you have to cut a line anywhere this would be one of the first to go. It may not be absolutely necessary to say that references are there for the asking, but those four extra words certainly don't do any harm and may help you stand out from the crowd. Including the phrase sends a little message: 'Hey, look, I have no skeletons in my closet.'

A brief but important aside: If you have ever worked under a different surname, you must take this fact into account when giving your references. A recently divorced woman I know of wasted a strong interview performance because she was using her maiden name on her CV and at the interview. She forgot to tell the employer that her references would, of course, remember her by a different last name. The results of this oversight were catastrophic. Three prior employers denied ever having heard of anyone by the name supplied to the references by the interviewer. She lost the job.

Written testimonials

It is best not to attach written testimonials to your CV. Of course, that doesn't mean that you shouldn't solicit such references for your files. Instead you might consider using them as a basis for those third-party endorsements we talked about earlier, then you can produce the written testimonials at the interview with the comment that they will support the claims made on your CV; this way you get to use them twice to good effect. This will be especially helpful to you if you are just entering the work force, or re-entering after a long absence, because the content of the testimonials can be used to beef up your CV significantly.

Marital status

If you think mention of your marital status will enhance your chances (if you are looking for a position as a long-distance truck driver, marriage counsellor, or travelling salesperson, for example), include it. In all other instances leave it out. Legally, your marital status is of no consequence.

Personal interests

A recent study showed that executives with team sports on their CVs were seen to be averaging £1,500 a year more than their more sedentary counterparts. Now, that makes giving a line to your hobbies worthwhile, if they fit into certain broad categories. These would include team sports, determination activities (running, climbing or bicycling), and 'brain activities' (strategy games such as chess). The rule of thumb, as always, is only to include activities that can in some way contribute to your chances.

Personal activities

Here and there throughout the CV section of this book you will see CVs that include – often toward the end – a short personal paragraph that gives you a candid snapshot of the CV writer as a person. Done well, these can be exciting, effective endings to a CV, but they are not to everyone's taste. Typically, they refer to one or two personal traits, activities, and, sometimes, beliefs. These are often tied in with skills required for the particular job sought.

The idea is to make the reader say, 'Hey, there's a real person behind this piece of paper, let's talk to them.' Of course, as no-one can be all things to all people, you don't want to go overboard in this area.

4

The ultimate CV

This is the part of the book that requires you to do some thinking. I will ask questions to jog your memory about your practical experience. The outcome will be a smorgasbord of your most marketable professional attributes. Whether you are a fast tracker, recent graduate, work force re-entrant, career changer, or what-have-you, if you are considering new horizons, you must take stock before stepping out.

People change jobs for a multitude of reasons. Perhaps your career isn't progressing as you want it. Perhaps you have gone as far as you can with your present employer, and the only way to take another career step is to change companies. Maybe you have been in the same job for three or more years, without dramatic salary increases or promotions, and you know that you are going nowhere, your having been stereotyped, classified, and pigeonholed.

You need to know where you've been, where you are, and where you're headed. Without this stocktaking, your chances of reaching your ultimate goals are reduced, because you won't know how best to use what you've got to get where you want to go.

Believe it or not, very few people have a clear idea of what they do for a living. Oh, I know; you ask a typist what he or she does, and you get, 'Type, stupid.' You ask an accountant, and you hear, 'Fiddle with numbers, what do you think?' And that is the problem. Most people don't look at their work beyond these simplistic terms. They never examine the implications of their jobs in relation to the overall success of the company. Most people miss not only their importance to an employer as part of the business, but also, their importance to themselves. Preparing your CV will give you a fresh view of yourself as a professional and your role in your chosen profession.

Employers all want to know the same thing: How can you contribute to keeping their ship afloat and seaworthy? Everyone who ever gets hired for any job gets hired because they are a problem solver. Companies hire only problem solvers. Look at your work in terms of the problems you solve in the daily round, as well as the problems that would occur if you weren't there.

The secret of CV writing

As a CV writer, you are going to have a lot in common with journalists and novelists. Beginners in each field usually bring some basic misconceptions about how writing is done: a novice writer may assume that Stephen King or John Grisham just sits down, writes 'Page 1,' and then three weeks later writes 'The End,' placidly returning the quill to the inkwell. In fact, many professional writers have a lot in common with the creative process employed by sculptors, who create beauty from a block of stone. Writers start the creative process by creating a mass of notes. This great mass is the raw material, like the sculptor's block of stone, at which they chip away to reveal the masterwork that has been hiding there all along.

The key is that the more notes you have, the better. Just remember that whatever you write in the note-making part of your CV preparation will never suffer public scrutiny; it is for your private consumption only. Don't let the 'need to get it done' or the fear of others' judgement cramp the creative process of capturing information: the final product can only ever be as good as the components from which you assemble it.

This process will help you:

- get a focus for your job search;
- prepare an effective CV;
- open doors for interviews;
- provide interviewers with a road map of your choosing;
- act as a positive spokesperson long after you have left the interview.

On top of all these benefits, this information-gathering process will also help you properly prepare for telephone and in-person interviews, as you will see over the following pages.

Questionnaire, part one: raw materials

First, set up a document titled 'CV Questionnaire' and save it to a CV subfolder within your career management folder. Add each of the following Steps into the document and then steadily work your way through them. Alternatively, you can come to *knockemdead.com* and download a PDF with the complete questionnaire ready to go in an electronic document.

Step 1: identify your target job

It's a misconception to think that a productive CV is a simple recitation of what you have done with your professional life. On the contrary, such a CV will seem unfocused and may well demand more effort on the part of the reader to determine if you are a worthwhile candidate.

Your CV will be incalculably more productive if you begin with defining a clear focus on a target job that you can land and in which you can be successful. Start with identifying this target job title.

Step 2: research the target job

Surf the web for an hour and collect as many job descriptions as you can with this target job title. Once you have a selection, deconstruct them into a series of bullets here as your answer for Step 2.

You should realize that:

● No-one is ever added to the payroll for the love of mankind.

● At some level all employees are hired to do the same job: Problem solution and problem avoidance within a specific area of expertise.

● No-one ever reads CVs for fun.

● CVs are always read with job titles in mind.

● CVs are always read with a job description in mind.

You can see the absolute necessity of beginning the evaluation of your background with an understanding of what potential employers will be looking for when they come to your CV.

Step 3: go through your recent work history

With the focus you have gained from Steps 1 and 2, understanding the sort of information those CV readers are going to be looking for, it is time to start working through your work history. In this process you'll not only be gathering all the information necessary for your CV, but reminding yourself of all kinds of data employers are likely to require at different stages of the selection cycle. This is a time when you are going to get completely immersed in your work history.

A. Current or last employer

Identify your current or last employer by name and location, follow it with a brief description (5–6 words) of the company's business/products/services.

> *Note:* This includes part-time or voluntary employment if you are a recent graduate or about to re-enter the work force after an absence. Try looking at your school as an employer and see what new information you can reveal about yourself.

For your current or most recent employer, write down the following:

Starting date: _____
Starting title: _____
Starting salary: _____
Leaving date: _____
Leaving title: _____
Reason for leaving: _____
Potential references for this job: _____
Leaving salary: _____

B. Deliverables

Make a bulleted list of the duties/responsibilities/deliverables in this position. Then arrange the elements from most important to least.

C. Skills and special knowledge

Now, for each of your identified deliverables, answer the following questions:

- What special skills or knowledge did you need to perform this task satisfactorily?
- What educational background and/or credentials helped prepare you for these responsibilities?
- What are your achievements in this area?

For each of your major areas of responsibility you should consider both the daily problems that arise and also those major projects/problems that stand out as major accomplishments. Think of each as a problem-solving challenge, and the analytical processes and subsequent actions you took to win the day. There is a four-step technique you will find useful here called PSRV:

P. Identify the *project* and the problem it represented, both from a company perspective and from the point of view of your execution of duties.

S. Identify your *solution* to the challenge and the process you implemented to deliver the solution.

R. What was the *result* of your approach and actions?

V. Finally, what was the *value* to you, the department, and the company? If you can, define this in terms of time saved, money saved, or money earned. This is not always possible, but it is very powerful whenever you can.

Step 4: Consider teamwork and your professional profile

Next within your information-gathering document, ask yourself and answer the following questions:

- What verbal or written comments did peers or managers make about your contributions in each area of your job?
- What different levels of people did you have to interact with to achieve your job tasks? What skills and methods did you use to get the best out of superiors? Co-workers? Subordinates?
- What aspects of your personality were brought into play when executing this duty?

Professional behaviours

To help you address that last question in Step 4, we're going to take a little break from the questionnaire (you've earned it, haven't you?). In order to identity which traits and abilities enabled you to perform well at your work in the past, look over the following list of twelve professional behaviours. These are behaviours that are in demand by all employers for all jobs at all levels. Going through the list, you will probably recognize that you already apply some or many of these behaviours in your work. As you read, come up with examples of your using each particular behaviour in the execution of each of your major duties at this job. The examples you generate can be used in your CV, in your cover letters, and as illustrative answers to questions in interviews.

1: Communication & listening skills: This covers your ability to communicate effectively to people at all levels in a company, is a key to success, and refers to verbal and written skills along with technological adeptness, dress, and body language. This is an especially important consideration when it comes to your covering letter and CV, because these written documents are the first means an employer has of judging your communication skills. You should demonstrate that you have to take the time to craft and edit, and re-edit your CV until it communicates what you want it to, and at the same time demonstrates that you have adequate communication skills.

Communication embraces *Listening Skills*: Listening and understanding, as opposed to just waiting your turn to talk; there is a big difference between the two. Consciously develop your 'listening to understand' skills and the result will be improved persuasive communication abilities.

2: Goal-orientation: All employers are interested in goal-oriented professionals: those who achieve concrete results with their actions and who constantly strive to get the job done, rather than just filling the time allotted for a particular task. Whenever possible, you should try to use an example or reference to this behaviour in your letters and CV.

3: Willingness to be a team player: The highest achievers (always goal-oriented) are invariably *Team Players*: employers look for employees who work for the common good and always with the group's goals and responsibilities in mind. Team players take pride in group achievement over personal aggrandizement; they look for solutions rather than someone to blame.

4: Motivation & energy: Employers realize a motivated professional will do a better job on every assignment. Motivation expresses itself in a commitment to the job and the profession, an eagerness to learn and grow professionally and a willingness to take the rough with the smooth.

Motivation is invariably expressed by the energy someone demonstrates in their work, always giving that extra effort to get the job done and to get it done right.

5: Analytical skills: Valuable employees are able to weigh the short- and long-term benefits of a proposed course of action against all its possible negatives. We see these skills demonstrated in the way a person identifies potential problems and so is able to minimize their occurrence. Successful application of analytical skills at work requires understanding how your job and the role of your department fits into the company's overall goal of profitability. It also means thinking things through and not jumping at the first or easiest solution.

*6: **Dedication & reliability:*** We are speaking here of dedication to your profession, with an awareness of the role it plays in the larger issues of company success, and of the empowerment that comes from knowing how your part contributes to the greater good. Dedication to your professionalism is also a demonstration of enlightened self-interest. The more you are engaged in your career, the more likely you are to join the inner circles that exist in every department and company enhancing opportunities for advancement; this dedication will therefore repay you with better job security and improved professional horizons.

Your dedication will also express itself in your *Reliability*: Showing up is half the battle; the other half is your performance on the job. To demonstrate reliability requires following up on your actions, not relying on anyone else to ensure the job is done well, and keeping management informed every step of the way.

*7: **Determination:*** Someone with this attribute does not back off when a problem or situation gets tough; instead, he or she is the person who chooses to be part of a solution rather than standing idly by and being part of the problem. Determined professionals have decided to make a difference with their presence every day and are willing to do whatever it takes to get a job done, even if that includes duties that might not appear in a job description.

*8: **Confidence:*** As you develop desirable professional behaviours, your confidence grows in the skills you have and in your ability to develop new ones. With this comes confidence in taking on new challenges. You have the confidence to ask questions, the confidence to look at challenges calmly, the confidence to look at mistakes unflinchingly, and the confidence to make changes to eradicate them. In short, you develop a quiet confidence in your ability as a professional who can deliver the goods.

*9: **Pride & integrity:*** Pride in yourself as a professional means always making sure the job is done to the best of your ability; paying attention to the details and to the time and cost constraints. Integrity means taking responsibility for your actions, both good and bad; it means treating others, within and without the company, with respect at all times and in all situations. With pride in yourself as a professional with integrity, your actions will always be in the best interests of the company, and your decisions will never be based on whim or personal preference.

*10: **Efficiency:*** Working efficiently means always keeping an eye open for wasted time, effort, resources, and money.

11: Economy: Most problems have two solutions – and the expensive one usually isn't the best. Ideas of efficiency and economy engage the creative mind in ways other workers might not consider; they are an integral part of your analytical proficiency.

12: Ability to follow procedures: You know that procedures exist to keep the company profitable, so you don't work around them. Following the chain of command, you don't implement your own 'improved' procedures or organize others to do so.

Employing these learnable behaviours is the key to long-term career success. If you can recognize the role each of these learnable behaviours play over the course of a successful career, you'll not only craft a better CV and land a better job, but you'll also be more successful in your new job and in all future ones.

And now, let's head back to the questionnaire.

Step 5: Add in your previous work history

It is not unusual to have held a number of different titles with a specific employer. If this applies to you, such professional progression needs to be identified on your CV, as it speaks to your competency and promotability. For each different intermediary title, repeat Steps 3 and 4. Do not skimp on this process. All you write may not go into the final version of your CV, but all your effort will reward you at some point during the selection process and lead to more and better job offers.

Next (and this may take some time), repeat Steps 3 and 4 for each of your previous employers. Most finished CVs place greatest emphasis on the last three jobs, or last ten years experience. In this developmental portion of the process, however, you must go back in time and cover your entire work history. Remember that you are doing more than preparing a CV here: You are preparing for the heat of battle. The work you do in a careful analysis of your career to date will help prepare you for interviews down through the years. One of the biggest complaints interviewers have about job candidates, and one of the major reasons for rejection, is unpreparedness: 'You know, good as some of this fellow's skills are, something just wasn't right. He seemed slow somehow. You know, he couldn't even remember when he joined his current employer!' You won't have that problem.

Step 6: Compile endorsements

Looking at each of your major areas of responsibility, come up with whatever verbal or written commentary on your performance you can.

Questionnaire, part two: details, details, details

The hard work is done, and it's all downhill from here. Step 7 (the last one!) of the questionnaire is to fill in the details concerning your abilities and experience in the following areas.

Military history

Include branch of service, rank, and any special skills that could further your civilian career.

Educational history

Start with highest level of attainment and work backwards. Give dates, schools, scholarships, and/or special awards.

List other school activities, such as sports, societies, and social activities. Especially important are leadership roles: any example of how you 'made a difference' with your presence could be of value to your future. Obviously, this is most important for recent graduates with little work experience, and those in the very early stages of a career.

Technological literacy

In this new era of work, every potential employer is concerned about your ability to work with new technologies. If you are technologically literate, let's hear the details. If not, it's time to catch up with today's technology – before you get left behind with the industrial-era dinosaurs.

Ongoing professional development

Identify all the classes and courses you have pursued during your career, including certification and accreditations; they all speak to your professional commitment and to employers' belief in your potential.

Languages

The ability to read and write foreign languages is always a plus; specify your fluency in each.

Personal interests

List interests and activities that could be supportive to your candidacy. For example, an internal auditor who plays chess or bridge would list these on a CV, because they support the analytical bent so necessary to work. Activities that challenge you physically, analytically, or as a member of a team are all regarded positively in the selection process.

Patents and publications

Include patents that are both pending and awarded. If you have published articles, list the name of the publication, title of article, and the publication date. If you have had books published, list the title and publisher.

Professional associations

Include membership and the details of any offices you held.

Civic affiliations and volunteer work

It isn't only paid work experience that makes you valuable, so include membership in community groups and any volunteer work you performed. Involvement in such activities has a variable value depending on the company and individual hiring manager; regardless it is always regarded as a positive commentary on your engagement.

Miscellaneous areas of achievement

All professions and careers are different. Use this section to itemize any additional aspects of your history where you somehow 'made a difference' with your presence.

Do your credentials warrant the target job?

We started the information-gathering process by focusing on a target job title and then researching recruitment advertising to come up with a clear idea of what employers are typically looking for under that job title. There is a simple check-and-balance step you can take here that will benefit you in some powerful ways. You'll remember that I advised you to make a bulleted list of the desired requirements from all the recruitment postings you discovered. Now go back to that list and reading each bullet, go through your answers in the questionnaire and proceed to cut and paste relevant information beneath each bullet. At the end of the process you can read the composite job description and your answers; you'll very quickly get a picture of your relative strengths and weaknesses. Hopefully this will tell you:

- I can do the job.
- I have a picture of what employers are going to ask me about.
- I have a blueprint for what I can talk about in response.

Being able to do 70 per cent or more of the job will usually get you in the running for the interview cycle. Less than this and you may need to re-evaluate your target job title. Most people don't get promotions to the next step up the professional ladder when they change jobs, because they are coming onboard as an unknown quantity. Typically, most professionals accept a position similar to the one they have now, one that offers the opportunity for growth once their mettle is proved. An exception might be when they are already doing that higher-level job but without the title; another might be the executive who is combining experience and credentials from a number of jobs into a new in-demand configuration.

5

Writing the basic CV

CVs depart from the rules that govern all other forms of writing. First and last they are an urgent business communication, and businesslike to get to the point.

You can assume that the potential employer has a position to fill and a problem to solve, and that he or she is buried in an avalanche of CVs.

For the next 15 minutes, imagine yourself in one of your target companies. You are in the personnel department on CV detail. Fortunately it is a slow morning, and there are only 30 that need to be read. Go straight to the example section now and read 30 CVs without a break, then return to this page.

Now you have some idea of what it feels like. Except that you had it easy – the CVs you read were well put together; CVs that got real people real jobs. Even so, you probably felt a little punch drunk at the end of the exercise. But I know that you learned a very valuable lesson: brevity is to be desired above all other things.

Choose a layout

You have seen the basic examples of chronological, functional and combination CVs in chapter 2, and certainly you have browsed through the CVs. Find one that strikes your fancy and fits your needs, and use it as your model. It need not reflect your field of professional expertise. Obviously, your template will need work; you will need to put in your own contact information and job objectives, add the details of each of your jobs and make any other changes necessary.

This first step is just like painting by numbers. Go through the model and fill in the obvious slots – name, address, telephone number(s), e-mail address, employer names, employment dates, educational background and dates, activities and the like. Shazam! You immediately have a document that is beginning to look like a CV.

Filling in the picture: chronological CVs

Objectives

You can have a simple non-specific objective, one that gives the reader a general focus, such as, 'Objective: Data Processing Management'. It gets the message across succinctly; and if there is no immediate need for someone of your background, it encourages the employer to put your CV in the file where you feel it belongs. That's important, because even if you are not suitable for today's needs, it increases the odds that the CV will be pulled out when such a need does arise.

If you choose to use an expanded, detailed objective, you will of course focus the objective on what you can do for the company and avoid mention of what you want in return. You can use the job description you developed in your information-gathering process (as described in chapter 4) to craft an objective in the language that employers use to describe your target job. This will help both human eyes and database spiders to find your CV attractive.

Company's business

Now, for each employer, edit your response from the Questionnaire in chapter 4 to outline that company's services or products. Make it one short sentence: this is not necessary if, like Microsoft, the company is a household name.

Job titles

Remember what we said in chapter 3. There is nothing intrinsically wrong with listing your title as 'Fourth-Level Administration Clerk, Third Class', as long as you are prepared to wait until doomsday for it to be considered by someone who understands what it means and is able to relate it to current needs. Make sure you use job titles that will be commonly understood.

Responsibilities

In a chronological CV, the job title is often followed by a short sentence that helps the reader visualize you doing the job. Get the information from the completed questionnaire and do a rough edit to get it down to one short sentence. Don't worry about perfection now; the polishing is done later.

The responsibilities and contributions you list here are those functions that best relate to the needs of the target job; if you have focused on a target job in which you can be successful, this should not be a problem.

They do not necessarily correspond with how you spent the majority of your working day, nor are they related to how you might prefer to spend your working day. It can perhaps best be illustrated by showing you part of a CV that came to my desk recently. It is the work of a professional who listed her title and duties for one job like this:

> Sales Manager: Responsible for writing branch policy, coordination of advertising and advertising agencies. Developed knowledge of IBM PC. Managed staff of six.

Is it any wonder she wasn't getting responses to her CV-mailing campaign? She has mistakenly listed everything in the reverse chronological order, not in relation to the items' relative importance to a future employer. Let's look at what subsequent restructuring achieved:

> Sales Manager: Hired to turn around stagnant sales force. Successfully recruited, trained, managed and motivated a consulting staff of six. Result: 22 per cent sales gain over first year.

Notice how this is clearly focused on the essentials of a sales manager's job:

> Hired to turn around stagnant sales force. (Demonstrates her skills and responsibilities.)

> Successfully recruited, trained, managed and motivated a consulting staff of six. Result: 22 per cent sales gain over first year. (Shows what she subsequently did about them, and just how well she did it.)

By doing this, her responsibilities and achievements become more important in the light of the problems they solved.

An important word about 'contributions'

Business has very limited interests. In fact, those interests can be reduced to a single phrase: making a profit. Making a profit is done in just three ways: by saving money in some fashion for the company; by saving time through some innovation at the company, which in turn saves the company money and gives it the opportunity to make more money in the time saved; or by simply making money for the company.

That does not mean that you should address only those points in your CV and ignore valuable contributions which cannot be quantified. But it does mean that you should try to quantify as much as you can.

Achievements

Pick two to four accomplishments for each job title and edit them down to bite-size chunks that read like a telegram. Write as if you had to pay for each entry by the word – this approach can help you pack a lot of information into a short space. The resulting abbreviated style will help convey a sense of immediacy to the reader.

> Responsible for new and used car sales. Earned 'Salesperson of the Year' awards, 2000 and 2001; Record holder for most cars sold in one year.

Here's another example from a fundraiser's CV:

- Created an annual giving programme to raise operating funds. *Raised £2,000,000.*
- Targeted, cultivated, and solicited sources including individuals, corporations, foundations and government agencies. *Raised £1,650,000.*
- Raised funds for development of the Performing Arts School facility, capital expense, and music and dance programmes. *Raised £6,356,000.*

Now, while you may tell the reader about these achievements, never explain how they were accomplished; the key phrase here is 'specifically vague'. The idea of your CV is to pique interest and to raise as many questions as you answer. Questions mean interest, and getting that interest satisfied requires talking to you!

You may have plenty of accomplishments to share with the reader that will tempt you to add a second page to your CV – and a third and fourth page. However, describing your achievements succinctly will not only leave room for further discussion at the hoped-for interview, but will also make it easier to scale down your CV to the preferred length of one page, or at most two.

Next, prioritize the listing of your accomplishments as they relate to your target job, and be sure to quantify your contributions wherever possible and appropriate.

If you can, now is the time to weave in some of those laudatory quotes. Put in all you have right now, but when you come to the final editing phase you will want to cut it back; one or two will be fine, although I have seen CVs where each job entry is finished with a complimentary quote. For example:

- Sales volume increased from £90 million to £175 million. Acknowledged as 'the greatest single gain of the year'.

- Earnings increased from £9 million to £18 million. Review stated, 'always a view for the company bottom line'.

- Three key stores were each developed into £30-million units. Praised for 'an ability to keep all the balls in the air, all the time'.

Functional or combination CV

In a functional or combination CV, you will have identified the skills and attributes necessary to fulfil the functions of the target job, and will high-light the appropriate attributes you have to offer. In this format, you will have headings that apply to the skill areas your chosen career path demands, such as. Management, Training, Sales etc. Each will be followed by a short paragraph packed with selling points. These can be real para-graphs, or an Introductory sentence followed by the bullets usually recom-mended for the chronological formats. Here are examples of each style.

COLLECTIONS
Developed excellent rapport with customers while significantly shortening pay-out terms through application of problem-solving techniques. Turned impending loss into profit. Personally salvaged and increased sales with two multi-million-pound accounts by providing remedial action for their sales/financial problems.

COLLECTIONS
Developed excellent rapport with customers while significantly shortening pay-out terms:

- Evaluated sales performance, offered suggestions for financing/merchandising.

> ● Performed on-the-spot negotiations; turned impending loss into profit.
>
> ● Salvaged two multi-million-pound problem accounts by providing remedial action for their sales/financial problems. Subsequently increased sales.

Keep each paragraph to an absolute maximum of four lines. This ensures that the finished product has plenty of white space so that it is easy on the reader's eye.

Editing and polishing

Sentences gain power with verbs that demonstrate an action. For example, a woman with ten years at the same law firm in a clerical position had written in her original CV:

I learned to use a computer database.

After discussion of the circumstances that surrounded learning how to use the computer database, certain exciting facts emerged. By using action verbs and an awareness of employer interests, this sentence was charged up, given more punch.

I analysed and determined need for automation of an established law office. Responsible for hardware and software selection, installation and loading. Within one year, I had achieved a fully automated office.

Notice how the verbs show that things happen when you are around the office. These action verbs and phrases add an air of direction, efficiency and accomplishment to every CV. They succinctly tell the reader what you did and how well you did it.

Now look at the above example when a third-party endorsement is added to it:

I analysed and determined need for automation of an established law office. Responsible for hardware and software selection, installation and loading. Within one year, I had achieved a fully automated office. Partner stated, 'You brought us out of the dark ages into the technological age, and in the process neither you nor the firm missed a beat!'

Now while the content is clearly more powerful, the presentation is still clunky and takes up too much space. Read on, and in the next few pages you will see how you can speed up and shorten paragraphs like this further.

Keywords

With the advent of electronic CV screening tools, it's become more and more important to use specific keywords in your CV. Internal job descriptions are usually built of nouns and verbs that describe the skill sets required for the job. Your CV should be built the same way, with nouns that identify the skill sets and verbs/action phrases that describe your professional behaviour and achievements with these skill sets.

This is an important distinction in the initial screening process. Screening software focuses on the skill sets, which invariably are nouns. If you are a computer programmer the screening device might search for words like HTML; if you are an accountant it might search for words like 'financial analysis'. Only when the computer has identified those CVs that include matching skills do human eyes enter into the picture; and only then can the verbs/action phrases that describe your competencies and achievements have the desired impact. With an electronic CV, the nouns/skill sets are the skeleton, while the verbs/action phrases are designed to put flesh on the bones – for human eyes hungry for talent.

For our purposes the keyword nouns are the words commonly used to describe the essential skill sets and knowledge necessary to carry out a job successfully They are likely to include:

- skill sets/abilities/competencies;
- application of these skills sets;
- relevant education and training.

You may also want to study the keywords that appear frequently in recruitment postings: if you have been following the programme outlined here, you have already collected these for your job description.

You'll want to weave these synonyms for job titles and skill sets into the main body of your CV as much as possible. However, that won't always be possible. The logical flow of your CV – or insufficient space might prevent you from using the keywords in place. That's where a separate keyword section comes in handy. It is the perfect spot to list the technical acronyms and professional jargon that you can't fit into the body copy.

Here's an example of a keyword box from a sales management professional:

SPECIFIC KNOWLEDGE AND SKILLS

- Market Trend Analysis
- Multi-Site Management
- Budget
- Business Savvy
- Performance Evaluations
- Technical Expertise

- Profit & Loss
- Needs Analysis
- Employee Motivation
- Sales
- Contract Negotiation
- Team Training

This innovation in CV writing allows you to add a host of additional information to your CV in a highly space-efficient way – usually in 20 to 60 words.

Using a core competencies keyword selection will increase the odds of an electronic screening agent making multiple matches between your CV and an open job requisition. Human eyes will view the list of keywords for topics for discussion.

This compels me to offer you a warning: don't use keywords to extend the 'reach' of your CV. You must have real experience in each of the areas you include. Including keywords for areas where you have no professional expertise may get you a telephone conversation with an employer, but it will also quickly reveal you as an impostor. End of story.

Where does the core competencies keyword section go? As far as the computer is concerned it doesn't matter. The computer doesn't care about the niceties of layout and flow. However, human eyes will also see this section so there is a certain logic in putting it front and centre, after any summary or objective or immediately after the contact information. The keyword section acts as a preface to the body copy, in effect saying, 'Hey, here are all the headlines. The stories behind them are immediately below.' To put it another way, the keyword section acts as a table of contents for your CV, with the body – with its action words and phrases – explaining and expanding on the list of topics.

Your keyword section can be as long as you require, though they typically don't run longer than 60 items and usually are a little shorter. There's no need to use definite or indefinite articles or conjunctions. Just list the word, starting with a capital and ending with a full stop: 'Forecasting', or a phrase, such as 'Financial modelling'.

You can also think of your keyword section as an electronic business card that allows you to network with computers!

Action verbs

Overleaf are over 175 action verbs: see which ones you can use to give punch to your CV writing.

Use these words to edit and polish your work, to communicate, persuade, and motivate the reader to take action.

Varying sentence structure

Most good writers are at their best when they write short punchy sentences. When writing a CV, where space is limited, this dictum is particularly true. Keep your sentences under about 20 words. If your sentence is longer than the 20 mark try to shorten it by editing out unnecessary words, or make two sentences out of one.

At the same time, you don't want the writing to sound choppy, so vary the length of sentences when you can. You can also start with a short phrase and follow with a colon:

- followed by bullets of information;
- each one supporting the original phrase.

These techniques are designed to enliven the reading process. Here's the example from a few pages back with the 'punching up' process taken a stage further:

> Analysed and determined need for automation of an established law office:
>
> - responsible for hardware and software selection;
> - coordinated installation of computer database and six work stations;
> - operated and maintained equipment, and trained other users;
> - achieved full automation in one year.
>
> Partner stated, 'You brought us out of the dark ages, and neither you nor the firm missed a beat!'

accepted	critiqued	increased	published
accomplished	cut	indoctrinated	purchased
achieved	decreased	influenced	recommended
acted	defined	informed	reconciled
adapted	delegated	initiated	recorded
addressed	demonstrated	innovated	recruited
administered	designed	inspected	reduced
advanced	developed	installed	referred
advised	devised	instigated	regulated
allocated	diagnosed	instituted	rehabilitated
analysed	directed	instructed	remodelled
appraised	dispatched	integrated	repaired
approved	distinguished	interpreted	represented
arranged	diversified	interviewed	researched
assembled	drafted	introduced	resolved
assigned	edited	invented	restored
assisted	educated	launched	restructured
attained	eliminated	lectured	retrieved
audited	emended	led	revamped
authored	enabled	maintained	revitalized
automated	encouraged	managed	saved
balanced	engineered	marketed	scheduled
budgeted	enlisted	mediated	schooled
built	established	moderated	screened
calculated	evaluated	monitored	set
catalogued	examined	motivated	shaped
chaired	executed	negotiated	solidified
clarified	expanded	operated	solved
classified	expedited	organized	specified
coached	explained	originated	stimulated
collected	extracted	overhauled	streamlined
compiled	fabricated	oversaw	strengthened
completed	facilitated	performed	summarized
composed	familiarized	persuaded	supervised
computed	fashioned	planned	surveyed
conceptualized	focused	prepared	systemized
conducted	forecast	presented	tabulated
consolidated	formulated	prioritized	taught
contained	founded	processed	trained
contracted	generated	produced	translated
contributed	guided	programmed	travelled
controlled	headed up	projected	trimmed
coordinated	identified	promoted	upgraded
corresponded	illustrated	proposed	validated
counselled	implemented	provided	worked
created	improved	publicized	wrote

Just as you use short sentences, you should also use common words. They communicate quickly and are easy to understand. Remember:

> *Short words for short sentences*
> *help make short, gripping paragraphs:*
> *good for short attention spans!*

Voice and tense

The voice you develop for your CV depends on a few important factors: getting a lot said in a small space; being factual; and packaging yourself in the best way.

The voice you use should be consistent throughout the CV. There is considerable disagreement among the experts about the best voice.

Sentences can be truncated (up to a point) by omitted pronouns – I, you, he, she, it, they – and articles – a or the. In fact, many authorities recommend the dropping of pronouns as a technique that both saves space and allows you to brag about yourself without seeming boastful. It gives the impression that another party is writing about you. Many people feel that to use the personal pronoun ('I automated the office') is naive. These experts suggest you use either the third person ('He automated the office') or leave the pronoun out altogether ('Automated office').

At the same time, there are others who feel that writing in the first person makes you sound, well, personable – and I have seen the odd CV like this that really does work. Use whatever style works best for you. If you do use the personal pronoun, though, try not to use it in every sentence – it gets a little monotonous and takes up valuable space on the page.

A nice variation I have seen is a third-person voice used through the CV and then a final few words in the first person appended to the end of the CV, to give an insight into your values. Here is an example:

Regular third person:
James Sharpe is a professional who knows Technical Services from the ground up. He understands its importance in keeping a growing company productive, and takes pride in creating order in the chaos of technology.

Abbreviated third person:
Responsible for machine and system design, production scheduling, procurement and quality control. Redesigned conveyors and

simplified maintenance while improving quality. Instituted a system of material control to account for all materials used.

First person:
I am accustomed to accepting responsibility and delegating authority, and am capable of working with, and through people at all levels. Am able to plan, organize, develop, implement, and supervise complex programmes and special projects. All of this requires a good sense of humour and a personal dedication to producing timely, cost-effective results.

Many people mistake the need for professionalism in a CV with stiff-necked formality. The most effective tone is one that mixes both the conversational and the formal, just the way we do in our offices and on our jobs. The only overriding rule is to make it readable, so that another person can see the human being shining through the pages.

Length

The accepted rules for length are one page for every 10 years of your experience. If you have more than 20 years under your belt, many of the skills from those early days are now irrelevant; so on the whole the 'two page maximum' rule is still a sensible guideline.

Now while the advent of electronic databases and the consequent tilt towards data heavy CVs (to maximize the keyword registers) is leading towards two-page CVs as the norm for all but entry-level professionals, never pad your CV to make it longer.

A note on executive CVs is necessary here. In my private consulting practice I work with executives around the world who are typically both seasoned professionals and earning over a quarter of a million dollars a year; they are relatively few in number, and they hold unrelentingly complex jobs.

With the increased complexity of these modern management jobs, the need to demonstrate competence, and the exigencies of electronic database manipulation, makes exceeding the traditional two-page mark not only necessary but often desirable. Now while brevity and focus are still the very soul of a productive CV, that £200,000-a-year Director of Marketing CV is going to have to be read by someone in a position to hire you. So squeezing everything onto two pages for the sake of accepted norms defeats your purpose. Assuming that the first page clearly demonstrates a thorough understanding and competency in the target job, you can feel comfortable taking that third and sometimes fourth page. In the chapter of sample CVs, you'll see two examples of justifiably longer executive CVs, starting on page 261.

You'll find that thinking too much about length considerations while you write will hamper you. Think instead of the story you have to tell, then layer fact upon fact until it is sold. When that is done, you can go back and ruthlessly cut it to the bone.

Ask yourself these questions:

- Can I cut out any paragraphs?
- Can I cut out any sentences?
- Can I cut out any superfluous words?
- Where have I repeated myself?

If in doubt, cut it out – leave nothing but facts and action words!

The proofreading checklist for your final draft

There are really two proofing steps in the creation of a polished CV. The first you do at this point, to make sure that all the things that should be in are there – and that all the things that shouldn't, aren't.

In the heat of the creative moment, it's easy to miss critical components or mistakenly include facts that give the wrong emphasis. Check your CV against these points:

Contact information

- Is the pertinent personal data – name, address, personal telephone number, and e-mail address – correct? (You will want to make sure that this personal data is on every page.)

Objectives

- Does your objective briefly state your employment goals without getting too specific and ruling you out of consideration for many jobs?
- If you gave a detailed objective does it focus on what you can bring to the employer, rather than what you want from the employer?
- Is your stated objective supported by the facts and accomplishments stated in the rest of your CV?

Summary

- If you choose to include a summary, is it no more than five lines long so that the block of type remains accessible?
- Does it include at least one substantial accomplishment that supports your employment goals?
- Does it include reference to some of your personality or behavioural traits that are critical to success in your field?

Keywords/core competencies

- If you include a keyword section do you have experience in each of the areas you've listed?
- Can you illustrate your experience in conversation?
- Does it include commonly used synonyms for your skill sets that you have not already used in the body of the CV?
- Are the spelling and capitalization correct? (It's easy to make mistakes here, especially with acronyms.)
- Are there any other justifiable keywords you should add?

Body of CV

- Is your most relevant and qualifying work experience prioritized throughout the CV to lend strength to your application?
- Have you avoided wasting space with unnecessarily detailed employer names and addresses?
- Have you been suitably discreet with the name of your current employer?
- Have you omitted any reference to reasons for leaving a particular job?
- Have you removed all references to past, current, or desired salaries?
- Have you removed references to your date of availability?

Education

- Is education placed in the appropriate position? It should be at the beginning of the CV if you have little or no work experience; at the end if you are established in your field and your practical experience now outweighs your degree.
- Is your highest educational attainment shown first?
- Have you included professional courses that support your candidacy?

Chronology

- If you've done a chronological CV, is your work history stated in reverse chronological order, with the most recent employment coming at the head of the CV?
- Within this reverse chronology, does each company history start with details of your most senior position?
- Have you avoided listing irrelevant responsibilities or job titles?
- Does your CV emphasize the contributions and achievements during your career?
- Can your body copy include one or more laudatory third-party endorsements of your work?
- Have you avoided poor focus by eliminating all extraneous information? This includes anything that doesn't relate to your job objective, such as captaining the tiddlywinks team in kindergarten.
- Have you included any volunteer or community service activities that can lend strength to your candidacy?
- Is the whole thing long enough to whet the reader's appetite for more details, yet short enough not to satisfy that hunger?
- Have you left out lists of references and only included mention of the availability of references if there is nothing more valuable to fill up the space?
- Have you avoided treating your reader like a fool by highlighting the obvious (ie, heading your CV, 'CV')?

Writing style

- Have you substituted short words for long words? And one word where previously there were two?
- Is your average sentence no more than 20 words? Have you made sure that any sentence of more than 20 words is shortened or broken into two sentences?
- Have you kept every paragraph under five lines, with many paragraphs considerably shorter?
- Do your sentences begin, wherever possible, with the powerful action verbs and phrases from earlier in the chapter and from the CV examples?

Crossing the T's, dotting the I's

Before your CV is finished, you have to make sure that your writing is as clear as possible. Three things guaranteed to annoy CV readers are incorrect spelling, poor grammar and improper syntax. Go back and check all these areas. If you feel uneasy about your CV, you had better get a third party involved and always use your spelling and grammar checker.

It simply isn't possible for even the most accomplished professional writer to go directly from final draft to print, so don't try it. Your pride of authorship will blind you to the blemishes, and that's a self-indulgence you can't afford.

You need some distance from your creative efforts to gain detachment and objectivity. There is no hard and fast rule about how long it takes to come up with the finished product. Nevertheless, if you think you have finished, leave it alone as long as you can – at least overnight. Then you can come back to it fresh and read almost as if it were meeting your eyes for the first time.

More than one CV

Do you need more than one type of CV? Probably. With just a few years' experience, most people have a background that qualifies them for more than one job. If this applies to you, the process is as simple as changing your format.

There is a case for having CVs in more than one format. I was once engaged in an outplacement experiment for a group of professionals. With just a little extra work, we developed chronological, functional and combination CVs for everyone. The individuals concerned sent out the CV of their choice. Then, in those instances where there was no response, a different version of the CV was sent out. The result from just a different format: 8 per cent more interviews. So if your chronological CV isn't getting results, maybe try a little reformatting and send it out as a combination style CV.

What's next?

Almost home now. Save your notes, early drafts and, of course, the completed Questionnaire. This 'legwork' represents essential material you'll need in updating or revising future versions of your CV.

6

The final product

By some accounts, upwards of 80 per cent of CVs are stored in and retrieved from electronic databases. Even if this number is unscientific, we can still accept that the percentage is substantial indeed. Your CV may be an aesthetic marvel, but if it goes into the computer as gobbledy-gook, it won't do you much good. This chapter will cover 'the traditional' CV – the CV designed for human eyes. The other kind, the 'computer-friendly' CV, is designed to get through a computer scanner with data intact. It is so vital in today's job market that I have devoted a separate chapter to it. Of course, the two kinds of CV do have certain basics in common. Let's start with those.

Avoiding the circular file

The average CV arrives on a desk with dozens of others. Your CV will only get a maximum of 30 to 40 seconds of initial attention. And that's only if it's laid out well and looks accessible to a tired pair of eyes.

What are the three biggest complaints about those CVs that reach the wastepaper basket in record time?

Impossible to read. They have too much information and are either too long or cram everything into the space with too small a font.

No coherence. Their layout is unorganized, illogical and uneven. They look shoddy and slapdash.

Typos. They are riddled with misspelings (see how annoying that is?).

Here are some tips that will help your CV rise above the rest.

Fonts

Business is rapidly coming to accept the likes of Bookman, New York and Palatino as the norm. When choosing your font, stay away from heavy and bold for your body copy (although you may choose to take a more dramatic approach with key words or headlines). Bold type takes up too much space, so use it sparingly to begin with. Use it for those things you want to jump out, and that would certainly include only words the company may have used in recruitment advertising. Avoid 'script' faces similar to handwriting; while they look attractive to the occasional reader, they are harder on the eyes of the person who reads any amount of business correspondence. Capitalized copy is tough on the eyes too; we tend to think it makes a powerful statement when all it does is cause eye strain and give the reader the impression that the writer is shouting at him or her.

How to brighten the page

Once you decide on a font, stick with it, because more than one on a page looks confusing. You can do plenty to liven up the visual impact of the page within the variations of the font you have chosen.

You will notice from the examples in this book that the best CVs pick two or three typographical variations and stick with them

Proofing

When you have the printed CV in hand, you *must* proofread it. Check everything, from beginning to end.

- Is everything set up the way you want it?
- Are there any typographical errors?
- Is all the punctuation correct?
- Has everything been underlined, capitalized, emboldened, italicized and indented exactly as you desire?

Once you read the CV, get someone else to review it. A third party will always provide more objectivity, and can catch errors you might miss.

Appearance checklist

- The first glance and the first feel of your CV can make a powerful impression. What's your immediate reaction to it?

- Have you used only one side of the page?
- If more than one page, did you paginate your CV ('1 of 2' at the bottom of the first page, and so on)?
- Does the first page of the CV clearly announce that you understand and can do the job?

Choosing your paper

Every CV should be printed on standard A4 paper. Paper can come in different weights and textures. Good CV quality paper has a weight designation of between 80 and 100g. Lighter, and you run the risk of appearing nonchalant, unconcerned. Heavier, and the paper is unwieldy, like light cardboard.

As for colour, white is considered to be the prime choice. Cream is also acceptable, and I'm assured that some of the pale pastel shades can be both attractive and effective. Personally, I think that most professionals just don't show up in the best light when dressed in pink – call me old-fashioned if you will. White and cream are straightforward, no-nonsense colours.

Cover letter stationery should always match the colour and weight of your CV. To send a white cover letter – even if it is written on your personal stationery – with a cream CV looks uncoordinated, and detracts from the powerful statement you are trying to make.

It is a good idea to print some cover-letter stationery when you produce your finished CV. The letterhead should be in the same font and on the same kind of paper, and should copy the contact data from your CV.

The final checklist

- Have you used a good-quality paper?
- Is the paper standard A4 size (210mm × 297mm)?
- Have you used white, off-white or cream-coloured paper?
- If your CV is more than one page, have you stapled the pages together (one staple in the top left-hand corner)?
- Is your cover letter written on stationery that matches your CV?

7

How to use the internet for your job search

The internet is especially effective in identifying all the target employers in a specific geographical area – whether it is where you live today or where you want to live as soon as possible. Its usefulness diminishes somewhat when you are only looking for jobs in your immediate area, and that area is a small town; even then there are still many useful ways you can use the medium.

From the corporate perspective, internet recruitment serves a dual purpose: a company's personnel openings are cost-effectively advertised to attract candidates, and the technologically challenged potential applicants screen themselves out.

How can the internet benefit your job search? It allows you to:

- research your industry and identify companies;
- create customized electronic documents and communicate with potential employers and recruiters pretty much instantly;
- find job openings through job banks and employers' job sites;
- have potential employers find you, whether you are currently looking for a position or just maintaining visibility for career growth opportunities;
- use database and networking sites to identify names and titles;
- pick up useful job search and career management advice.

You can post your CV on the internet so that companies and recruiters can find you; you can surf for job openings and you'll have access to more information about prospective employers, making you a better-informed candidate. The internet offers you access to millions of job openings, and tens of thousands of companies and recruiters. Of course, they are not all going to be in your town, so the wider your geographical parameters, the more useful the tool will become.

The electronic CV

Whether electronic or a paper, companies increasingly store CVs received in electronic databases. You need to create a database-compatible CV – one that can be stored in a public job site or corporate database, where Human Resources people and recruiters can have quick access to it.

Because of competition and the growth of the internet, CV scanning and searching capabilities are now available to virtually all companies and recruiters. When an employer needs to sort through CVs for likely job candidates, they go to the keyboard, type in a job title, and are presented with a list of descriptors and choose those most relevant to the job being filled (*descriptors* are keywords describing different aspects of a particular job). The selection of keywords having been chosen, the software program searches in the company's database and ranks the documents containing any of the selected keywords. The more keywords your CV matches the better your chances are of having it read, because the program not only looks for CVs that contain those keywords, it also ranks the generated list and puts the most keyword-heavy CVs at the top. As you use the internet and recruitment ads from newspapers and the professional press to find open positions, pay attention to the keywords that you see repeated. If you see keywords in job descriptions for positions that interest you and fit your qualifications, add these keywords to your CV.

Making your CV scannable

In today's electronic world, you need both a 'keyword conscious' paper CV that is scannable as well as an electronic CV that can be sent via e-mail and is database compatible. When you mail your CV to a company it is a paper document. In order for a company to quickly and effectively transform your CV to an electronic format they can scan, or digitize, it.

Here's what happens behind the scenes: a company receives your paper CV and they place it in a scanner that takes a picture of your CV. When you fax your CV to a company, the fax machine will act just like a scanner and create a file with a picture of your CV. A software program called OCR (optical character recognition) is then applied to that picture of your CV. The OCR software tries to identify parts of that picture that represent letters, numbers, and symbols. Knowing that recruiters and employers use this technology means that you must create your print CV to operate within the technical capabilities of the software. The software capability improves almost by the month, but that doesn't mean that every company always has the latest version of the best program, so we will err on the side of conservatism. Here are some general rules to follow to assure that your print CV is indeed scannable:

- Always avoid paper with a dark or even medium colour, a coloured border, heavy watermark, or graining – plain white paper is best.

- Be circumspect about adding borders around a document or around a section of text in the CV. The OCR software could identify the outline as a single character and omit the entire content of that section.

- Do not use columns – when scanned, the order of words will be out of sequence and that could hurt the effectiveness of your keyword sections.

- Do not use fonts smaller than 10 point; 12 point is ideal. If the employer experiences difficulty in scanning your CV you will not receive a polite phone call asking you to resubmit.

When should you use a scannable CV?

Anytime you are mailing or faxing your CV to a company, assume that it will be scanned. Always use the 'fine mode' setting when faxing your CV. This will result in better resolution and allows the OCR to optimize the digital conversion. Many companies do not print faxed CVs, but instead convert them directly to digital. Also, most PCs now come with standard software that allows the user to fax and receive documents without ever having to print them.

The difference between scannable and electronic CVs

An electronic CV is one built solely on a computer, sent via e-mail to the recipient, and, once received, usually downloaded directly into an employer's CV database. Whereas an electronic CV is only digital, a scannable CV is a paper CV that is converted to digital. There are three different ways you can send your CV electronically:

1. ASCII or plain text;
2. Formatted, usually as a Microsoft Word document;
3. Web-based/HTML.

You may not need all three, but you will definitely need at least the first two. Here are descriptions of all three:

1. *Plain text or ASCII:* This is the simplest version of the three. We're talking just the basics: only text; letters, numbers and a few symbols found on your keyboard. ASCII (American Standard Code for Information Interchange) CVs are important because this is the only format that any

computer type, whether PC or Macintosh, can read. The reader will not need a word processing program such as Microsoft Word or Word Perfect, and their software or printer compatibility needn't be considered. An ASCII CV looks like the average e-mail message you receive.

2. *Formatted Electronic CV:* This is a CV that is also sent via e-mail, but as an attachment. A formatted electronic CV is usually your CV as created in a word-processing document, most often in MSWord, which has become the standard WP format. It is normal when sending CVs, without a prior conversation to determine that the recipient expects the attachment, to paste your CV into the body of your email with a notation that a copy is also attached. You paste into the body of the email and attach as an MSWord document because many will not open attachments from people they do not know, for fear of viruses. It is sensible to work with Microsoft Word, which is the world's word processing program of choice.

3. *Web or HTML CV:* A Web CV is not a 'must have' for everyone. Essentially, a Web CV is an electronically formatted CV housed on the internet. There are some advantages; for example, you can include audio and video clips, music, and pictures. If you are in a creative profession and would typically have a portfolio, a Web CV can allow access to your work samples. Likewise if you are a Web page design professional or HTML guru, then, by all means, use the internet to show your creative and electronic abilities. Otherwise a Web-based or HTML CV is a nice thing to have but not mandatory. My advice is to get your MSWord CV completed along with a text version, get your job search up to speed, and then decide if you need to develop this third variation.

How to convert your formatted CV to ASCII

Converting your CV into a text or ASCII version is simple. To start the ASCII conversion process, go to your 'My Documents' or 'My Briefcase' folders and create a series of new folders to store the various documents you will be creating.

Job search folders

The first thing to do is to create a section within the 'My Documents' folder and then create a series of folders within that to hold your 'CVs', 'Cover Letters', 'Job Descriptions', etc. Within each of these folders, you will need to name your documents appropriately – even creating additional sub-folders.

Next, open your CV using your word processing program. The most widely used is Microsoft Word, so that's what we'll use in our example. Copy the entire document by choosing 'select all' from the 'edit' pull-down menu then, by choosing 'copy' from the 'edit' pull-down menu or Ctrl+C for Windows.

Converting your CV

Then, open a new document in your word processor. Set the margins to 1.5 inches on both right and left sides, which equates to about 60 characters per line depending on type size and font. The number of characters in each line must be limited because electronic screens are restricted to that viewing width; consequently you do not want text to 'wrap off the screen.'

Setting margins

Next you are going to paste the CV you just copied into this new document. Simply choose 'paste' from the 'edit' pull-down menu, or Ctrl+V for Windows. Initially, the document will look very similar to your previous CV, but we will modify it further. Do not panic if your one-page CV just became two pages. If you had small margins, the shorter line length will create a longer CV.

Go to the 'edit' pull-down menu and choose 'select all.' Now you are going to change the font type and size. To do this, choose 'font' from the 'format' pull-down menu and change the font type to Times New Roman or Courier. Change the size to 12 point.

Changing the font

Now, we need to save this new document using the 'save as' command. Select the document type as 'text only,' and rename the document. Let's call it 'Text CV 1' and even put it in a new folder.

Pay attention: you will get a message box saying that you will change your formatting that asks if you want to continue. Answer 'yes.' An ASCII or text-based CV strips out formatting that could make your document difficult to read. Notice that the file name of the CV no longer ends with .doc; it now ends in .txt, meaning text-based document.

The document has lost many of its features and 'pretty looks.' Spacing is also altered considerably. You will want to spend time proofreading this new document, and making necessary adjustments. Any tabs, tables, or columns that you used in your formatted version may wreak havoc on your new text version. In order to prevent lines from wrapping or flowing down to the next line, you need to make your document flush left by removing empty spaces and tabs.

A text-only CV

You will need to use ALL CAPS for section headers and to replace things that were in bold or underlined. Likewise, all of your bullets will be gone and you will have to adjust the spacing to create a new type of emphasis, or use characters on your keyboard such as '*'. Remember that the goal is to get your CV downloaded into the databases of potential employers and then retrieved by the software. A better-looking paper CV can be sent after your first electronic contact with the manager, Human Resource professional, or recruiter.

A properly edited text CV

Before you send your CV, take time to save and proofread it carefully. Send your electronic cover letters and CV attachments to yourself, and to a friend, or a family member. Ask them for printouts of your practice e-mail messages and CVs to ensure that what you intended to send is actually what was received. Often this exercise will help you find mistakes, bloopers, or larger problems incurred during the conversion process; you shouldn't be finding spelling errors at this stage, and if you do, reward yourself with a smack on the side of the head for being sloppy.

Posting your CV, and tricks to online questionnaires

Job sites have evolved tremendously over the last few years. There are literally thousands of job boards on the internet, from mega sites to very focused sites that cater to a specific geographical location or profession.

Most of the larger sites offer free job delivery and CV posting services. You just select a few criteria, and job listings matching your specifications are automatically sent to your inbox. With the CV banks, your CV goes into a database for employers and recruiters to search by keywords, when there is a match you will be notified. If you are already employed, these sites allow you to stay on top of your career by keeping abreast of available opportunities in your direction of choice.

If you are currently in a full-blown job search, spend plenty of time browsing the job site itself. Keep your search criteria broad-based; you might even eliminate salary or geographical requirements when you begin. This enables you to uncover the maximum number of companies and recruiters in your industry. Even if the specific job opening isn't a great match or you aren't planning to relocate, you'll be able to check your CV against the requirements being advertised and the keywords being used to describe them; additionally, you'll become aware of these companies for future reference.

Internet CV posting allows an employer to find you while you are sleeping, playing, or working – it never sleeps. It sounds great and it works – if you understand the rules of the game.

Not all job sites and CV banks work the same way. On some sites, you simply copy and paste your CV like we've done in the previous examples. On other sites, you'll have to complete a profile or questionnaire that creates your online presence at that site.

These sites are usually free for job hunters, though an exception would be the executive sites, which typically charge a monthly membership fee. The job sites work with prospective employers to develop better screening tools, since the employers are the paying clients. By making job seekers fill out very specific profiles and questionnaires, employers have more specific data with which to screen.

When filling out a profile or questionnaire, keep these two things in mind:

1.   What is my audience? Who will be reading this?
2.   What are they really asking me?

When a site or a company does not want your CV, but does want you to complete a registration or profile process, they are looking to provide employers with effective screening tools. Let's take a closer look at the Monster.co.uk CV builder as an effective screening tool, and what you can do to make it work to your benefit.

Setting up a new account at Monster.co.uk

Once on the site, follow the buttons for new users, and begin to set up your free 'My Monster Account,' filling out your name, address, career level, and degree, which are all required fields. When a field is required, it must be completed or your enrolment process stops. These are the hardest fields to complete, as they can force you to divulge more information than you want.

As with most 'free' sites, you will immediately be asked to sign up for newsletters and advertisements.

One of the nice features of Monster.co.uk is that it allows you to maintain five different CVs/profiles; this is particularly useful when you have a broad background and can do a number of different jobs. Use this opportunity! Make some of your profiles very specific, and make others very broad in order to increase your visibility.

The Monster CV builder is typical in that it breaks up the CV, and, in this case, a profile, into a number of specific topics. Topics include things like Career Objective, Target Job, Target Location, Salary, Work Status, Skills, References, and Education. These are all common topics covered in most online profiles and registrations.

One of the very first screens you will be asked to complete includes your 'Title' and 'Career Objective.' The site offers examples to help you fill in answers to these questions – but their advice is not in your best interest. Remember, the employer pays the job sites for advertising space and they are trying to help the employer screen you out. Monster advises you to list a specific position title and, in the 'Career Objective' field, write out a short professional profile and list your career goals.

If you want to increase your visibility, then you need to think beyond these questions. This is all about keywords. Instead of completing the 'Title' field, as this field holds up to 60 characters, you have the opportunity to add more detail besides your actual title. The best way to make use of that space is to list any special skills or qualifications you may have.

A Monster.co.uk online CV

According to the comments under the 'Objective' field, Monster tells us that it holds up to 2,000 characters. Following the site's examples by listing a two- or three-sentence objective would be wasting an opportunity to inundate employers with favourable keywords. Remember, it is not just the mention of a keyword that is counted by the software; the number of times they are repeated counts into the grand total. So, from your CV, pick and choose keywords that highlight your skills, experience, qualifications and technical knowledge. When answering these questions, you are building your CV all over again, so describe past successes that will attract the attention of database search software and, consequently, prospective employers.

As you continue to complete your profile, you will come to a section that breaks down your 'target job.' The important element to notice here is that you are not always limited to one answer – even in the case of checkboxes. For your desired job type, you may be able to select both *Employee and Temporary/Contract/Project*, and even *Intern* if you want. It's a good idea to test the site to see if you can select more than one answer. Never assume you are limited – not even if the directions on the screen indicate that you are.

Choosing a target job

You will also be asked about your salary requirements. We all dread this question in a pre-employment screening. Although the salary question is sandwiched between 'required' fields, it is not required. So you can, and should leave it blank. In instances where you are forced to answer the question, answer in terms of a range as you would in an interview situation.

The last question on this screen allows you 500 characters to describe your ideal job. This is not a space to really answer that question; it is more an opportunity to use keywords to describe the kind of job you can land and in which you can succeed. Remember that the more keywords that appear in your profile, the higher on the list it will appear; and the more likely it is to be read by a sentient human being.

Now the dreaded relocation question – check to make sure that this is a required field. If it isn't, don't answer it. If it is, keep your answer broad. Any company or recruiter only interested in local candidates will use the address on your CV as the search parameter.

Here's the rule: you can always say 'no,' but you can't say 'yes' unless you've been asked. For the right job, the right opportunity, and the right money, we all might move to Timbuktu. Besides, what isn't right for your career today may be tailor made for your situation a year from today; you never know what the future may hold and you need to be prepared.

Choosing a company

Notice that while the page is optional, the 'Company Category' field is designated 'required' by the red asterisk. Most people have probably completed this screen assuming that it is required. Read every word to distinguish between what is optional and required and how much information can be included or excluded.

You are most likely to come across online questionnaires and profiles in these situations:

- registering with a job site;
- posting with a job site;
- applying for a job within a company;
- registering with a recruitment firm.

In each case, you must always consider who is asking you the question and why. They are trying to screen you in or out, so consider your responses carefully. Always read the instructions, avoid questions on salary and relocation if possible, and add as many keywords as possible. Proofread and spell-check everything you enter, and only post to sites that allow editing and updating.

Sending your CV directly to companies and recruiters

The third way to distribute your CV via the internet involves direct contact with companies and recruiters. There are a number of ways to use the internet to help you locate companies and recruitment firms and appropriate executives within them. Once you are aware of a company in your industry or a recruitment firm that makes placements within your profession, why not make contact? You do not need a recruitment ad to have a reason to get your credentials in front of hiring eyes.

The internet is a particularly useful information resource – provided you know where to look. Luckily, sites and services exist to simplify our search.

Just because you do not see a job advertised with your name on it where you happen to be looking today, that does not mean that particular company is not looking for someone like you. You can look at job postings simply as a way of identifying companies so that you can apply to them directly whether or not you have seen a relevant job posting. Instead of replying directly to the job postings, visit the company websites and browse there. Send a cover letter and your CV to specific individuals, or, failing that, send one blind into the HR department. Add this contact information to your database for future job-search efforts.

Many job sites offer pages listing all companies posting jobs with them. Usually, these lists link to those companies' job openings, or directly to their home pages. Look for this feature on every job site you enter; it can help you build your job search database and will serve to stop you relying solely on visible job postings.

There are many database sites that exist to help develop corporate intelligence, allowing you to search entire industries and develop long lists of companies and their executives.

A second use for this data is accumulating e-mail addresses in an address book or even in a Word document. Assemble an electronic cover letter suitable for a mass distribution to go with it, and 'blast' your CV out there yourself. By using the bcc (blind copy) feature on your e-mail software, you can e-mail 100 letters at a time – far more productive than individually.

A third option is hiring a company to do it for you. Several years ago, 'CV blasting' services came into being. Their results are not too bad. Companies will distribute your CV electronically (via e-mail). The cost depends on the number of people you intend to contact. It is important to receive a copy of the list of addresses being sent to, even if it adds to the cost of the service. This list allows you to follow up after the 'blast', and you can enhance your career management database with it.

Keep in mind that whether you do the research on your own, or purchase it from another company, either process involves time or money – probably a bit of both. Treat it as an investment in your career management. While CV blasting companies were hot news when they first appeared, the promise hasn't always lived up to the hype; consider the option carefully. To my mind, just blasting CVs and cover letters out blind to companies doesn't provide a worthwhile return on the time and cost involved. The only situation where this is viable is mass e-mailing to the headhunting community.

Internet job search strategies

The internet is a powerful job search tool, and your approach in using it will make a difference to your success. No single job search method guarantees this success. The best approach is one that integrates networking, online job search. The following list is a brief overview of strategies for internet-based CV distribution.

- *The blitz* – You are unemployed (or soon to be unemployed or graduating) and need a job ASAP. In this case, you have no concern for confidentiality and want maximum exposure and results. You should visit and post your CV to a selection of job sites including the majors, and also professional association and profession specific sites. You should 'blast out' CVs to all the companies and recruiters on the databases you have accumulated from your research or purchase.

- *Focused attack* – a much more focused version of the Blitz. Employed or unemployed, you will want to use a couple of the major job boards with more specialty sites, associations, and specific company site research. The focused attack could be as confidential as you decide to make it. It can also work well for those pursuing multiple potential career paths, or for those interested in a career/industry change. If you are still employed but have informed your employer that you are looking for a change, then this is the perfect strategy for you.

- *Stealth mode* – There are two types of job seekers fitting this strategy. The first is the employed seeker who understands the value of keeping a pulse on the job market. Only post confidential CVs, if any, and only use sites that deliver jobs to you. The second type of job seeker using this strategy is one who has identified his or her dream company or geographic area to work in. You are employed, and are using the internet to monitor sites that this dream company posts to, in order to send them confidential CVs, research their executive bios, association members, and like information, to find an open door.

Whichever strategies you use, make the commitment and follow through. Remember, no single strategy is an absolute, sure-fire way to find a suitable job. Always use an integrated approach employing all of your online and offline resources.

The internet encourages three primary methods of CV distribution:

1. responding to recruitment ads (job postings);
2. posting your CV and credentials;
3. sending your CV directly to companies and recruiters.

Any time you can grab human attention before the electronic system takes over, it is to your advantage. Two elements will help to get you there: the ability to use your cover letter and the subject line to garner attention, and circumventing the electronic system by sending your documents to specific individuals.

Since all e-mail messages you send are electronic versions of your cover letter, you may want to take a look at the companion book *Ultimate Cover Letters*. Electronic cover letters are similar, but don't take the availability of unlimited space to make them longer, just as you would limit a paper cover letter to one page or three to five paragraphs, do the same with your e-mail cover letter.

Use keywords that illustrate your potential and examples of your accomplishments to prospective employers in this document as well. With a little practice, you can write short, powerful sentences, which will get your e-mail messages and attached CVs read. It's a smart idea to create cover letter templates that you can easily customize for each response.

The subject line is your first, and possibly only, chance to interest the initial reader enough to read your CV instead of forwarding it directly to a database. The key is to focus on a clear message stating the nature of your contact, hopefully giving them some incentive for interest. If you are responding to a job posting or print advertisement state the job posting number or job title, and where possible take an extra step to get yourself noticed.

Let's look at an example. Susan O'Malley has been using the Society for Human Resource Management career site and has found an appealing job posting. A holiday resort developer is seeking a Regional Human Resources Manager.

The job posting

This position requires ten years of experience, and the job description says that knowledge of employment law is important. Susan is a good match.

This position has requested that correspondence be sent in the following manner:

> 'Candidates may apply by sending their CV to Trendwest Resorts, Willows Road, Exeter, Devon EX4 2BH or by e-mail to pamelae@trendwestresorts.com.'

Responding by e-mail suggests technological adeptness, while a regular mail response offers another opportunity to get your CV brought to the top of the pile. You should do both.

Since the employer did not provide any additional directions, it is best for Susan to paste it into the body of the e-mail and also attach it as an MSWord document.

We want our electronic cover letter example to do three things: identify the purpose of sending this CV; emphasize why it deserves to be read; and get you an interview or next contact. Susan has accomplished these things with her cover letter.

An e-mail compatible cover letter

She succinctly states the purpose of her e-mail, hits her 'hot points' to get the reader's attention, and requests the follow-up information. Before closing this document, Susan needs to copy the entire letter. She does this by choosing 'select all' from the 'edit' pull-down menu, then, by choosing 'copy' from the 'edit' pull-down menu or Ctrl+C for Windows.

The next step is to create the e-mail, insert the cover letter text and the text only version of her CV, and then attach the formatted MSWord CV. From her inbox, Susan will create a new message by choosing 'compose' from the tabs along the top of the page. By placing her cursor within the message of the newly created e-mail, Susan can then paste the contents of her custom electronic cover letter in the message box. Simply choose 'paste' from the 'edit' pull-down menu or Ctrl+V for Windows.

With the cover letter safely pasted, turn your attention to addressing the e-mail to the proper recipient and establishing your subject line. From the job posting, you can copy and paste the e-mail to the address provided by the company. The subject line needs to be factual, professional, and intriguing. How about 'Your next Reg HR Manager – empl. law exp' or 'Reg HR Candidate – 10 yrs exp. w/empl. law.' Remember, the subject line may get your CV an immediate review instead of automatic computer upload. Give it adequate thought; subject lines usually accommodate about thirty characters, so take advantage of this.

Keep copies of all your correspondence. It's a good idea to keep track of exactly what you've sent out to avoid unnecessary repetitions. It also allows you to move messages from a general folder to a specific company-named folder once you have started a communication stream with an interested corporation.

Under the subject line of the new e-mail Susan created, there is a button for 'Add/Edit Attachments.' All programs will have a menu choice to insert documents; for example, in Microsoft Outlook, the paper clip icon designates the button for this function. Once you select this menu choice, you need to find the document that you want to attach. Follow the instructions on the screen. Once you have 'browsed' to locate the file, it may have you select 'open.' In Hotmail, once you've browsed and found the file you must then select 'attach.' The name of your file will then appear in the attachment box.

Attachments

Before you send a message, recall the two points made earlier when Susan came across this job posting. First, the employer did offer a suggested CV format. The most popular format is the one we have chosen, but it is not 100-per cent effective in the rare instances when an employer doesn't use Microsoft Word, or for some reason, cannot open the attachment. The sensible precaution you can always take is to paste your ASCII CV into the body of the e-mail, and attach your formatted Microsoft Word document, noting that you have done both in your e-mail cover letter.

Sending the message

Your goal is not so much to get your CV launched into cyberspace, but to get it read by a human being. With company e-mail addresses, the website name of the company is often the part that comes after the person's username and the '@' symbol. In this case it is safe to assume that if we break up the e-mail address of *pamelae@trendwestresorts.com*, we can probably find the company's home page at www.trendwestresorts.com. If that doesn't work, you can use Google or another search engine to look for 'Trendwest Resorts' (putting it in quotes will work best). You can then surf the site to look for a company career centre, the bios and contacts for company executives, and press releases about their business.

Your mission here is finding other potential inroads, other people to whom you can pitch yourself. With a little effort, you could make a direct connection to your next potential boss, gather information that will help you ace an interview, and garner you your dream job. As they say, luck comes to those who make it happen.

Now if you see a job posting that requires you to blindly respond to the HR department, but through your research have been able to identify specific executives likely to be involved in the hiring cycle: you can approach them directly. When you do this, it is best not to note that you are attempting to circumvent established procedures. You can achieve your ends by any number of ways you will find in my cover letter book, and you'll see an example in just a couple of paragraphs.

8

Cover letters

Tons of junk mail has probably made it through your letterbox over the years. Now, what do you do with the stuff marked 'Occupant'? Either bin it without reading, or after a quick glance. If you don't want this to be the fate of your CV, your covering letter is the best preventive tool you can employ.

The days when you could dash your CV off to 'Personnel', with a clear conscience and no personal note, are long gone. It will be read by the lowest of the low, someone who probably can't even spell 'professional'. You will be consigning it to the mass graveyard that all other impersonally addressed CVs reach.

Your cover letter is the personalizing factor in the presentation of an otherwise essentially impersonal document – your CV. A good cover letter sets the stage for the reader to accept your CV as something special.

The best way to start a cover letter is with someone's name, which alone dramatically increases the chances of it being read. It shows you have focus, and guarantees that a specific individual will open and read it. It also means you have someone to ask for by name when you do your follow-up – important when you are interview hunting.

Your target is someone who can either hire you or refer you to someone who can; a management title always offers you a more direct contact with the ultimate decision maker, but an HR name is good for different reasons. The HR contact can't make the hiring decisions (although he or she can have a strong influence), but their pivotal position makes them aware of other areas of the company that could use your skills. The moral is that any name is better than no name.

Your cover letter will either be sent to someone as a result of a prior conversation, or sent 'cold' – with no prior conversation. You will see how to handle both these eventualities as we progress through the chapter. When the envelope is opened, your cover letter is the first thing seen. It can make an indelible first impression. Of course your cover letter sets the tone for your candidacy, and done properly it will get your CV a careful examination.

You can find a wealth of practical advice on all the different letters you can use in an effective job hunt in this book's companion volume *Ultimate Cover Letters*.

Cover letter rules

The following four steps will help you create the body of the letter.

Step one

There are four basic building blocks to creating a productive cover letter, and the underlying rules of effective written communication embodied in these four steps can be applied to any memo or business letter you ever write.

Your first step is to grab your reader's ATTENTION. You do this with the appearance of your letter: the type is large and legible enough for others to read, it is free of misspellings and it is well laid out so that it is easy on the eye; and if that letter is going by mail rather than e-mail you grab attention by using quality stationery, and matching envelopes. This way your letter and CV will match and give an impression of balance and continuity (see chapter 6 for details on paper choice). When your message is crafted with this attention to detail, and convenience for the reader, it reflects the kind of professional who just might have something to say. Here is an example:

[YOUR ADDRESS/LETTERHEAD
AND TELEPHONE NUMBER]

[DATE]

[ADDRESSEE ADDRESS]
[SALUTATION]

Recently I have been researching the leading local companies in data communications. My search has been for companies that are respected in the field, and who provide ongoing training programmes. The name of DataLink Products keeps coming up as a top company.

I am an experienced voice and data communications specialist with a substantial background in IBM environments. If you have an opening for someone in this area you will see that my CV demonstrates a person of unusual dedication, efficiency and drive.

My experience and achievements include:

- The complete redesign of a data communications network, projected to increase efficiency companywide by some 12 per cent.
- The installation and troubleshooting of a Defender II call-back security system for a dial-up network.

I enclose a copy of my CV, and look forward to examining any of the ways you feel my background and skills would benefit DataLink Products. While I prefer not to use my employer's time taking personal calls at work, with discretion you can reach me at 020 8123 4567 to initiate contact. Let's talk!

Yours,

[SIGNATURE]
[TYPED NAME]

Step two

Generate interest with the content. You do this by addressing the letter to someone by name and quickly explaining what you have to offer: the first sentence grabs attention, the rest of the paragraph introduces your candidacy. The secret is to introduce yourself with conviction. If you don't believe in the professional product that is you, how can you expect anyone else to?

A little research, for example, can get your letter off to a fast start; with Google and other search engines, anyone can search the web for articles and visit the employer's own site. For example:

> *'I came across the enclosed article in Newsweek magazine and thought it might interest you. It encouraged me to do a little research on your company. I am now convinced of two things: You are the kind of people I want to be associated with, and I have the kind of qualifications you can use.'*

On a company's website you will find lots of eye-opening information, including news and press clippings. You can also use search engines to find interesting info about the company by typing in the company name as a keyword. Once you find a relevant article, you can use it in the following ways:

- with an e-mail, you paste the article and attach it;
- with a traditional letter, you enclose a copy of the article.

Of course, not every company you approach will have been mentioned in *Newsweek*, but even if there is no mention in the press, the chances are still good that their website can give you some insight that can be turned to your advantage. Here are some real-life examples that you can adapt to your own needs:

> I have been following the performance of your fund in *Mutual Funds Newsletter*. The record over the last three years shows strong portfolio management. Considering my experience with one of your competitors, I know I could make significant contributions.

> Recently, I have been researching the local _____ industry. My search has been for companies that are respected in the field and that provide ongoing training programmes. The name _____ keeps coming up as a top company.

> Within the next few weeks I will be moving from London to Edinburgh. Having researched the companies in my field in my new home town, I know that you are the people I want to talk to.

> The state of the art in _____ changes so rapidly that it is tough for most professionals to keep up. I am the exception. I am eager to bring my experience to bear for your company.

Step three

Now turn that INTEREST into DESIRE. First, make a bridge that ties you to a general job category or work area. It starts with phrases like:

> I am writing because …

> My reason for contacting you is …

> … should this be the case, you may be interested to know …

> If you are seeking a _____ , you will be interested to know …

> I would like to talk to you about your personnel needs and my ability to contribute to your department's goals.
>
> If you have an opening for someone in this area, you will see that my CV demonstrates a person of unusual dedication, efficiency and drive.

Then call attention to your merits with a short paragraph that highlights one or two of your special contributions or achievements.

> I have an economics background (LSE) and a strong analytical approach to market fluctuations. This combination has enabled me to consistently pick the new technology flotations that are the backbone of the growth-oriented mutual fund.

Similar statements applicable to your area of expertise will give your letter more personal punch. Include any qualifications, contributions and attributes that qualify you as someone with professional commitment and talent to offer. If an advertisement (or telephone conversation with a potential employer) revealed an aspect of a particular job opening that is not addressed in your CV, it can easily be covered in the cover letter. For example:

> I notice from your advertisement that audio and video training experience would be a plus. In addition to the qualifications stated in my enclosed CV, I have over five years' experience writing and producing sales and management training materials in both these media.

It is through this third step that you want the reader to say 'Wow, this man/woman really understands the job. I need to read on and learn more.'

Step four

Here's where your letter turns that DESIRE into ACTION. You want to make the reader dash straight to your CV, then call you in for an interview. You achieve this with brevity – always leave the reader wanting more. Offer too much information and you could be ruled out of consideration, so whet the reader's appetite, but leave them asking questions.

Make it clear to the reader that you want to talk. Explain when, where and how you can be contacted. You can also be proactive by telling the reader that you intend to follow up at a certain point in time if contact has not been established by then. Just as you worked to create a strong opening, make sure your closing carries the same conviction. It is the reader's last personal impression of you, so make it strong, make it right and make it obvious that you are serious about entering into meaningful conversation.

Useful phrases include:

- I look forward to discussing our mutual interests further.
- It would be a pleasure to give you more information about my qualifications and experience.
- While I prefer not to use my employer's time taking personal calls at work, with discretion I can be contacted at _____.
- I will be in your area around the 20th, and will call you prior to that date to arrange a meeting.
- I hope to speak with you further and will call the week of the 20th to follow up.
- The chance to meet with you would be a privilege and a pleasure. To this end I will call you on the 20th.
- I look forward to speaking to you further and will call in the next few days to see when our schedules will permit a face-to-face meeting.
- May I suggest a personal meeting where you can have the opportunity to examine the person behind the CV?
- My credentials and achievements are a matter of record that I hope you will examine in depth when we meet.
- I look forward to examining any of the ways you feel my background and skills would benefit your organization. I look forward to hearing from you.
- CVs help you sort out the probables from the possibles, but they are no way to judge the true calibre of an individual. I should like to meet you and demonstrate that I have the personality that makes for a successful _____ .
- After reading my CV, you will know something about my background. Yet you will still need to determine whether I am the one to help with the current problems and challenges. I would like an interview to discuss my ability to contribute.
- I expect to be in your area on Tuesday and Wednesday of next week and wonder which day would be best for you. I will call to find out. In the meantime I would appreciate your treating my application as confidential, since I am currently employed.
- With my training and hands-on experience, I know I can contribute to your company, and want to speak with you about it in person. When may we meet?

- You can reach me at 020 8123 4567 to arrange an interview. I know that your time investment in meeting with me will be amply repaid.
- Thank you for your time and consideration. I hope to hear from you shortly.
- May I call you for an interview in the next few days?
- A brief phone call will establish whether or not we have mutual interest. Recognizing the demands of your schedule, I will make that call within the week.

Some people think that it is powerful in the closing to state a date – 'I'll call you on Friday if we don't speak before' – or a date and time – 'I'll call you on Friday morning at 10am if we don't speak before' when they intend to follow up with a phone call. The logic is that you demonstrate that your intent is serious, that you are organized and that you plan your time effectively (all desirable behavioural traits).

On the other hand, at least one 'authority' has said that an employer would be offended by being forced to sit and await your call. Frankly, with thirty years of involvement in the hiring process, I have never met anyone who felt constrained to wait by the phone for such a call. What sometimes does get noticed though, is the person who doesn't follow through on commitments as promised. Therefore, if you use this approach keep your promise.

Writing the cover letter

Keep your sentences short – an average of 20 words per sentence is about right. Likewise, your paragraphs should be concise and to the point. In cover letters, paragraphs can often be a single sentence, and should never be longer than five lines. This makes the page more inviting for the harried reader, by providing adequate white space to ease eye strain.

Short words work best as they speak more clearly than those polysyllabic behemoths that say more about your self-image problems than your abilities. A good approach is to think in terms of sending a telegram, where every word must work its hardest.

While abiding by accepted grammatical rules, you should punctuate for readability rather than strictly following E. B. White or the *Oxford Manual of Style*. Get by on commas, dashes – and full stops. And in between the punctuation marks use the action verbs and phrases that breathe life into your work.

The executive briefing

The executive briefing is a different and dramatically effective form of cover letter, whenever you have some information about a job opening from a recruitment ad, an online job posting, or a prior conversation. This kind of letter gets right to the point and makes life easy for the reader. Why send an executive briefing?

1. It quickly matches stated requirements against the skills you bring to the table, making analysis much easier for the reader.
2. The initial CV screener in Human Resources (HR) might not have an in-depth understanding of the job or its requirements, so the executive briefing helps match an open requirement directly to your abilities. This can be a real help to someone working on fifty or more different openings at a time.
3. Your general CV invariably needs customizing for any specific job. (Overly broad CVs are like 'one-size-fits-all' clothes – one size usually fits none.) The executive briefing allows you to fill in the gaps in a succinct and helpful manner.
4. Imagine for a moment that a great opportunity comes your way, but your CV is somewhat (or more than somewhat) out of date and you have to send something out immediately to take advantage of the opportunity of a lifetime. The executive briefing allows you to bring that work history right up to date.

An executive briefing can also help you through a screening and multiple interview cycle. Let me explain: you will be interviewed by a number of people, not all of whom can be expected to have a thorough understanding of the needs of the job – perhaps surprising but nevertheless true. When this happens, the problems begin.

A manager says, 'Spend a few minutes with this candidate and tell me what you think.' This means that sometimes other interviewers do not have any way to qualify you fairly and specifically for the needs of the job. While the manager will be looking for specific skills relating to projects at hand, the personnel department will be trying to match your skills to the vagaries of the job-description manual.

Also, by taking multiple copies of your CV and the briefing, carefully stapled together, you guarantee that everyone with whom you interview will have the job's specific requirements and your matching skills front and centre when they sit down with you.

The executive briefing, which introduces your CV, as well as customizing and supplementing it, solves the above problems with its layout. It looks like this:

From: top10acct@aol.com
Subject: Re: Accounting Manager
Date: February 18, 2005 10:05:44 PM EST
To: rlstein@McCoy.com

Dear Ms. Stein,

I have nine years of accounting experience and am responding to your recent posting for an Accounting Manager on Careerbuilder. Please allow me to highlight my skills as they relate to your stated requirements.

Your Requirements	My Experience
Accounting degree, 4 years exp	Obtained a C.A. degree in 2000 and have over four years' experience as an Accounting Manager.
Excellent people skills and leadership	Effectively managed a staff of 24, ability to motivate staff including supervisors.
Strong administrative and analytical skills	Assisted in the development of a base reference skills library with Microsoft Excel for 400 clients.
Good communication skills	Trained new supervisors and staff via daily coaching sessions, communication meetings, and technical skill sessions.

My CV, pasted below and attached in MSWord, will flesh out my general background. I hope this executive briefing helps you use your time effectively today. I am ready to make a move, hope we can talk soon.

Sincerely,

Joe Black

The executive briefing assures that each CV you send out addresses the job's specific needs and that every interviewer at that company will be interviewing you for the same job. It provides a comprehensive picture of a thorough professional, plus a personalized, fast, and easy-to-read synopsis that details exactly how you can help with an employer's needs.

The use of an executive briefing is naturally restricted to jobs you have discovered through your own efforts or seen advertised. It is obviously not appropriate when the requirements of a specific job are unavailable.

James Sharpe   16 November 20__
123 Anystreet, Anytown AT1 0BB

Dear Mr Bell,

Recently, I have been researching the leading local companies in data communications. My search has been for companies that are respected in the field, and who provide ongoing training programmes. DataLink Products keeps coming up as a top company.

I am an experienced voice and data communications specialist with a substantial background in IBM environments. *If you have an opening for someone in this area you will see that my CV demonstrates a person of unusual dedication, efficiency and drive.*

My experience and achievements include:

- complete redesign of a data communications network, projected to increase efficiency companywide some 12 per cent;
- the installation and troubleshooting of a Defender II call-back security system for a dial-up network.

I enclose a copy of my CV, and look forward to examining any of the ways you feel my background and skills would benefit DataLink Products. While I prefer not to use my employer's time taking personal calls at work, with discretion I can be reached at 020 8123 4567 to initiate contact. Let's talk!

Yours truly

James Sharpe

James Sharpe

In response to the advertisement, here is an example using a different selection of phrases.

Jane Swift   16 November 20__
123 Anystreet, Anytown AT1 0BB

Dear Ms Pena,

I have always followed the performance of your fund in *Mutual Funds Newsletter.*

Recently, your notice regarding a Market Analyst in Investors Daily caught my eye – and your company name caught my attention – because your record over the last three years shows exceptional portfolio management. With my experience with one of your competitors, I know I could make significant contributions.

I would like to talk to you about your personnel needs and how I would be able to contribute to your department's goals.

An experienced market analyst, I have an economics background and a strong analytical approach to market fluctuations. This combination has enabled me to consistently pick the new technology flotations that are the backbone of the growth-oriented mutual fund.

For example, I first recommended Fidelity Magellan six years ago. More recently, my clients have been strongly invested in Pacific Horizon Growth (in the high-risk category), and Fidelity Growth and Income (for the cautious investor).

Those following my advice over the last six years have owned shares in funds which consistently outperformed the market.

I know that CVs help you sort out the probables from the possibles, but they are no way to judge the personal calibre of an individual. I would like to meet you and demonstrate that, along with the credentials, I have the personality that makes for a successful team player.

Yours sincerely

Jane Swift

Jane Swift

As you can see, the letter is a variation on a theme, and as such might have a place in your marketing campaign.

Here is an example of a cover letter sent as a result of a conversation.

Dear Ms _____ ,

I am writing in response to our telephone conversation on Friday the 10th regarding a new- and used-car sales management position.

   With a successful track record in both new- and used-car sales, and as a sales manager, I believe I am ideally suited for the position we discussed. My exposure to the different levels of the sales process (I started at the bottom and worked my way up) has enabled me to effectively meet the challenges and display the leadership you require.

   I am a competitive person professionally. Having exercised the talents and skills required to exceed goals and set records as a Sales Manager, I believe in measuring performance by results.

   I would appreciate your consideration for a meeting where I could discuss in more detail my sales and management philosophy, and capabilities. Please call me at your earliest convenience to arrange a personal meeting.

Sincerely yours,

James Sharpe

James Sharpe

Finally, here is an example of the somewhat different cover letter you would send to a corporate headhunter:

Dear Mr _____ ,

As you may be aware, the management structure at XYZ Ltd will be reorganized in the near future. While I am enthusiastic about the future of the company under its new leadership, I have elected to make this an opportunity for change and professional growth.

My many years of experience lends itself to a management position in any medium-sized service firm, but I am open to other opportunities. Although I would prefer to remain in Liverpool, I would be amenable to relocation if the opportunity warrants it. I am currently earning £65,000 a year.

I have taken the liberty of enclosing my CV for your review. Should you be conducting a search for someone with my background – at the present time or in the near future – I would greatly appreciate your consideration. I would be happy to discuss my background more fully with you on the phone or in a personal interview.

Very truly yours,

James Sharpe

James Sharpe

9

A balanced job search

Companies are always looking for employees. Even a company with no growth rate can still be expected (based on national averages) to experience a 12 per cent turnover in staff over the course of a year. In other words, every company has openings.

A man who goes fishing and puts one hook in the water has only one chance of catching any one of the millions of fish in the sea; a man with two hooks in the water has double the chances of getting a bite, so the more hooks you have in the water, the better your chances of getting bites.

There are many, many ways to get interviews using the internet, apart from responding to job postings; there are proven and effective techniques for networking, tools to research and approach employers directly, productive ways to use newspapers and magazines, techniques for tapping into the different headhunter communities, and many more, but no single channel of search is a guaranteed silver bullet. Any one of them could turn up the ideal opportunity for you and your future, so your plan of attack should embrace as many of these approaches as is practical to your situation.

I have touched on distribution of your CV as much as space will allow me in these pages. Your CV is an integral part of every single approach to job search approach and continues its job throughout the interview and selection cycle.

It may surprise you that the role of your CV doesn't end with helping you get a foot in the door. If you followed my advice to focus your CV first on a specific target job, and then went about deconstructing the deliverables of that job from relevant recruitment advertising, you will have a CV that not only opens doors, but one that helps you prepare for the interview cycle.

After all, you created a job description based on those developed by employers and your CV reflects this focus. Consequently you already know the areas that employers are going to want to discuss and you know what you have to offer in these areas; with this blueprint you can set about preparing for the toughest of interviews with a degree of self-confidence.

Because your CV has been built with the end user in mind, tailored to their needs and reflective of their language, there is a much greater likelihood that your CV will already have set a positive tone for your meetings and may well be used as a roadmap for the interviewers' questions.

Always take multiple copies of your CV with you to interviews. Often you can attach it to those annoying application forms and then just write on the form "See attached CV." You can have one on your lap during the interview to refer to, as the interviewer has one on his desk; it makes you look organized and helps to keep you from doing anything awkward or socially unacceptable with your hands. You can also offer copies to subsequent interviewers.

Your CV will even work for you long after the last interview is finished. Before the hiring decision is made, hiring managers usually sit down with the dossiers on leading candidates as a last refresher, so that a properly constructed CV can indeed not only open doors, prepare you for the interview and guide the course of the interview, it can also be your last and most powerful spokesperson. It is this agglomeration of reasons that makes the careful development of a properly focused CV such a valuable exercise for your future.

Your CV's impact goes far beyond opening doors and is well worth the investment of time it will take to get it right. Now take a little of that time to read through all the samples with your highlighter, flagging those phrases, words and layouts that you feel might work for you, when adapted to your profession and particular work experience.

This probably won't be the last time you execute a job search, but invest yourself properly in understanding all the component parts of a successful plan of attack, and your future steps up the ladder of success will be the better for it.

10

The CVs

The CVs on the following pages are based on the genuine articles, the ones that really did the trick for someone who had to translate his or her fantastic skills and background into a single, compelling document. Whether or not your background is represented in the following samples, use the CVs reproduced here as a starting point for composing your own.

Registered nurse

To emphasize Chantile's objective, a title was used in place of a statement along with a tag line to highlight the medical units where she has worked. Her jobs are grouped together to make it easier to read while allowing the CV to remain on one page.

CHANTILE FAUSETT

1 ANY ROAD, ANYTOWN, ANYSHIRE AX0 0AA • 020 8123 4567 • ERNurse@med.net

REGISTERED NURSE
ER...Shock/Trauma...Immediate Care...Triage

- Two years experience as a Registered Nurse in ER, Shock/Trauma, Immediate Care and Triage units.
- Hardworking and energetic; adapt easily to change, stressful environments, and flexible work schedules.
- Maintain strong observation, assessment, and intervention skills essential to providing competent patient care.
- Advocate for patients/family rights; effectively communicate a patient's needs and concerns to medical team.

Education

Western Community College, Brentwood, Essex
Currently enrolled in Graduate Medical Programme with a concentration in Nursing, 2005–Present
Coursework: Anatomy and Physiology, Chemistry, Psychology, Sociology, Statistics

Diploma in Nursing 2006
North Brentwood School of Nursing, Brentwood, Essex
Clinical Skills Upgrade Programme 2007

Licences & Certifications
Registered Clinical Nurse Assistant, 2006
Basic EKG and Phlebotomy

Professional Experience

Registered Nurse, North Brentwood Hospital, Brentwood, Essex	4/04–Present
– prior positions: Hospital Attendant; Pharmacist Assistant	Evening/Night Shifts
Pharmacist Assistant, One Way Pharmacy, West Islip, Essex	6/02–10/03
Customer Service Representative, Safeway Transportation, Islip, Essex	5/02–6/03

- Work with a team of nurses and physicians throughout Emergency Room, Shock/Trauma, Immediate Care, and Triage departments for Brentwood Hospital, one of the only Level 1 Trauma hospitals in Essex.
- Care for up to 200 patients per shift within a 29-bed Emergency Room Unit, and for patients in a 7-bed Trauma Unit; assist with intubating of patients, life support systems and general post mortem procedures.
- Provide direct patient care in areas of vital signs, phlebotomy, EKGs, treatment of surgical wounds, gynaecological examinations, Activities of Daily Living, and patient transportation within the hospital.
- Prepare patients for transfer to all critical care units, demonstrating quick thinking skills and ability to multitask while remaining focused and calm under pressure.
- Under the direction of the staff nurse, perform initial assessments of patients upon admission within a fast-paced Triage unit, and establish a Plan-of-Care for all patients.
- Assist orthopaedic physicians with splinting, casting, positioning, and set up of tractions.
- Closely monitor and report changes in patients' conditions and malfunctioning of medical equipment.

Registered nurse

Cheryl used this CV to land her first RN position straight out of college.

Cheryl Bloom, RN

1 Any Road, Anytown, Ayrshire AX0 0AA • 020 8123 4567

Registered Nurse

✔ Strongly motivated graduate with experience in hospital, sub-acute and other health care settings.
✔ Clinical skills combine with dedication to excellent patient care, compassion, and professionalism to integrate patients' medical and emotional care.
✔ Able to relate to patients quickly and work effectively with physicians, peers and other health care professionals. Conscientious, team-oriented and eager to learn.

Education, Licensure and Certification

B.Sc in Nursing, 2005
Chenneworth College, Croton, Northamptonshire

Registered Nurse, 2006

Basic Life Support with Automatic External Defibrillator, British Heart Association
COR, British Heart Association
Certified Nursing Assistant, 2003

Additional: Maths and Science courses, Flynn Community College

Areas of Knowledge & Skills

- Physical Assessments
- Vital Signs/Blood Glucose
- Catheter Insertion
- Finger Sticks
- Patient & Family Education

- Dispensing Medications/Intravenous Therapy
- Documentation/Care Maps
- Nasopharangeal & Oral Suctioning
- Application of Dressings/Wound Care
- Cast Care/Pin Care/Traction Care/Tracheotomy Care

Clinical Training

Acquired hands-on clinical experience and knowledge in nursing procedures while completing several rotations at the following facilities. Experience with patients ranging from paediatric to geriatric.

Medical-Surgical Rockport General Hospital
OB/GYN Melville Memorial Hospital
Paediatric Montessori School
Gerontology Evergreen Health Care Centre, Mediplex, Kimberley Hall, Northampton

Employment in Health Care

Patient Care Technician – Jackson Memorial Hospital, Croton   2003–present
Provide post-operative care to patients on an 80-bed Medical-Surgical Unit. Diverse responsibilities include: monitoring vital signs, blood glucose and tube intake/output, collecting specimens, assisting with personal hygiene and feeding, and recording patient status. Transport patients to medical procedures and operating portable electrocardiogram. Educate patients and family members on home care.

Prior Employment

Waitress, Calinda's Restaurant, Preston   1998–2005
Earned reputation for dependability, accuracy and delivering superior customer service by providing well-timed, professional service. Demonstrated skills in communication, organization and problem solving, as well as ability to work efficiently in a fast-paced environment. Gained computer skills.

Registered nurse

Kate-Lynne went back to college for RN certification and needed a CV to highlight her new degree as well as her previous experience as an LPN and Certified Nurses' Aide.

Kate-Lynne Kennedy, RN

1 Anystreet
Anytown, Ayrshire AX0 0AA

Tel: 020 8123 4567

PROFILE

Recent RN graduate with over 10 years experience in healthcare and nursing profession. Comprehensive knowledge of nursing procedures and committed to delivering quality patient care. Successful in managing time and prioritizing tasks. Communicate well with staff, family, and patients. Punctual, reliable, and able to be counted on in a crisis.

Awarded scholarship from the Long-Term Care Federation for continued studies in nursing.

EDUCATION

Bachelor of Science in Nursing, May, 2007
University of South London, School of Nursing

CPR, The British Heart Association, 1997

PROFESSIONAL EXPERIENCE

Mendelsohn House – London   2001–2004

Charge Nurse
Provided quality patient care in a 200-bed residential nursing facility. Supervised Certified Nursing Assistants, Rehabilitation Aides, and assisted in training new licensed staff. Performed patient assessments, developed care plans, and coordinated with other disciplines including: physical therapy, occupational therapy, dietary, activities, and consult with psychologists, pharmacists, and social workers regularly. Distributed medications, as indicated by physicians; order and document labs by lab cards.

- Supervised night-shift as the one licensed nurse on duty.
- Provided patient care in Unit, observing patients' progress with medication, treatment and rehabilitation; revised shift documentation, ensuring accuracy and completeness of forms and monthly summaries.
- Resolved pharmacy problems relating to delays and reimbursement issues and ensured compliance with documentation requirements.
- Received rarely issued management recognition award for excellence in nursing, flexibility, and willingness to work varied shifts to accommodate scheduling needs.

UNITY HEALTHCARE – Mountain View, Cardiff   1999–2001

Nurse
Provided outsourced nursing care in various settings: Medsurg, Detox, Special Needs School, Long-term Care, Group Home, Adult Care.

CITY INFIRMARY, Birmingham   1993–1999

Charge Nurse (1997–1999); ***Certified Nurses' Aide***   (1993–1997)
Supervised staff of six CNAs, and one Rehabilitation Aide, in providing nursing care for two floors, 35 patients each. Monitored blood glucose, labs, therapeutic drug levels and equipment; performed assessments, treatments, and documentation. Organized staff/patient assignments and patient care.

Hospital nurse

Stephanie recently completed a special programme allowing LPNs to earn RN status by completing just two terms of college. She is looking to make the leap to an RN position in a hospital.

Stephanie A Monaco

1 Anystreet, • Anytown AX0 0AA • 020 8123 4567 • sam862@yahoo.com

SUMMARY:
Graduate Nurse with over 12 years' healthcare experience, which includes patient care in long-term care facilities and private homes. Experience dealing with a broad range of medical conditions, including ventilator-dependent, dialysis, cardiac rehabilitation, post-operative orthopaedic, emphysema, heart failure, and Alzheimer patients. Outstanding interpersonal skills, including strong patient rapport, excellent ability to relate to patient families, and capacity to interact with nurses, physicians, and other providers. Demonstrated leadership skills, including directing activities of nursing aides and fulfilling other supervisory functions.

PROFESSIONAL EXPERIENCE
Staff Nurse, Strong Memorial Hospital; Rochester, Kent   **Jan. 2006–Present**
– Provide direct patient care for two to five patients in a critical care step-down unit.
– Address patients' respiratory needs, including ventilator care.
– Implement treatment plans consistent with directions of physicians and RNs.

Team Leader, The Hemlock Hills Living Centre; Mendon, Wilts   **2002–2005**
(An Affiliate of Highland Hospital & Strong Health)
– Accountable for day-to-day care of up to 50 residents in a long-term care setting.
– Supervised and delegated duties to six Certified Nursing Aides.
– Addressed treatment needs of Alzheimer, kidney dialysis, and cardiac/orthopaedic rehab. patients.
– Conferred with physicians, therapists, and other providers to develop and implement care plans.
– Assessed residents on a daily basis and reported changes to physicians and/or Nurse Practitioners.
– Interacted with families of residents to discuss care plans and otherwise address any concerns.
– Assisted Registered Nurse in fulfilling 'Charge Nurse' duties on a recurring basis.

Nurse's Aide (Private Duty), The Collins Family/William R Jeffords; Rochester, Kent
1997–2002
– Addressed daily living needs of geriatric patients in their homes.
– Under direction of RNs and physicians, administered medications for heart failure and hypertension.
– Assisted clients with nutrition, ambulation, and daily exercise regimes.
– Conferred with nurses, physicians, and family members to discuss care plans and other issues.

Personal Care Assistant (Private Duty), Emerline VanderGelder; Rochester, Kent **1986–1987**
– Fulfilled the daily living needs of patient with emphysema and congestive heart failure.

page 1 of 2

Stephanie A Monaco
page 2 of 2

EDUCATION:
Associate of Applied Science, Nursing   **May 2005**
Monroe Community College; Rochester, Kent
Enrolled in Advanced Standing Two Term Option

BSc Nursing Practice   **2002**
Isabella Graham Hart School of Practical Nursing; Rochester, Kent
Clinical Rotations at The County Hospital

CERTIFICATIONS:
Registered Nurse/CPR Certified/Basic Life Support (BLS)/Telemetry Certified

References Available Upon Request

Trauma treatment

Richard is leaving the Navy, where he gained a great deal of experience in trauma treatment and crisis management

RICHARD P ISAACS, RN, BSN

1 Anystreet • Anytown, Any County AX0 0HA • 020 8123 4567 • Richi@cs.com

....

DISASTER RESPONSE • ACUTE & CRITICAL PATIENT CARE • MEDICAL/SURGICAL CARE
Paediatrics/Geriatrics/Post-Surgical/Nuclear & Biological Hazards

Health care professional with over eight years' intensive experience in fast-paced military hospital environments. Demonstrated capacity to provide direct patient care and effectively supervise support staff in a variety of clinical settings. Specialized training in dealing with nuclear and biological exposure, as well as experience treating patients with infectious diseases including Typhoid, Meningitis, AIDS, and other contagions. Proven capacity to function well in crisis situations, plus excellent ability to relate to patients from diverse cultural backgrounds and various age groups.

....

PRIMARY CLINICAL EXPERIENCE

LIEUTENANT, Royal Navy (2003–Present)
UK Naval Hospital; Gibraltar
Patients encompass infants through geriatrics, with conditions including a broad range of infectious diseases and physical injuries.

Staff Nurse/Charge Nurse – Adult & Paediatric Care   **May 2007–Present**
- Provide bedside care to patients; administer medications and implement physician orders.
- Confer with physicians and other care team members on treatment plans for various patients.
- Address the needs of patients in isolation with Typhoid, Meningitis, and other contagious diseases.
- Train and provide leadership for staff of seven RNs and LPNs in Charge Nurse role.
- Participate in field exercises to maintain readiness for combat deployment in support of Marine units.

Key Accomplishment:
Restructured medical supplies inventory and wrote new Standard Operating Procedures (SOPs) to improve departmental efficiencies.

Staff Nurse/Division Officer – Post Anaesthesia Care Unit   **May 2006–May 2007**
- Served needs of post-operative patients, addressing special concerns of post anaesthesia recovery.
- Otherwise supported surgical teams in treating patients with a broad range of medical conditions.

Naval Hospital, Plymouth
Patient base included military dependents and retirees, as well as active military personnel; including several 'VIP' patients.

Staff Nurse – Medical/Telemetry Acute Care Unit   **April 2003–April 2006**
- Addressed acute care needs of medical patients, including oncology and infectious disease patients.
- Cared for patients in isolation wards with tuberculosis, AIDS, and other contagious diseases.
- Monitored cardiac activity of patients using state-of-the-art telemetry technology.

Richard P Isaacs, RN
Page Two

Accomplishment:
Selected to serve as part of Humanitarian Relief Response Team.

PRIMARY CLINICAL EXPERIENCE *(continued)*:

STOCKPORT GENERAL HOSPITAL; Cheshire

Staff Nurse/Charge Nurse – Medical/Surgical Unit   2000–2003

- Provided direct patient care including telemetry monitoring.
- Served needs of incarcerated individuals in conjunction with police service.

ADDITIONAL CLINICAL EXPERIENCE:

EXPOSERVE MEDICAL SERVICES; Yorks.

Per Diem Registered Nurse – York Children's Centre   2003–2006
- Served the needs of paediatric patients in a clinical outpatient setting.

HEARTLAND NURSING SERVICES; Riverhead, Yorks.

Per Diem Registered Nurse   2002–2003
- Cared for burn victims, cardiac patients, post-surgical patients, ICU patients, and the terminally ill.

EDUCATION:

NORTH YORKSHIRE UNIVERSITY
Master of Science, Community Service   May, 2007

NORTH YORKSHIRE UNIVERSITY
BSc (Hons), Nursing   May 2001

UNIVERSITY OF WALES
Associate of Science, Hotel & Restaurant Management   June 1986

CERTIFICATIONS/SPECIALIZED TRAINING:

Registered Nurse
Advanced Cardiac Life Support (ACLS); Basic Life Support (BLS)
Paediatric Advanced Life Support (PALS I)
Intravenous Conscious Sedation (IVCS)

Nuclear & Biological Hazard Medical Training
Mass Casualty Training; Field Hospital Training; Shipboard Hospital Training
Suturing; Chest Tube Insertion

References Provided On Request

Nurse

Sarah Vincent
1 Anystreet, Anytown, AX0 0AA
Phone: 020 8123 4567 Email: svincent@yahoo.com

NURSING PROFESSIONAL
Registered Nurse

EDUCATION

BSc (Hons) Nursing Studies – Current
Kaplan College, West Somerset

Advanced Diploma in Nursing – 2000
St. Petersburg Community College, Wilts.

CERTIFICATIONS/TRAINING

Advanced Cardiac Life Support (ACLS)
Paediatric Advanced Life Support (PALS)
EMT-Tactical, Counter-Narcotics Tactical Operations
Introduction to Chemical, Biological & Radiological Defence

Associate in Science in EMS Management – 1995
EMT and Paramedic Certification Programme
St. Petersburg Community College, Wilts.

PROFESSIONAL EXPERIENCE

Registered Nurse – Emergency Room, Radiology Specialist
MEASE HOSPITAL, Cardiff
Current
General nursing duties within a critical care setting.

SWAT Paramedic
MEASE HOSPITAL, Cardiff
1993 to 2003
Directed field medical patient care and supervision.

Medical Assistant, 2nd Class,
NAVAL RESERVE, Plymouth
1994 to 2002
Provided field medical patient care and coordinated
urinalysis, immunization, and annual medical/dental
screening programmes.

Emergency Medical Services to Lab Supervisor
HILLSBOROUGH COMMUNITY COLLEGE, Hillsborough
1999 to 2002
Monitored and assessed student progress.

QUALIFICATIONS SUMMARY

Competent and knowledgeable medical professional with more than 10 years of increasingly responsible experience. Effective critical thinking, problem solving, and interpersonal skills.

EXPERTISE

Legal Nurse Consultant

- Direct initial client assessments to identify potential liability

- Organize and review medical charts and records

- Review surgeons and expert witness depositions

Nursing Expertise

- Direct patient care and advocacy

- Triage

- Intubation and airway management

- Medication administration

- Cardiac monitoring and EKG rhythm interpretation

- Conscious sedation

- Counselling and education

- Chart review quality assurance

Occupational therapist

A great combination style CV for a recent master's degree graduate

EVELYN WILLIAMS   ewilliams@earthlink.com

Value to your organization   426 Lincolnshire Lane
Bowling Green, Oxford OX1 7LE
020 8123 4567

- **Interpersonal skills** achieved by successfully communicating with physicians, patients, professors, co-workers, visitors, hospital personnel, and other agencies.

- **Leadership skills** displayed by developing and directing groups related to stress management, substance abuse awareness, assertiveness training, and self-awareness; volunteer assistant basketball coach.

- **Problem-solving skills** gleaned by determining and providing individualized care and rehab to patients with neurological, orthopaedic, and generalized diagnoses in home and clinical settings, and by visualizing and preparing goals with functional outcomes to maximize patient independence level.

- **Organizational skills** as evidenced by the ability to manage and prioritize tasks in a fast-paced environment, co-organized EMU Reach Out 'Run for the Homeless.'

EDUCATION

EASTERN UNIVERSITY, Norwich
Master of Occupational Therapy, 2006

EASTERN UNIVERSITY, Norwich
Bachelor of Arts in Psychology, 2004

WORK EXPERIENCE

1/06–Present   **PRIVATE RESIDENCE**, Birmingham
Home Health Aide
8/04–12/05   **EVERGREEN CARE & REHABILITATION CENTRE**, Birmingham
Certified Nursing Assistant
9/03–8/04   **RAINBOW REHABILITATION CENTRE**, Chester
Rehab Assistant –Traumatic Brain Injury

CLINICAL/PRE-CLINICAL EXPERIENCE

3/04–6/04   **ST. VINCENT MEDICAL CENTRE**, Chester
Physical Dysfunction, Inpatient Acute Care Setting
1/04–3/04   **HERITAGE HOSPITAL**, Cheltenham
Psychosocial Dysfunction, Inpatient Psychiatric Hospital
9/03–12/03   **McPHERSON HOME SERVICES**, Howell, Cheltenham
Occupational Therapy in Home-Based Community Setting
1/03–4/03   **INTENSIVE PSYCHIATRIC COMMUNITY CARE**, Gloucester
Intensive Clinical Case Management, Department of Health

ACTIVITIES & AFFILIATIONS

UK Occupational Therapy Association; EMU Stoic Society Member.

ADDITIONAL SKILLS

- First Aid • NeuroDevelopment Techniques • CPR • MMT
- Bloodborne Pathogens • ADL • Adaptive Equipment
- Pre-fabricated Splinting • Spanish • Microsoft Office XP

Ophthalmic doctor assistant/technician

Career transition: This former sales representative attained her ophthalmic certification and then obtained successful employment in her new field.

THERESA R KEEBLER
020 8123 4567 48 Derry Lane, Anytown, Any County AX0 0AA

OPHTHALMIC DOCTOR ASSISTANT/TECHNICIAN
Building organizational value by assisting with diagnostic and treatment-oriented procedures

Technical Skills:

Precise Refracting/
  Work Up
Scribing
Goniometry
Sterile Techniques

*Procedures and
  Treatments:*

Chalazion Surgery
Glaucoma Treatments
Conjunctivitis
Diabetes Monitoring
Retinopathy of
  Prematurity
Macular Degeneration
Strabismus
Cataracts
Palsy
NLD Obstruction
Blepharoplasty

Equipment:

A Scans
Lasers
Tonometry
Slit Lamp
Lensonetry
Keratometer
Visual Fields
Topography

QUALIFICATIONS SUMMARY

Personable and capable professional experienced in conducting diagnostic tests; measuring and recording vision; testing eye muscle function; inserting, removing, and caring for contact lenses; and applying eye dressings. Competently assist physicians during surgery, maintain optical and surgical instruments, and administer eye medications. Extensive knowledge in ophthalmic medications dealing with glaucoma, cataract surgery, and a wide variety of other diagnoses.

PROFESSIONAL EXPERIENCE

AUGUSTA EYE ASSOCIATES, Bristol – since 2005
Hired as a **Technician/Assistant** for a cornea specialist in a large ophthalmic practice. Performed histories, vision screenings, pupil exams, and precise manifest refractions. Assisted with a variety of surgical procedures. Quickly build trust and rapport and streamline processes to ensure physician efficiency.

GUGGINO FAMILY EYE CENTRE, Bath – 2004 to 2005
Taught customer service techniques and promoted twice within two months to an **Ophthalmic Doctor Assistant** for a paediatric neurology ophthalmologist performing scribing, taking histories, preparing patients for examination, and educating patients on treatment procedures.

DAVEL COMMUNICATIONS, Bath – 2001 to 2003
Recruited as a **Regional Account Manager** and promoted within 3 months of hire to **National Account Manager**. Contributed to the company doubling in size within 10 months; maintained a 100% satisfied customer retention rate.

CHILI'S BAR & GRILL, Neath – 1995 to 2000
Hired as a **Hostess** and quickly promoted to Server.

EDUCATION

Bachelor of Science, Organizational Communication – 2001
University of Wales

CERTIFICATION

Certified Ophthalmic Assistant (COA) – expected July 2008

Dental assistant

Burton wanted a position with a larger practice. The CV highlighted his extensive training and certifications as well as experience. It contains lots of information, in a great layout

Burton Roberts, CDA

Dental Assistant • CDA, EFDA, CPR Certified

GENERAL OR SPECIALITY PRACTICE
ORAL SURGERY • PERIODONTICS • ENDODONTICS • ORTHODONTICS

Highly skilled, energetic and flexible dental professional with experience in 4-handed dentistry, radiology, sterilization, laboratory, and office duties. Adept at earning patient's trust and confidence. Demonstrated initiative and commitment, and a proven asset to a growing practice.

DENTAL SKILLS SUMMARY

- 4-Handed Dentistry
- Preventive Care
- Instrument Sterilization
- Diagnostic X-Rays
- Infection Control
- Oral Surgery/Extractions
- Emergency Treatment
- Prosthetics/Restorations
- Teeth Whitening
- Casts/Impressions
- Root Canals
- Patient Education

CHAIRSIDE EXPERIENCE
- Prepare tray setups for dental procedures. Obtain dental records prior to appointment.
- Prepare patients for procedures – ensure comfort and develop trust; calm distressed patients; instruct patients on postoperative and general oral health care; take and record medical and dental histories.
- Oversee cleanliness of operatories and instruments; ensure safe/sanitary conditions using autoclave, ultrasound, and dry heat instrument sterilization.
- Assist dentist with extractions, fillings, and sealants. Take casts and impressions for prosthetics/restorations.

LABORATORY EXPERIENCE
- Prepare materials for impressions and restorations.
- Pour models and make casts.
- Expose radiographs and process X-ray film.

OFFICE EXPERIENCE
- Greet patients; arrange and confirm appointments; keep treatment records.
- Order dental supplies and materials; maintain stock in accordance with monthly budgets.
- Develop and document office policies and procedures. Share best practices with staff.

PROFESSIONAL HISTORY
Chairside Assistant, Dr. George Rose, Dublin   January 2005–Present
Student Intern/Chairside Assistant, Dr. Victoria Mercer, Dublin   September 2004–December 2004
Student Intern/Nitrous Oxide/Oxygen Administration, Dr. John Mann, Belfast   October 2004

EDUCATION AND PROFESSIONAL DEVELOPMENT

CPR Certification – Adult, Infant, and Child, Red Cross, January 2005–January 2007
Tooth Bleaching, Home Study Educators (Continuing Education Recognition Programme) 2006
Certified Dental Assistant, Community College, 2005
Expanded Function Dental Assistant (EFDA), University of the South School of Dentistry, 2005
Schuster Centre for Professional Development, 2005
Radiology Certification, 2004
Nitrous Oxide/Oxygen Administration Certification, 2004
ADA Midwinter Dental Conventions, 2003–2006
Photocopier Technician Certification, 1996

BBA University of the South, May 1993

---

1 Anystreet, Any town, AX0 0AA • 020 8123 4567 • burtrob@aol.net

Medical assistant

LINDA BLACK

1 Anystreet
Anytown, Any County, AX0 0AA
Home Phone 020 8123 4567

OBJECTIVE

To secure a position with a company that affords me the opportunity for advancement.

QUALIFICATIONS

Receiving a Certificate in Medical Assisting gave me knowledge of front office and back office skills. One of my strong points is working with numbers; I am also a fast learner. I also enjoy phlebotomy. I feel I would be able to perform any duty for which my education has prepared me.

EDUCATION

1997   7 GCSEs including Maths, English and Biology, Western Community School
1998–1999   Medical Assistant Certificate, Western College Plymouth

EMPLOYMENT

2004–2006   *Self-Employed Child Care Provider*
Provided daily basic care for children.

4/03–6/03   *Bureau of Census, Assistant Team Leader*, Plymouth
This was a temporary job that included the duties of door-to-door interviews, distributing, collecting, and reviewing interviews from other enumerators. Reassigning those interviews or following up on them if necessary.

1999–2000   *Manpower, Accounts Receivable and Payable*, Plymouth
For a brief period, I gained employment through a temp agency that enabled me to perform various tasks in accounts receivable and accounts payable for two different medical affiliated facilities at separate times.

1/99–2/99   *Full-Time Assistant, Internal medicine office*
Duties included basic front office skills, patient care and communication, assisting the doctor, and performing lab work.

Medical assistant

Jennifer's actual paid experience was minimal and dated; her skills needed to be brought to the forefront. This new CV was presented at a job fair where she was hired on the spot.

Jennifer Martin
020 8123 4567
email@address.com
1 Anystreet
Anytown AX0 0AA

MEDICAL ASSISTANT

Triage	Injections	Patient Scheduling
Medical Terminology	Phlebotomy	Chart Updating
Patient Intake	Vital Signs	ICD and CPT Coding
Dosage Calculations	Infection Control	Insurance Claims
Sterilization Procedures	Urinalysis	Accounts Payable/Receivable
Blood Smears and Blood Tests	Hematocrit	Collections
Lab Equipment Operation	EKG	Data Entry

EXPERIENCE

Patient Care
- Cared for in-home patients with complex, multi-symptom illnesses for three years
- Eased patient discomfort by conducting accurate assessment and drawing techniques
- Fostered healthy environment for diabetic patient through meal preparation, medication dispensing, and glucose level monitoring

Administrative
- Improved cash flow by recovering uncollectable accounts in excess of £1,000.00
- Increased accuracy of patient files by designing and implementing new patient update sheet
- Exceeded daily quotas and minimized overhead expenses with effective scheduling and management of part-time employees

Computer Skills
- Microsoft Windows, Word, Excel, and Works
- Corel Word Perfect
- Medical software including Medical Manager and Great Plains

---

EDUCATION

Western College of Exeter
Medical Assistant Certificate, 1999

Community High School, Anytown
A levels: Biology; Physics; Sociology

RELATED EMPLOYMENT HISTORY

Billing Specialist, Bookkeeper, Medical Assistant (various – Wiltshire and Somerset)	1999–2000
Medical Assistant (Internal Medical Office – Anytown)	1999
Long-term/Acute Care Provider (self-employed – Anytown)	1995–1998

Occupational health services manager

Susan was successful in finding an Occupational Health Services management position in another industry after being a casualty of airline downsizing.

SUSAN BROWN, RN

Manchester
Mobile: 07850 515536   •   Pager: 800-726-3642 PIN#1937761
E-mail: susanbrown81@hotmail.com

OCCUPATIONAL HEALTH SERVICES MANAGER

Certified Occupational Health Nurse Specialist/Certified Case Manager/Certified Occupational Hearing Conservationist/Case Management/OSHA & DOT Compliance/Ergonomics/Worker's Compensation/Corporate Safety/Training/Customer Service/Problem Solving/Quality Assurance/Sales & Marketing

- 10 years direct experience developing innovative occupational health programmes and establishing clinics.
- 14 years experience in trauma centres and critical care units.
- Success in driving revenue stream and cost-saving initiatives through strong combination of business management and clinical skills.
- Registered Nurse
- Proficient in Sign Language, Microsoft Office, and Outlook.

PROFESSIONAL EXPERIENCE

Supervisor, Occupational Health Services, Southwest Air Lines, Manchester   2001–Present

Recruited to implement and manage Southwest's first onsite employee health clinic in eight years. Accountable for care of work-related and non-occupational injuries and illnesses for 5000 airport employees (from baggage handlers to pilots). Coordinated care for another 1500 employees in Rochdale and 1000 employees at Gatwick. Hired and directly supervised 13 registered nurses. Managed £1,000,000 budget. Assisted with the launch of new Southwest clinics in four other airports. Standardized policies and procedures and created training programmes.

Developed position to also encompass system-wide responsibilities, and established self as the resource for HSE related matters, insourcing opportunities, ergonomic issues, and post-job offer testing programmes. Updated operational managers on daily events, occupational health programme progression, new programmes, ongoing testing, compliance achievement, drug testing programme etc.

Achievements
- Overcame resistance and established first-ever Manchester airport onsite clinic as an integral part of operations. Planned the department design, oversaw the architect and contractors, hired and trained staff, and developed an orientation manual from scratch.
- Conceived and implemented matrix to document value of occupational health services to Southwest. Demonstrated an average of 55% ROI each month.
- Generated annual revenue of £120,000 by spearheading a drive to insource business from other airport companies, promoting the utilization of the Southwest clinic instead of an off-site clinic.
- Initiated joint venture with Comair and opened a lucrative satellite clinic in Manchester for Comair employees.
- Innovated a post-job offer functional testing programme to address the high percentage of injuries among new hires. Worked closely with Southwest Legal and Human Resources and researched vendors.

SUSAN BROWN   **PAGE TWO**

- Negotiated inpatient services volume discount with most utilized hospital system that will save £60,000 + per year.
- Developed an improved nurse orientation process and a charting quality assurance programme.
- Coordinated availability of appropriate emergency care for passengers aboard flights that were diverted on 9/11. Arranged for medical providers to meet over 17 staggered flights and 1100 passengers that arrived over the course of the next 6 days following the event.

Trainer, Manchester   1999–Present
Provided continuing education, with CEUs approved by Hampshire Board of Nurses, on Workplace Violence Guidelines for Health Care Workers, Nuts and Bolts of Occupational Health Nursing, HSE Compliance and the Occupational Health Nurse, and Worker's Compensation Fraud Prevention and Update.

Programme Supervisor, Allied Health Corporation, Boston, Lincs   1998–2001
Accountable for providing a broad range of quality services in a convenient, efficient, and cost-effective manner for this 8,000 employee Hospital Based Occupational Health Services Programme dedicated to 'Business Health'. Supervised staff of 50 at 35 different companies.

- Managed successful start up of 8 freestanding occupational medicine walk-in clinics.
- Instrumental in winning £600,000 in new business through marketing the placement of clinics, doctors, and/or nurses at company sites.

Manager, Occupational Health Services, Cumberland Farms, Cumbria   1995–1998
Managed department, worker's compensation benefits, HSE compliance issues, and health and wellness initiative for this multi-million pound division of ABC Industries with 1,000 employees.

- Decreased compensation costs by 66% over three years.

Occupational Health Nurse, Granite Industrial Constructors, Boston, Lincs.   1994
Provided occupational health and case management services to this large construction company.

Previous experience working at several medical centres and a trauma centre providing direct emergency nurse care as a lead trauma nurse and charge nurse.

EDUCATION & TRAINING

BSc (Hons) Nursing, University of Durham   1983

Select Ongoing Professional Development (attended numerous occupational health and case management continuing education programmes):

- 28 hours toward Bachelor of Science, Nursing Practice, Manchester Community College
- Certification Programmes for Occupational Health Nurse Specialists, Certified Case Manager, and Occupational Hearing Conservationist
- 50 hours of HSE Training

PROFESSIONAL MEMBERSHIPS

- Member, Association of Occupational Health Nurses (AOHN)–10 years
- International Airline Occupational Health Nurse Association
- Board of Occupational Health Nurses (BOHN)

COMMUNITY SERVICE
Manchester Association for the Hearing Impaired (1995–Present)

Pharmaceutical sales and service

Catherine was a bright sales and service specialist who was growing in her career responsibilities and accomplishments and wanted to move into more advanced management positions.

Catherine Atree

1 Anystreet, Any Town AX0 0AA • 020 8123 4567 • catherineatree@yahoo.com

EXPERTISE:

PHARMACEUTICAL SALES AND SERVICE

High energy sales professional with experience developing product awareness through building business relationships. A proven performer with a track record of outperforming sales goals, delivering high levels of customer service, and achieving successful sales results built on key strengths of:

- **Consultative Sales Skills** – experience and education involving custom pharmaceutical and consumer products
- **New Business Development/Territory Management** – prospecting and building a territory; identifying and capitalizing on opportunities, knowledge of sales cycles
- **Customer Retention/Relationship Building** – excellent communication (listening, speaking) and interpersonal skills
- **Goal Setting** – experience in setting and achieving both independent and team-driven targets

PROFESSIONAL EXPERIENCE

ABC HEALTHCARE INCORPORATED; Coalport
Largest domestic contractual sales and marketing partner providing solutions to pharmaceutical & healthcare industries
Pharmaceutical Sales Specialist, 2003–current
Manage team-driven pharmaceutical sales responsibilities in southeast territory. Interact with physicians, nurses, physician assistants, and medical professionals to represent a premier product line. Interact with other sales reps to do strategic planning, problem solving, and collaborative thinking. Manage 35–40 weekly calls on physicians to increase market share in territory.

- Coordinated product launch for new acid reflux drug.
- Petitioned physicians to contact their HMOs and recommend formulary status: received formulary standing in January 2005.
- Member of market-leading Prilosec sales team.
- Consistently over sales quota; won highest call activity contest. Regional sales leader for hypertensive drug.

OFFICE MAX (2000–2003); Oldham
Multibillion-pound global retailer of office supplies, furniture, and technology
Business Development Specialist, 2001–2003
Promoted to develop new business while maintaining current business in competitive southeastern and central territories; focused on small to medium-size companies. Managed complete sales cycle from initial contact, through presentation and consultation, to close of sale. Acted as liaison between sales centre rep team and corporate office in London.

Catherine Altree
Page 2 of 2

- Consistently maintained above expected goal percentage in regional and corporate sales.
- Trained new reps in all areas of product presentation, solution selling, and customer service.

Sales Representative, 1998–2000
Managed sales and account maintenance with companies. Independently maintained relation-ships with company personnel to increase visibility and credibility. Developed leads through cold calls; met with customers to identify needs.

- Developed new customers; maintained high goal percentages; recruited to higher position.

EDUCATION & TRAINING
UNIVERSITY OF MANCHESTER
Bachelor of Science degree in Interdisciplinary Studies/Social Science with a focus in Health & Humanities; 1998
Vocational courses: Leadership Sales, Presentation Skills

References available on request

Medical sales representative

Jennifer went out of her way to display her yearly achievements right up front.

Jennifer J Rogers

1 Any Street
Anytown AX0 0AA

020 8123 4567
jrogersmed@earthlink.com

Medical Sales Representative

Professional Profile
Impressive 17-year *Medical Sales Representative* career with proven track record in prospecting, consultative sales, new business development and account retention. Proficient in sales presentations, introducing and detailing products, conducting inservices with physicians and nursing staffs. Strong assessment abilities with outstanding perception of customer needs and ability to recommend effective solutions. Well-developed closing skills for large capital purchases. Experienced sales trainer providing training classes in a corporate setting as well as field training. Highly motivated, enthusiastic, and committed to professional excellence.

Achievements – percentage of plan by year

2004 – 183%	2001 – 105%	1998 – 90%	1995 –164%
2003 – 78%	2000 – 159%	1997 – 92%*	1994 – 110%
2002 – 100%	1999 – 138%	1996 – 111%	

*started new territory

Professional Experience
Experience includes the sales of medical supplies and capital equipment. As a Senior Monitoring Consultant, worked with sales representatives throughout the West to assist in the presentation and closing of large systems deals. Outstanding achievements include securing multiple orders for patient monitoring systems in excess of £1 million. Possess excellent product knowledge with quick learning abilities. Demonstrated a commitment to long-term customer relationships evidenced by strong repeat business.

Career Progression
ABC Monitoring • prior to 2003 known as XYZ Systems • Exeter

Senior Representative • *1999–Present*
Position achieved by recommendation of Sales Director and MD

Sales Trainer/Sales Representative • Northwest Region • *1997–Present*
Territory includes North West and Scotland

Medical Sales Representative • South East Region • *1993–1997*
Co-Medical
Medical Sales Representative • *1985-1993*
ABC Hospital Pharmacy Department • Nottingham
Technician Coordinator • *1981–1985*

Honours & Awards
- Six Award Trips
- Multiple Sales Awards
- National Accounts Award Winner • *2001*
- Monitoring Consultant of the Year • *1999; 2001*

Education
BSc Biological Sciences • Medical Assistant Programme
Nottingham University

Medical equipment sales

Erik is seeking to move from pharmaceutical sales to sales of medical equipment.
The CV demonstrates a track record of accomplishments and outstanding sales and account
development capabilities.

ERIK CLAYTON

erikclayton@email.com

1 Any Street
Anytown AX0 0HA

Home 020 8123 4567
Mobile 07850 515536

MEDICAL EQUIPMENT SALES

Top-producing sales professional with five years' progressive experience, including three years in pharmaceutical sales. Natural communicator with expertise in forging solid working relationships with professionals at all levels. Proven ability to identify and capitalize on market opportunities to drive revenues and capture market share. Strong closer who consistently exceeds targets in a consultative sales environment.

– Core Competencies –

Sales & Marketing • Business Development • Account Development & Retention
Client Relations • Team Building & Leadership • Training & Educating
Prospecting & Closing Negotiations • Consensus Building
Problem Solving • Presentations • Public Speaking

PROFESSIONAL EXPERIENCE

Sales Representative • 2003 to Present
INDUSTRY-LEADING PHARMACEUTICAL CO., York.
Represent leading pharmaceutical company in consultative sales of select medications to GPs, Pharmacists, Pharmacy Technicians and Pharmacy Managers throughout UK.

- Call on 250 accounts monthly; consistently exceed company targets.
- Increased product market share from 25%–46%
- Educated clients on launch of product, achieving 35% market share within three months.
- Selected by District Manager, out of 12 representatives, to anchor and train new hires.
- Placed #2 in nation for sales of main product out of 2,500 reps.
- Achieved #1 in district two consecutive years, 2005, 2006.
- Nominated for Representative of the Year award (2005).
- Nominated for company's most prestigious award (2004).

Account Executive • 2001 to 2003
ABC COMPUTERS, York.
Gained valuable sales and client relations experience with £5 million computer sales company.

- Serviced existing accounts and developed new business, including several major corporations.
- Increased territory gross sales by 20%.

EDUCATION
BSc Communications
York University, 2001

Professional Development
Company Sponsored Sales Training; 2005
Team Train the Trainer (Company home office, one week); 2005

Computer Skills: Windows, Microsoft Word, PowerPoint

Pharmacy technician

OLIVIA S KOSTER, CPhT

1 Any Street
Any Town AX0 0HA
020 8123 4567

PROFILE

A focused and disciplined **Certified Pharmacy Technician** with more than eight years of retail experience, reflecting:

- ability to read/understand/dispense prescriptions
- knowledge of drugs and drug strengths
- sound judgement, seeking professional assistance when needed
- outstanding communication/customer service skills
- awareness of legality issues
- experience with inventory control and stocking
- proficiency in computer operations/data entry

Well-developed communication skills, interacting effectively with people on all levels; speak English. French, Spanish and Hungarian.
Conscientious and detailed-oriented with an earned reputation for dependability, integrity, efficiency and professionalism.

EXPERIENCE

1998–   ABC Pharmacy, 2/03–8/06   Wellingborough
2006   XYZ Pharmacy, 5/98–12/02   Wellingborough
Senior Certified Pharmacy Technician

Provided assistance to registered pharmacist and pharmacy customers, managing up to 700 prescriptions daily:

- Answered phones for orders and repeats; answered questions on pricing.
- Contacted physicians to verify prescriptions/repeats and address third-party issues; communicated with warehouse and wholesalers for inventory information; followed up with customers.
- Filled prescription under guidance of registered pharmacist; prepared labels using InterCom Plus system.
- Worked with customers at Drop Off Window, ensuring optimum customer service to generate repeat and referral business.
- Entered prescriptions into computer system's patient profiles and checked for drug allergies.
- Managed special orders; received and stocked inventory, maintaining appropriate documentation.
- Received outstanding ratings from Safeway Secret Shopper Programme.

EDUCATION

South West College
- Pharmacy Technician Liability Controlling Errors
- Civil Liability and the Evolving Role of Pharmacy Technician

XYZ Drug Stores
Pharmacy Technician Training – OJT

Scottsdale Community College   Scottsdale
NVQ level 3 Pharmacy Services

Medical technology sales

Jane Petroski

1 Any Street
Any Town AX0 0HA
020 8123 4567

MEDICAL INDUSTRY PROFESSIONAL
Training Specialist/Pharmaceutical Sales/Medical Software Support

Radiography Technology graduate integrating work and education to achieve career goal. Ability to communicate highly technical medical information to professionals, as well as to patients and their families. Persuasive public speaker delivering high-impact presentations to diverse audiences including board of instructors. Expert time manager with tenacity and perseverance to handle rejection without taking it personally. PC proficient in MS Office, Lotus and industry-specific software.

EDUCATION
BSc Diagnostic Radiography with Biology, University of the South, 2005
Courses: Medical Terminology, Physics, Microbiology, Human Anatomy and Physiology

Radiography Placement, Chapman General Hospital, London
Studied all Radiography modalities by rotating through areas of CV, Mammography, CAT Scan, Special Procedures, Ultrasound, Radiation Oncology, Diagnostic, Surgery, Nuclear Medicine and Patient Care. Observed procedures and participated in hands-on training; completed detailed patient histories.
Established network of physician contacts by demonstrating exemplary performance and providing competency/reliability in the operating room and at clinical sites.

Bedford Community College, 2000
A levels: A* Sociology, Psychology, Biology

CONTINUING PROFESSIONAL DEVELOPMENT
Emergency and Triage Seminar, Chapman General Hospital, London, 10/01
Trauma Seminar, Chapman General Hospital, London, 7/01
Caring for Customer Service, A. D. Banker & Company (8-week course), Reading, Berks, 8/90

PROFESSIONAL EXPERIENCE

CHAPMAN GENERAL HOSPITAL, London   2/01 to Present
CAT Scan Technician (Part Time)
Administer quality CAT Scans for outpatients and inpatients, plus emergency and trauma patients, while pinpointing immediate problems to provide patient care. Trained on operation of G.E. and Phillips machines, acquiring knowledge of physics principles. Assess and triage patients according to procedural priorities. Facilitate communication between doctors and patients. Interact with patients' families in crisis situations. Delegate tasks, as necessary, to maintain homeostasis.
Dispense correct patient contrast and radiation dosage to prevent contraindications. React quickly and accurately in trauma situations using critical thinking and reasoning.

Continued on Page 2

ADDITIONAL EXPERIENCE

Accounts Clerk, RYAN & FESTER, Bedford   6/96 to 1/00
   Performed general accounting functions for tax and litigation law firm.

Office Manager/Secretary, AUTO SUPPLY OUTLET, Bedford   4/96 to 6/96
   Supported six outside account representatives, assisting with direct sales and customer service.

Accounts/Shipping/Line Manager, C&B EMBROIDERY, Bedford   11/94 to 4/96
   Supervised quality control and resolved problems as liaison between employees and owners.

Data Entry Clerk, XYZ BANK, Brighton   2/94 to 11/94
   Rewarded several times for speed and accuracy with large return items.

Office Manager, ABC CONSTRUCTION, Brighton   11/91 to 9/93
   Established business relationships with vendors and HSE.

Accounts Clerk, CPA FIRM LTD, Portsmouth   5/90 to 11/91
   Assisted Department Supervisor in this CPA firm: performed A/P, A/R and data entry.

Customer Service Manager, BANKS & COMPANY LTD, Portsmouth   6/88 to 5/90
   Delivered train-the-trainer presentations on customer service techniques.

EARLY POSITIONS
Accounts Assistant/Secretary to Owner, 3/88 to 6/88
Reproduction Department Head/Relief Receptionist, 6/87 to 3/88
Store Manager, 8/86 to 6/87
Dental Assistant, 6/85 to 8/86

PROFESSIONAL AFFILIATIONS/CERTIFICATIONS

Member: Society of Radiographers, 2 years
CPR and Advanced Lifesaving Certificates, 2002
Radiologic Science Club, Charitable Volunteer Coordinator, Member, 2 years

COMMUNITY INVOLVEMENT

Famine Relief: Prepared and served dinner to families through class project, 2004.
Hope House: Collected and delivered clothing and home products through class project, 2003.
Angel Tree: Collected gifts for children of incarcerated parents through community project, 2003.

Pharmaceutical sales representative

Melanie Moore

1 Any Street, Any Town
AX0 0AA
020 8123 4567 mmoore@yahoo.com

WHAT I CAN OFFER CROSLEY AS YOUR NEWEST PHARMACEUTICAL SALES REPRESENTATIVE

Meeting demanding customers' needs • 'Selling' ideas to doctors • Communicating to get results under tough conditions • Using creative ideas to solve problems on my own

RECENT WORK HISTORY WITH EXAMPLES OF PROBLEMS SOLVED

Promoted from six eligibles to **Hospital Liaison***; promoted to* Training Supervisor and Hiring Manager, XYZ Pharmaceuticals Ltd.   00–Present

CAPABILITY: Well informed, senior, **doctors usually approve my recommendations quickly because I've built their trust** without the benefit of formal training.

CAPABILITY: Regularly **win the day** with my ideas, even **after** penetrating **cross-examination** by some of the best doctors in the business.

CAPABILITY: Persuaded senior decision makers to help us deliver better quality, reduce turnover, and make our employees more effective. Our **clients were served even better**.

CAPABILITY: My new training programme lowers **costs**, **despite our diverse workforce**. **Team members** now **master training** that once intimidated them.

Child Specialist, Family Services, Northampton   99–00

CAPABILITY: Convinced a decision maker that **my plan would help his patient stay with a demanding treatment protocol**. Patient and her unborn child protected.

Account Manager, XYZ Staffing, Northampton   98–99
XYZ provided temporary clerical and light industrial workers to local employers.

CAPABILITY: Boosted our client's productivity and made us more productive at the same time. **Complaints fell to zero** and stayed there.

EDUCATION

BSc Biology, North East University   97
Earned this degree while working up to 20 hours a week.

COMPUTER SKILLS

Expert in Word and Excel; proficient in proprietary customer information software suite and Outlook; familiar with Internet search protocols

Preschool teacher

A new mother moving back into the workforce as a preschool teacher.
She sent out one CV and received an offer.

PENNY R HAYES

020 7446 7124 • phayes@email.com
8 Sunset Drive, London E4 9XU

PRESCHOOL TEACHER
qualified by more than 10 years experience working with children. Possess ...

Solid *organizational skills* for planning and follow through and maintaining control of the classroom.

A *genuine love of children* and a desire to see each child succeed.

Superior *written and verbal communication skills*, with an ability to meet diverse personalities at their level.

Flexibility in dealing with the unpredictability of children in classroom situations.

A *willingness* to learn and improve skills and give whatever it takes to accomplish the goal.

'She tutors children who are in academic need and also works as an advocate for them with their teacher. I don't believe there is any task too big or too small for Penny to undertake as long as it will benefit students.'
Head
Local Primary School

RELATED EXPERIENCE
Reading Tutor
School Volunteer
Assistant Cub Scout Leader
Sunday School Teacher
Substitute Teacher

SELECTED RELEVANT HIGHLIGHTS

Reading Tutor ... Selected by teachers and parents as a tutor for two Year One students failing in reading. Planned the agenda, selected age-appropriate reading and supplemental materials, liaised with teachers and parents, and supported and encouraged both students in their successful reading efforts.

Co-ordinator ... Maintain a database of parent volunteers and ensure the appropriate items and volunteers necessary for special events and class parties. Act as the class representative for PTA functions.

Assistant Cub Scout Leader ... Stepped in to assist the Leader, preventing the dissolution of a 12-boy troop. Facilitate meetings and manage all the paperwork and records for the troop and each scout individually.

Sunday School teacher ... Use the 'Exploring Faith' early elementary curriculum to teach up to 100 children. Plan weekly lessons, arts and crafts projects, story time, and games with an emphasis on good classroom behaviour.

School Volunteer ... contributed 800+ volunteer hours over the past four years including reading to children, chaperoning field trips, assisting aides and teachers, tutoring, helping PTA with hospitality, leading fundraising events, and maintaining the Book Resource Room.

EDUCATION & TRAINING

BSc Psychology – 1995
South of England University

Leadership Training – 2005
Scouts Association

Building Better Readers – 2004
Southeast Regional Vision of Education and the County Education Foundation

Volunteer Orientation – 2003 and 2004
Local Primary School

Educational programme manager

Teresa moved from working in daycare and preschool to working with special needs children. Her programmes were later adopted throughout her district.

Teresa H Long

1 Anystreet, Any Town, AX0 0AA

020 8123 4567
E-mail: THLong@zero.net

Programme Management/Administration/Leadership Development

My professional career reflects over 15 years of education, training, administration, and programme management in the highly visible and uniquely challenging environment of Special Education. I possess a demonstrated record of success to customize learning programmes for students in all grades and performance levels. Have built positive working relationships with support staff, administrators, parents, paraprofessionals and students. These skills and experience provide the foundation for my service to West Central Joint Services as **Programme Coordinator**.

Selected Accomplishments:

- Sought by Special Education Director to serve on team to create standards, protocols, and framework for assessing ED teachers and programmes
- Administrated programme needs for students and coordinated the interactions of support professionals, including but not limited to: Programme Directors, Building Administrators, School Psychologists, Physical Therapists, Occupational Therapists, Speech/Language Pathologists, Autism Consultants, Orthopaedic, Visual, Hearing and other health-impaired service coordinators
- Effective facilitator of case conferences, that fosters a productive partnership between parents and school personnel, and ensures that the individual needs of each student are met
- Excellent oral and written communication skills with the ability to speak on a broad range of topics; reflecting depth and understanding of the resources and programmes available to the special needs community
- Designed preschool programme with overall responsibility for recruiting, training, curriculum development and the establishment of 'hands on' learning centres
- Created 'behaviour system' for County ED Classrooms, that was used as a 'foot-print' for other programmes and buildings throughout the district
- Possess a solid working knowledge of Local Education Authority requirements that enable students to participate in programmes and services for special needs
- Experienced with the implementation and evaluation of a wide range of assistive technology, programmes have included but are not limited to: Boardmaker, PECS, Writing With Symbols, Kurzweil, and Alpha Smart
- Customized curriculum for LD, ED, and MiMH students and coordinated performance standards against individual Education Plans
- Thoroughly communicate the change plans and service modifications following IEP Conferences, to ensure timely implementation of new and effective educational strategies
- Established thorough working knowledge and practical understanding of various academic assessment tools
- Functioned as department and building mentor to supervise new teachers and student teachers, helping them to increase competence and adapt quickly to school policies and procedures

Teresa H Long   020 8123 4567

- Participated in two building wide 'Climate Audits', as a staff member providing input and feedback to the review committee, and as an audit team member interviewing staff to develop a written review of results for school administration
- Recipient of the Shining Star Award, and two consecutive awards for Excellence in Education of Students with Autism

Academic Credentials:

Currently in pursuit of a **Master of Science** degree in **Education Administration**, as part of the **EPPSP (Experiential Programme for Preparing School Principles)** at Butler University.

Awarded a **Bachelor of Science** degree in Special Education from University of London. Certified in Mildly Mentally Handicapped, Seriously Emotionally Handicapped, and Learning Disabled.

Professional Development:

Formal academic training and personal experience has been enhanced with additional training from:

- The **Lindamood-Bell Institute**. Course of study included Lindamood Phoneme Sequencing Programme Visualizing & Verbalizing for Language Comprehension & Thinking, Seeing Stars – Symbol Imagery for Phonemic Awareness, Sight Words & Spelling, On Cloud Nine Maths – Visualizing and Verbalizing for Maths and Drawing with Language. Certified LAC Test Administrator; Lindamood Auditory Conceptualization Test.
- **ADOS** – Autism Diagnostic Observation Schedule, Butler University (2006)
- **Differentiating Curriculum** – Birmingham University – University of Kent
- **Multi-Cultural Education**, **Cooperative Learning**, **Applied Behaviour Analysis**, and **Effective Goal Writing** – Birmingham College

Career History:

Primary/Intermediate ED Teacher
Hamilton Primary School 2002–present

Private Tutor and Assessor
Lindamood-Bell Process. 2001–present

Executive Director/Teacher
The Child Connection Preschool. 1998–2002

Middle School Special ED Teacher
Pike Middle School. 1996–1998

Learning Disabled Teacher
ABC School. 1993–1994

Learning Disabled Teacher
XYZ School. 1993

Secondary Teacher of Severely Emotionally Handicapped (Alternative School)
XYZ School. 1990–1992

Direct Care Staff/Programme Coordinator
Northern Hills Group Homes 1989–1990

Teacher (entry-level)

ALEKSANDER GRINKOB

1 Any Street, Any Town, AX0 0AA   020 8123 4567 • alek_g@rochester.rr.com

GOAL   To secure a Social Studies teaching position at the secondary education level, 11–16

CERTIFICATIONS Provisional Certification in Social Studies, 2004

EDUCATION   SOUTH EAST UNIVERSITY
                  Currently pursuing Masters of Arts in Teaching Social Studies Anticipated May 2005

                  Bachelor of Science, Business and Economics, concentration in History Graduated May 2002

Appointments **Teaching Assistant**, North East College
- Selected to teach Advanced Labour theory and Microeconomics curricula.
- Collaborated on the development/implementation of challenging undergraduate lectures.

Internships   **Financial Analyst**, Strategic Systems, XYZ Bank, York   2000

Activities Co-founder/Captain. Farmingville Volleyball Team   1998–2002
Planned and coordinated off-site tournaments, handled group transportation and lodging arrangements, and resourcefully managed an annual budget of £10,000.

STUDENT   Brittonswoods School, Brittonwoods
TEACHING   Combined knowledge and experience in the following positions:
                  Brittonwoods High School, year 12
                  Brittonwoods Junior School, year 7

Year 12
- Team teach and observe the instruction of Advanced Placement students, as well as class discussions on current events presented by community leaders Steve Israel and scheduled guest, Rick Lazio, centred on terrorism and related issues.
- Foster a stimulating learning environment that integrates cooperative learning, role-playing, critical debates, graphic organizers, primary sources, and lesson review.
- Promote higher-level thinking skills through development of reinforcement-based mastery learning techniques modelled for students' individual learning styles.

Year 7
- Held full responsibility for all aspects of instruction and classroom management activities for five daily Social Studies classes over a one-month period.
- Taught comprehensive Social Studies units on Anthropology, Archaeology, Economics, and Political Science, providing students with an understanding of past civilizations' traditions, religions, agriculture, technology, military, government, and social structures.
- Formulated, administered, and graded lesson-specific tests.
- Participated in weekly Parent-Teacher conferences.

                  WESTFIELD SCHOOL, Westfield
                  Per-diem Substitute Teacher, Years 7–12
- Effectively taught regular and special education while demonstrating an ability to manage classroom responsibilities and easily establish rapport with students.

WORK HISTORY **Customer Relations Manager**, *Food & Country Magazine*, London
                  1999–2003

Teacher (experienced)

ROBERT A DOWNEY
1 Any Street, Any Town AX0 0HA • 020 8123 4567 • rad24@aol.com

---

OBJECTIVE To secure a position teaching English at the secondary education level, 11–16

EDUCATION SAINT JOHN'S UNIVERSITY
Bachelor of Arts in English, 2004

SELDEN COMMUNITY COLLEGE
Diploma, Applied Science, 2000

CERTIFICATIONS CPR/First Aid for Adults and Children

TEACHING EXPERIENCE CALVERTON MIDDLE SCHOOL, Brentwood

2004–present   **Replacement Computer Lab Teacher, Sixth Form**
- Facilitate the interactive learning process in a virtual classroom setting, using the School Vista program to teach lessons and basic Internet navigation/keyboarding skills
- Implemented an English/Social Studies interdisciplinary unit incorporating the use of the Internet, spreadsheets, Web diagrams, and creative writing exercises to research, organize, and depict their understanding of King Arthur and the Middle Ages

2003–2004   **Permanent Substitute Teacher, Years 6–8**
- Managed classroom responsibilities and maintained continuity of the learning process
- Incorporated cooperative education and role-playing activities to establish a relationship between course material and students' life experiences
- Devised a mock English Language Arts (ELA) test based on previous testing methodologies and content-specific rubrics; co-selected multiple choice questions for short stories; administered and proctored ELA standardized/mock tests
- Encouraged critical thinking skills through the use of challenging debate

2003   **Replacement English Teacher, Year 7**
- Worked collaboratively with English, Science, Maths and History teachers to implement an interdisciplinary unit on heritage, incorporating the use of essay writing, laboratory experiments, graphing, and historical research on family roots
- Taught students to formulate DBQs, enabling students to develop an understanding of diversity, individualism, and creativity through short story multicultural literature:
  - 'Aida,' authored by Leontyne Price (Egyptian and Ethiopian)
  - 'The First Flute,' authored by Dorothy Sharp Carter (Central American)
  - 'L.A.F.F.,' authored by Lense Nemioka (Asian)
- In participation with the cooperating Social Studies teacher, implemented an interdisciplinary poetry unit to develop students' creative/critical thinking skills, and an appreciation for the causes/effects of war through the use of personification, simile, and metaphors illustrated in war-related poetry
- Assisted in the planning and coordination of the 2003 Year Book, providing consultation on layout, and supervised the collection of student photographs, poetry, and song lyrics
- Interfaced with Guidance Counsellors, Teachers and Parents at BPST and Parent/Teacher meetings to discuss and review curriculum development and student progress

2003   WESTFIELD SCHOOL, Westfield
2003   **Substitute Teacher, Student Teacher**

DIRECTOR SAINT JOHN'S SUMMER SCHOOL, 1998–Present

SKILLS Windows 95; MS Word/Excel 97; Word Perfect 6.0; School Vista; Claris Works; Internet

Teacher (specialist)

CHARLENE WILSON

1 Any Street, Anytown AX0 0AA
020 8123 4567
cwilson@aol.com.

'Choose a job you love, and you will never have to work another day in your life

—Confucius

PROFILE
A detail-oriented, high-energy ART TEACHER with the ability to motivate students to work at optimum levels while maintaining a comfortable, creative environment, and keeping a clear perspective of goals to be accomplished. Extensive experience in helping students broaden perspectives for personal expression through visual artistry. Qualified by:

Technical Skills	Self-Management Skills	Transferable Skills
Ceramics/Handbuilding	Resourcefulness	Perception & Enthusiasm
Collage	Creativity & Flexibility	Personal Expression
Paintings/Oils	Productive Competence	Artistic Impact

PROFESSIONAL EXPERIENCE
2003–2005   LIBERTY-BENTON PRIMARY SCHOOL, *Art Teacher*   Findlay
Instructed years 4 and 5 in Art Studio and Art History; created weekly art lessons with a variety of subject matters and mediums in both two-dimensional and three-dimensional projects. Instructed a small group of students in a gifted art programme; selected artwork throughout the year and facilitated the annual student art show.

2002–2003   NORTHTOWN CITY SCHOOL, *Art Teacher*   Northtown
Full-time substitute for year 12 in the Northtown City School; part-time art teacher for years 1–5 at Woodward Primary.

COMMUNITY INVOLVEMENT
SUMMER 2002 ARTS FESTIVAL, *Table Leader*   Findlay
Collaborated in meetings throughout the year to organize an art activity table.
Recruited community volunteers to assist children with art projects.

AUTUMN 2003 ARTS PARTNERSHIP   Findlay
Bank One Student Art Exhibit
Entered 5 students' artwork: 4 students received honourable mentions and 1 student received third place.

SUMMER 2002 RIGHT TO READ, *Committee Member*   Findlay
Helped organized a week of activities to promote the importance of reading.
Designed theme T-shirts worn throughout the Right-to-Read Week.

2005   MOTHER HUBBARD'S LEARNING CUPBOARD   Findlay
Commissioned by local store to design logo 'character' to be imprinted on bags, keyrings, bookmarks, and signs.

EDUCATION
SOUTH WEST UNIVERSITY
Bachelor of Science in Education Degree, 2000

International Scholarship Recipient to SACI School of Art In Florence, Italy, 1999

Network administrator/programmer

Richard needed a CV that showcased his education and certification in networking systems and programming.

Richard Hall, MCSE, CCNA

1 Any Street, Any town AX0 0AA • 020 8123 4567 (h) • 07850 515536 (m)

NETWORK ADMINISTRATOR/PROGRAMMER

QUALIFICATIONS SUMMARY

Certified Network Systems Specialist with extensive technical experience in network administration and programming. Skilled in all areas of computer technologies including: installation, configuration, maintenance, troubleshooting, design and conversion. Successful in implementing £3000,000+ cost reduction programme and improving operational efficiencies. Excellent organizational, team-building and communication skills.

TECHNICAL SKILLS

- MCSE+1
- Certified Linus Administrator
- Network Administrator
- LAN/WAN
- Network Firewalls
- Router Configuration
- Workstations

- CCNA
- C Programmer
- Windows NT/2003
- Software and Hardware Configuration
- System Integration
- Internet
- MS-SQL

PROFESSIONAL EXPERIENCE

Network Administrator/Programmer
CW Associates, York, January 2003–Present
- Researched and implemented £300,000+ cost-saving technology programmes and operating systems; Oversaw and supervised network conversions from FileMaker Pro, Lasso and Webstart to MS-SQL, Php and Apache; Customized and monitored company search engines; Configured, installed and maintained Company VPN, Cisco Pix Firewalls and Routers; Updated company electronic mail system from QuickMail to CommuniGatePro.

Network Administrator
Networking Worldwide, York, February 2002–October 2002
- Designed, installed and configured computers and peripherals; Maintained and repaired hardware, software and operating systems; Troubleshot and resolved application and electronic mail system issues; Managed four domain servers.

EDUCATION & TRAINING

North West University
MSc in Computer Science, 2005
BSc in Computer Science, 2004

Microsoft Systems Certified Engineer, 2003
Cisco Certified Network Associate, 2003

Computer support technician

Joshua is a recent graduate of a computer help desk/computer support technician programme, and his CV demonstrates commitment to excellence, team spirit, and customer focus – all qualities needed in his new line of work.

Joshua Michael Peterson

1 Any Street, Any Town AX0 0AA • 020 8123 4567 • petersonjm22@aol.com.

OBJECTIVE   HELP DESK/COMPUTER SUPPORT TECHNICIAN

PROFILE
- **Recent computer centre graduate with proven technical abilities.**
- Demonstrated track record of achieving goals in a team environment.
- Highly motivated and dependable. Proven skills in problem solving, customer relationship management, and organization.

EDUCATION
The Computer Learning Centre, **Skillman**   2005–2006
Computer Coursework completed in:
- **Networking Essentials**
- A+ Certification
- Intermediate Word 2003
- Beginning Word 2003
- Beginning Access 2003
- TCP/IP Protocol
- Beginning Windows NT
- Administering Windows NT
- Windows NT Core Technologies
- Windows NT Support by Enterprise
- Beginning Business on the Internet
- Beginning FrontPage 2003

Southampton University   2003–2004

General first-year courses in Bachelor's Degree programme

EMPLOYMENT
A Cut Above, **Southampton**   2002–2006

Receptionist/Cashier
- Successfully handled front desk and three incoming telephone lines for busy, upmarket hair salon. Greeted and logged in steady stream of customers, coordinating appointments with hairdresser availability.
- Developed cooperative, team-oriented working relationships with owners and co-workers in this 12-station salon.
- Managed customer problems and complaints with tact and attention to prompt customer service. Received team and customer service awards.
- Experience gained in opening and closing procedures, cash register receipts, counter sales, light bookkeeping and telephone follow-up.

Sport-for-all programme   **Summers 1999–2002**

Trainer/Coach
- Assisted Women's Football Coach in 200-participant sports camp. Asked to return as trainer for 3 seasons. Worked with individuals, as well as teams, to improve their attitude and resulting performance.

ACTIVITIES
Football Semi-Pro Team   1999–2003
- **Team consistently ranked in top 10 semi-pro teams in the nation.**

Washington Crossing High School Football Team   1998–2001
- Captain of team that won Regional Title in 2000
- Recognized as one of the top two mid-fielders in the state in 2001

Software developer/project manager

Jackson A Lewis

1 Any Street, Any Town AX0 0AA • 020 8123 4567 • Email: jacklew@sbc.global.net

SOFTWARE DEVELOPMENT/PROJECT MANAGEMENT

Expertise
Software Development Life Cycle, Process Automation, Vendor Management, Software Interfacing Systems and Hardware Analysis, Maintenance, Upgrade, Customization and Modification Client and Vendor Presentations/Employee Recruiting/Employee Mentor and Trainer, Improved Efficiency

Operating Systems
UNIX, Solaris, IBM AIX, HP-UX, DOS, Windows 95/98/NT/2003/XP

Languages
Java (JSP, Servlets, Applets, EJC, J2EE), JavaScript, Visual Basic, HTML, XML, C/C++, COBOL, PL/SQL

Databases
Oracle, SQL, JDBC, ODBC, Microsoft Access

Software/Programs
Weblogic Application Server, Websphere Studio Application Developer. Eclipse, Forte for Java (Sun One), NetBeans, Visual Age for Jva, MQ Series, ROPLink, CVS, RCS, Visual Source Safe, Dreamweaver, Microsoft Project, Word, Excel, Outlook, PowerPoint, FrontPage

SUMMARY OF EXPERIENCE

SBC Corporation, Gloucester
Software Engineer IV, April 2003–Current
Software Engineer III, October 2001–April 2003
Software Engineer II, July 2000–October 2001

Integrated communications provider serving 85 Million customers, and employing a workforce of 90,000 worldwide.

- **Lead Analyst** for **multiple projects** and **sub-projects** (with Regional, National, and International clients and vendors), performing supervisory functions, including task assignment, quality assessment, scheduling, and employee evaluation.
- Vendor development and management, including **Cingular Wireless**, **Telcordia**, and **RLG Systems**.
- Designed and developed Web-based production job scheduling system with multi-threaded server component, **automating scheduling process**.
- Managed Customer Records Database project, interfacing with vendor software, affecting **1 Million+** SBC customers and 700 internal personnel.
- **Improved** operational **efficiency** of Sierra Online Scheduling, **reducing personnel by 50%**.
- **2004 SBC Award of Distinction.**
- **Multiple Monthly SBC Awards of Distinction**, including May 2006, December 2005, March 2005, April 2004, August 2003, November 2002, July 2001, and September 2000.
- Developed **configuration management process** allowing multiple team members to access systems without interference to other users.
- Created and presented seminar for EDP (Enterprise Development Project) process to client and software team. Implemented **customization or updating processes** to meet team needs.
- **Trained** over **40 employees** in use of systems and processes.

Page One of Two

Page Two of Two – Jackson A Lewis

- **Mentored 20 employees** in technical and professional business aptitude, including associates in Sales and Marketing Systems, Operational Systems Support, and Resolution Support Services departments.
- Experienced in managing hardware-related projects.
- Maintain existing systems, upgrade existing hardware and operating systems, establish new hardware, and provide on-call support.

XYZ Ltd, Exeter
Programmer/Analyst, May 1998–July 2000

Medical-based applications company marketing software to healthcare industry, including hospitals, laboratories, pharmacies, and doctors.

- 24 hour **on-call crisis management** for all client accessing Patient Management Systems.
- **Enhanced Patient Management software** with additional functionalities, using COBOL, and Discern Explorer.
- **Modified** Patient Management software to correct flaws/errors.
- Planned and executed all phases of project management, including design, coding, testing, and implementation.
- Analysed and resolved client software issues.
- Educated clients during **troubleshooting** process in **resolution of software issues**, while preparing them to independently repair similar issues in the future.
- Assisted management team in **selection of new associates**, including interview process.
- **Lead Developer** for Patient Management Team, guiding other developers and software specialists.

CIVIC CONTRIBUTIONS

Habitat for Humanity, May 2006

Grande Point Homeowners Association, Vice President 2004, Member 2002–Present

EDUCATION & PROFESSIONAL DEVELOPMENT

South West University, London

BA Business Administration – Computer and Office Information Systems, May 1998

Exeter College

'Advanced Project Management' April 2004
'Project Management Principles and Practices' May 2003
'Negotiations' August 2002
'Process Analysis and Maturity' January 2002
'Advanced C++' December 2001
'C++' November 2001
'Conflict Prevention and Resolution' October 2001
'Presentation Skills' March 2001
'Managing Basic Projects (Project Management)' February 2001
'Seven Habits of Highly Effective People' January 2001
'Java Workshop' December 2000
'Visual Basic' December 2000
'UNIX: Advanced Shell Programming' November 2000
'UNIX: Shell Programming' November 2000
'Oracle for Application Developers' September 2000

Network administrator

David wants to change his impressive and broad experience from technical consulting with the military to commercial endeavours in the corporate sector.

DAVID J WAGNER, MCP

1 Any Street, Anytown AX0 0AA • 020 8123 4567 Home • 07850 515536 Mobile • djwagner@csn.com

Networks/Systems
Hardware Configuration:
Windows, UNIX, Cisco
Software Configuration
Systems Integration
Systems Configuration
Route Configuration
Intrusion Detection
Systems
Frame Relay Networking
Network Planning
Network Firewalls
Peer-to-peer Networks
Ethernet Networks
Telephony & Fibre
Optics
Internet Information
Server
Switches & Hubs
ISDN/T1 Lines

Media & Peripherals
Voice & Data
TCP/IP

Project Management
Technology Consulting
Technology
    Management
Networking
    Infrastructures
Systems
    Implementation
Virtual Team Leadership
Relationship
    Management
Advanced
    Communications
Telecommunications
Security Analysis
Security Development
Applications
    Development
Evaluation & Testing
Troubleshooting
Resource Utilization

TEAM LEADER • PROJECT MANAGER • DEPARTMENT MANAGER
Network Administration • Systems Security Technology

● **Microsoft Certified Professional. A+ Certification.**
Accomplished technology consultant and project manager adept in desktop and network security/systems architecture planning, design, installation, configuration, maintenance and smooth project delivery.
● Accustomed to supporting multi-user networks, as well as leading high-performance technology and telecommunications solutions. Successfully employ technology to improve operations efficiency, reduce costs, and meet reliability and security goals and deadlines.
● Proven track record in team leadership and training, supplying a balanced mix of analytical, management, coaching and technical skills.

PROFESSIONAL EXPERIENCE
Senior Computer Scientist   2003–present
AA Systems Group (Army technology consulting firm), Stockton

Technical Lead – Army Computer Systems Office (2004–present)
Focus: Rollout of Army Partnership Tool Suite (APTS) system, implementing new functionality into live networks and systems.

● Lead Consultant and liaison (chosen by government project manager) in 7-member cross-functional team deploying integrated networks, systems, and technologies. Introduced real-time, peer-to-peer collaboration via new application, bringing far-flung team together and eliminating disconnects.
● Key player in development, testing, and implementation process, including custom tool suite development, to fit client needs. Integrate configuration, and supply installation support for pioneering technology collaboration.

Lead Network Engineer
Information Systems Engineering Office   (2003–2004)
Focus: £24 million Communications Update & Planning System (CUPS). Evaluated, selected, and integrated advanced communications and networking products for the Communications Collaboration Team.

● Key role (network engineer/administrator/technician) leading 6-member team. Honed end-to-end project management and presentation skills.

continued

DAVID J WAGNER, MCP   *Page 2*
020 8123 4567 Home • djwagner@csn.com

Inventory Management
Technology Training
End-User Training
Knowledge Transfer
Executive Presentations
Strategic Planning
Project Team
   Development
Team Building
Client Relations
Quality Assurance
Problem Solving

HARDWARE:
Sun Microsystems
IBM PCs & compatibles
SCSI & IDE Hard Drives
Cisco Routers &
   Switches
3COM Switches & Hubs
Ascend Pipeline Series
Netgear Hubs
RAID Arrays (Sun)
Ethernet NICs
Printers, Scanners
CD-ROMs, Modems
CD-R & CD-RW Drives
Sound Cards, TV Cards
Tape Drives

Software (UNIX):
Solaris, Linux
HP UNIX, SCO UNIX
Cisco Works Essentials
BIND 4 & 9 (DNS)
X-Windows, Open
   Windows
SSH, Lynx, Pine, ELM
sh, csh, bash
ftp servers & clients
Eagle Raptor Firewall
Apache, Sendmail, IRC

Software (PC):
Windows, DOS
Novell Netware
MS Office, MS Outlook
WordPerfect, FrontPage
IRC, IE, Netscape
FTP Servers & Clients
Norton, Cisco

- Pioneered first-ever use of security hardware/software, including intrusion detection systems (IDS), Cisco routers, and network management apps.
- Designed robust, mobile communications (and upgrades) to facilitate efficient network convergence and bandwidth utilization. Developed network management tools for real-time monitoring and troubleshooting.
- Field-tested flying local area network (FLAN), utilizing wireless Ethernet technology, which interconnected enroute aircraft to ground based units
- Proposed equipment purchasing savings of £2.5–£6 million through service analysis, reducing duplication of physical space and equipment.
- Introduced new traffic routing method (tech) using a defence satellite channel for communications, enabling netmetting in worldwide locations.

Signal Officer   1994–present
113th Signal Battalion, Stockton

- Platoon Leader   Mobile Subscriber Equipment Company. Lead, develop and motivate 40 soldiers. Oversee inventory management of £4.8 million in vehicles, weaponry, security, and communications equipment.
- Mission – establish mobile subscriber equipment network (mobile phone network for combat soldiers in the field).

Computer Scientist   2001–2003
Computer Development Services, Amberley

- Lead technical consultant – Computer Services Security Branch (Army) for setup, testing, and evaluation of networks/systems security technologies. Established configuration, installation procedures, and network topologies for all support tasks. Tech reports used as management measurement tool.
- Designed secure test bed networks/domain on UNIX, Windows, and Cisco IOS providing e-mail, DNS, firewalls, routing, file serving, and accounting.
- Selected to serve as test bed manager for dry run and official testing, personally resolving testing challenges and intrusion issues.

Systems Administrator   2000–2001
Technical Solutions & Services Ltd

- Installation, configuration, and troubleshooting software (UNIX, Linux, Windows, Solaris) on HP workstations, Toshiba laptops, and servers (Compaq, Diversified, HP, Sun). Prepared backups on multiple platforms and provided 24/7 technical support to data warehousing centre.

continued

DAVID J WAGNER, MCP   *Page 3*
020 8123 4567 Home • djwagner@csn.com

Hyper Terminal, Kermit
HP Openview
Cisco Works Essentials
Carbon Copy
Seagate Backup Exec.
SCO Xvision

Software (Cisco IOS):
Internetworking OS
Network Address Trans.
Access Lists
Context Based Access
Intrusion Detection
Remote Syslog Logging
Routing Protocols

● Oversaw corporate telecomm system, LAN physical extension, and technical purchasing (POs, quoting, authorizations, and receiving).

Technology Consultant   1999–2000
Campbell & Cohen (legal firm), Trenton

● Systems and network troubleshooting (Windows & Novell Netware) at multiple locations. Peer-to-peer training. Proposed LAN and equipment recommendations to stay ahead of the curve, which were implemented.

Systems Instructor/Client Support   1998–1999
Healthcare Information Group, Humberside

EDUCATION & CERTIFICATIONS
MSc Telecommunications Management, North East University – in progress
BSc Accounting, Eastville College – 1998

Microsoft Certified Professional – Windows NT, Network Essentials
A+ Certification – Computer and Network Repair
Cisco Switching 2.0 & Routing 2.0 – towards CCNP in progress
Building Scalable Cisco Networks (BSCN) course – in-house training

PROFESSIONAL ASSOCIATION
Institute of Electrical & Electronics Engineers (IEEE)

Software designer

Regina updated her CV after being off from work for quite some time due to surgery following an accident. She wanted an updated CV just in case (after being away from work for over a year) the company decided to demote her.

Regina Pierce

1 Any Street, Anytown AX0 0AA
Phone: 020 8123 4567 • Email: reginapierce@msn.com

SOFTWARE DESIGN ENGINEER
DELIVERING SOFTWARE TO REDUCE COSTS AND INCREASE EFFICIENCIES

Detail-oriented, highly motivated SYSTEMS SOFTWARE CONSULTANT with 8+ years of successful experience in designing, developing, and implementing software solutions to support strategic business objectives. Keen **problem-solving skills** evidenced by the implementation of innovative technologies across dissimilar architectures and multiple platforms to provide quality product functionality. An **effective communicator** who can easily interface with end-users, technical teams, and professionals on all levels.

Technology Expertise Includes:

- Astute strategic understanding of mainframe, client/server, and Internet environments.
- Experience in Object-Oriented design and development.
- Empirical knowledge of all systems development life cycle phases and a structured approach to project management. Accurately develop end-user documentation.
- Proven ability to acquire knowledge rapidly and to apply new technologies for process improvement.
- Functional knowledge of the finance, billing, and operations areas of **Customer Information Systems**.

KEY PROJECT MANAGEMENT & LEADERSHIP

ERNST & YOUNG – *LEAD TECHNICAL ANALYST*
Customer Information System for South Eastern Utility Company

Challenge: To identify and resolve critical errors of newly developed software in the Primary Test region before migrating online and batch programs to Regression Testing region.

Action: Extensively used problem-solving skills while interacting with eight-member team, Software Engineers, Data Conversion, project manager, and end-users to understand client requirements. Executed and analysed test suites resulting in quality assessments that verified product requirements and high quality code.

Result: Delivered high quality software that exceeded client expectations and was specifically required to stay on as Technical Analyst of the Regression Test Team, supporting both test teams through first-site implementation.

ERNST & YOUNG – *CUSTOM DEVELOPMENT LEAD/ SUPERVISOR*
Customization of Client/Server Customer Information System

Challenge: To resolve technical issues of the Open Client architecture that were slowing progress on the development of a £1.8M CIS system at a Canadian utility company. To develop a detailed design of Powerbuilder software modifications in the Operations area.

Action: (1) Supervised two developers in identifying the cause of the Open Client issues and in the completion of software modifications to resolve those issues.
(2) Developed detailed design of Powerbuilder software modifications to increase functionality and efficiency.

Result: My team successfully identified and resolved the Open Client Issues ahead of schedule, streamlining the rest of the project back to schedule.

Regina Pierce (page 2 of 2)   **Phone: 020 8123 4567**

COMPUTER TECHNOLOGIES

Languages: SQL, SQL*Plus, PL/SQL, Transact SQL, C, Java, HTML, COBOL, Pascal, Scheme •
Databases: Oracle 8.x, DB2, Sybase, MS Access • **Environments:** Microsoft Windows
95/98/NT/2003, DOS, UNIX, VMS, CICS • **CASE Tools:** ADW 1.6, ADW 2.7 • **Development Tools:**
JDeveloper v.2.0, Oracle Designer v.6.0, Oracle Developer 2003 v.2.0, Oracle Forms v.5.0, Oracle
Reports v.2.5, Dreamweaver 3.0 • **Methodologies:** Oracle's Applications Implementation
Methodology (AIM) & Custom Development Methodology (CDM): Ernst & Young's Application
Implementation Methodology (SMM).

PROFESSIONAL EXPERIENCE

*Corporate Affiliations: Oracle, Healthnet, Bell South, Eaton Corporation, Kellogg Company, Kelly
Services Corporation, Price Waterhouse, XYZ Power Co., ABC Gas, Atmos Energy, Consumers
Gas, Consolidated Natural Gas*

ORACLE CORPORATION, **Senior Consultant/Technical Analyst**   2000–2006
Installed and configured Oracle Financial Applications at five large UK companies to enhance
the accuracy, availability, and timeliness of financial data for strategic planning and reporting.
Identified, designed, developed, and documented customizations and interfaces to Oracle
applications. Delivered excellent results to each client. Consistently commended for ability to
work independently or as a team member to complete assignments on time and under budget.

● Designed and developed on-line Help for a customized installation or Oracle's iBill – iPay
  system, of a £1.2M Oracle initiative. Extensive use of Dreamweaver 3.0 to develop 16 HTML
  Web pages.
● Developed work plans for a £2.5 million implementation of the Oracle CPG/Oracle Financials
  solution using Project Workbench and Microsoft Project '98.
● Developed Configuration Management Standards for a £1.50 million global implementation
  of Oracle Applications at a large international temporary services agency. Developed initial
  template of the project's global work plan.

ERNST & YOUNG LLP. **Consultant/Programmer Analyst**   1996–2000
Demonstrated outstanding technical skills in design, development, and implementation of a large
Customer Information System package at five UK companies.

● Conducted analysis of Finance System on the CIS project of a large utility holding company.
  Prepared and presented Joint Application Design sessions, creating modification control
  reports, and proposing and estimating solutions for complex system enhancements in the
  following areas of Finance: Credit and Collections, Accounts Receivable, and Payment
  Processing.
● Programmer/Analyst Modified existing batch and on-line (CICS) programs and constructed
  new programs to support general ledger journalling and credit collection processes in the
  implementation of a COBOL/DB2 Customer Information System at a northeastern electric
  and gas company.

EDUCATION & TRAINING

LONDON UNIVERSITY – **BSc in Computer Information Systems**
ORACLE PRODUCT TRAINING
Oracle CRM eCommerce 3i (iStore)
Java Programming with JDeveloper v.2.0
Developer/2003 Release 2: Build Forms I and Report Builder v.3.0
Oracle Receivables Release II
Oracle Financials 10.7 SC Bootcamp: General Ledger, Purchasing, Payables, Receivables, &
Application Implementation Methodology (AIM) 2.0
Ernst & Young MCS Information Technology Individual Study (MITIS 1) & Study 2 (MITIS 2)

Technical support specialist

Gloria needed to present her technical, project management, and technical training/supervisory qualifications for an upcoming promotion possibility within her department.

GLORIA BARTLETT

1 Any Street, Anytown AX0 0AA
020 8123 4567 Home • 07850 515536 Mobile • gloriabar@bol.com

Application Support Administrator/Technical Support Specialist/Desktop Support
Technologically sophisticated, bilingual (Spanish/English) IT Support & Training Specialist with hands-on experience in project lifecycle management for technical and intranet applications, Web site development and maintenance, and workgroup support. Proven desktop and network troubleshooting skills. Expertise in:

- Help Desk & Hardware Support
- System Upgrades/Conversions
- Peer-to-Peer User Groups
- First-level PC Support
- LAN/WAN Architecture
- Web Content Upgrades
- Project Management
- Escalation Resolution
- Customer Service

TECHNOLOGY SUMMARY
Networking – LAN/WAN, Windows 2000/NT 4.0 Server, TCP/IP, SQL Server

Operating Systems – Windows 95/98, 2000/ XP, Windows 2003/NT 4.0 Server, DOS 6.0

Applications – MS Office Suite 97/2000/2002 (Word, Access, Excel, PowerPoint), MS Front Page 2003, Macromedia Dreamweaver 3.0, Adobe Acrobat 5 and PDF, Flash 4.0, Novell GroupWise 5.5, Adobe Pagemill 3, Lotus Suite 96, Corel Suite 96, Corel 9, Adobe Photoshop, Kodak digital software, Symantec pcAnywhere 32, Internet Explorer, Netscape Communicator, and WinZip

Programming – HTML code, CGI, Java, JavaScript, C Programming, RPG 400, SQL, Visual Basic 5.0, Visual InterDev 6.0, AS/400, ASP code

Professional Experience

XYZ Ltd, Northampton   (1998–present)
Senior Technician, MIS – Technical Support Activity (2004–present)
Promoted to provide help desk support for 2003+ end-users (including remote users) in 9 locations throughout the UK, as well as project management team leadership for special technical assignments. First-point-of-contact (Tier 1 Help Desk Technician) for support incidents, as well as end-user training.

- **Help Desk.** Ensure effective 'one-stop' technical support for mainframe, WAN, LAN, and remote system. Install and update software, and set up, configure, and troubleshoot Reach Centre equipment. Track and de-escalate technology and workflow problems, and assist Desktop Support Group and other IT groups.
- **Web site Development.** Project managed company Web site redesign to text-only version, enabling fast and easy access for all users, including vision impaired. Supervised staff of 8.
- **Intranet Development.** Key player in creation, launch and maintenance of Division intranet site, providing management with easily retrievable, up-to-date information for operations decisions. Initiated, created, and maintain Access users group intranet to facilitate information sharing and learning.
- **Project Management.** Led WIX CD-ROM project for 2 years, delivering interactive CD-ROMs with 1000+ documents for simplified presentation.
- **ASP Development.** Played pivotal role in beta-test programming and development of causal sales application (upgraded Alpha 4 database into back-end of Access 2000 and SQL Server, front-end into Internet Explorer via ASP programming).
- **End-User Training.** Expanded Reach Centre offerings by designing, developing, and delivering advanced programs and manuals for MS Office, GroupWise, Novell Network, and Internet, making information easily understood and usable. Manage all Access courses, training and supervising 5 adjunct team instructors.

Gloria Bartlett
020 8123 4567 Home • 07850 515536 Mobile • gloriabar@bol.com   Page 2

XYZ LTD continued
Technical Assistant, MIS – Technical Support Activity   (2002–2004)
First level technical support for software installation, as well as set up and configuration of new equipment (PCs, laptops, printers, scanners, projectors, digital & video).

- **IT Software Training.** Designed curriculum and materials, and delivered technical training, for introductory programs in Microsoft Office Suite (Word, Excel, Access), as well as Windows 95, keeping staff motivated and focused while improving job satisfaction and productivity.
- **Web site Support.** Functioned as Web Editor for Internet/intranet Web site, proofing and updating Web site information on a daily basis.
- **Database Maintenance.** Upgraded and maintained link-shared employee Access database, ensuring data integrity for training. Created database reports for management evaluation.
- **Technical Development Project.** Pioneered development and implementation of storage, archive, and retrieval system for electronic presentations used throughout company.

Principal Clerk – Technical Education   (2000–2002)
Promoted to provide installation, configuration, and troubleshooting support for new equipment and software, as well as evaluation and modification of skills assessment.

- **Training Centre Database.** Initiated and implemented data gathering system in Access to compile, store, and retrieve statistics on computer training classes. Researched and wrote monthly reports used to evaluate training trends and staff training needs.
- **WI Saver Rebate Programme.** Key team participant in initial, large-scale data compilation for WI Saver Rebate Programme, including retrieval, distribution, quality control, and storage of data.

Senior Clerk Typist, Clerk Typist – Corporation Business Tax   (1998–2000)
Assisted auditors by researching information on mainframe, ordered work files for Supervising Auditor using HLLAPI information system, and prepared report statistics using Excel spreadsheets.

XYZ ACCOUNTING (temp contract)   (1997–1998)
Data Entry Specialist/Legal Secretary
Front office support for accounts: records management, legal document preparation, purchasing, and equipment maintenance. Used software for research and to process complaints.

ABC BANK, Stevenage   (1993–1996)
Customer Service Representative/Supervisor Teller
Instructed employees in use of computerized banking systems and procedures. Verified and audited financial reports and balance sheets. Cash management responsibility exceeded £100,000.

EDUCATION

Instructor Certification, **HRDI** 2003
Courses: Curriculum Design, Performance Consulting, Training Presentations, Design Surveys and Questions, Determining Training Needs, and Active Techniques for Teaching.

Certificate in Computer Programming, The Computer Institute, London 2002
Courses: HTML, CGI, Java Programming, JavaScript Programming, RPG 400,
C Programming, SQL, Visual Basic 5.0, AS/400 Subfiles & Common Language Queries,
MS Office, Windows NT 4.0

Ongoing Professional and Technical Development in-house and at vendor locations
     (1998–present)

Web developer/programmer

Here's an example of a young technologist creating a powerful one-two punch:

Kelly L Hillman
1 Any Street, Anytown AX0 0HA • 020 8123 4567

Web Developer/Programmer or Database Programmer

Highlights of Qualifications

Accomplished and innovative Web Development/Programming Professional with a proven track-record of effective database/Web page design for high-profile, technical companies and governmental organizations. Experienced in all aspects of architecture and accessibility techniques; hands-on working knowledge of Section 508 and W3C Standards. Skilled analytical problem-solver with the ability to quickly learn new technologies. Polished communication, presentation, training, and client relations skills; able to relate effectively to people at all levels and convey complex technical information in an understandable manner.

Technical Skills

Programming/Scripting Languages: HTML, XHTML, DHTML, CSS Stylesheets, ColdFusion, Fusebox, Perl, JavaScript, CGI Scripting, XSSI, Java, Java Servlets, JSP, JDBC, Swing
Database Applications: SQL, SQL/PL, Oracle, Access, Database Design and Architecture
Software Applications/Programs: Dreamweaver, Flash, Fireworks, Adobe Photo Shop
Operating Systems/Platforms: UNIX and Windows 95/98/2003/NT

Professional Experience

Web Developer/IT Specialist, EXCEL SYSTEMS/EPA (Formerly LOCKHEED-MARTIN) – RESEARCH Swindon (2005 to Present): Manage the maintenance, development and enhancement of a Coldfusion application that interfaces with an Oracle database. Create, update, and maintain 11,000 Web pages/templates while ensuring compliance with section 508 and EPA Web guidelines. Perform Java Script and PDF conversions; resize, create, and maintain high quality graphics; compile a monthly report listing all Web pages, URLs, titles, and updates; produce content; integrate dynamic popup menus; and update employee Web-based information. Trained a temporary employee in all aspects of conversion operations and Dreamweaver applications.

Managed the complete conversion of 20,000 EPA Web pages to meet section 508 Web site guidelines in both appearance and compatibility.
Instrumental in successfully meeting all critical and stringent deadlines.
Recognized by management for advanced skill level and efficiency.

Web Development/Maintenance – Newbury (2004 to 2005): Oversaw all aspects of client Web site development. Performed a wide range of design and coding projects using HTML, DHTML, XHTML, JavaScript, and Flash. Updated and maintained content and graphics for both new and previously existing sites.

Spearheaded and managed all business, technical, and client relations functions.
Developed and launched numerous high-impact Web sites in addition to successfully re-designing existing sites to create additional market exposure.

Junior Systems Programmer/Analyst, MCTC – Swindon (2002 to 2004): Hired to develop and code Web-based applications and user interfaces in transmitting/integrating data with Oracle databases for a comprehensive government occupational network database. Served as a member of a technical team in developing multiple Web, database, data search, and retrieval applications.

Recruited for a part-time position, promoted to full-time.
Pioneered the research and development of guidelines for people with disabilities.

Marketing/Technical Support Assistant, XYZ CORPORATION – Swindon (2000 to 2001)

Educational & Training – MSc Computer Information Technology, UNIVERSITY OF ESSEX

BA in Sociology (2000), UNIVERSITY OF ESSEX
Information Systems Programming (2002), DURHAM TECHNICAL COMMUNITY COLLEGE –
Durham, HTML_Advanced HTML_Advanced Online Java Script Training_Sun's sl285 Hands-on
Java Workshop_XML Certification Training_Applied Systems Analysis and Design_Object-
Oriented Software

Network architecture specialist

John had just been laid off and needed to find another job. He is looking to stay in his field, and he wants a position that will use his Cisco Networks Certification and experience.

JOHN A CHRISTOPHER
1 Any Street, Anytown AX0 0AA • 020 8123 4567 • fax 020 8123 5678 • jacla@aol.com

Applications
Adaptec Easy CD Creator
Adaptec Direct CD
Carbon Copy
Cc Mail
Clarify
HP Colorado Backup
MS Active Sync
MS Office Professional
MS Outlook 98 and 2003
MS Internet Explorer
NetAccess Internet
Netscape
Norton Ghost
Partition Magic
PC Anywhere
Rainbow
Reflection 1
Reflection X
Remedy-ARS
Symantec Norton Antivirus
Visio
Windows CE

Operating Systems
Microsoft Windows 2000
Microsoft Windows NT 4.0
    Workstation and Server
Microsoft Windows ME
Microsoft Windows 95, 98
Cisco Router/Switch IOS
MS-DOS
UNIX

Hardware
Intel-based Desktops
Intel-based Mobile Computers
HP Colorado Tape Backup
Cisco 2500 Series Router
Hewlett Packard Pro Curve
Switches
CD Writer

Network Architecture Specialist
Cisco Certified Network Associate

Results-driven, self-motivated professional with solid experience supporting hundreds of users in multiple departments in the corporate environment. Recognized for outstanding support and services, process development, and project management. Able to manage multiple projects simultaneously and to move quickly among projects. Capable of leading or collaborating. Areas of expertise include:

● Network architectures and networking components
● Software and operating system deployment in corporate environments
● PC hardware installation/repair and disk imaging
● Troubleshoot complex operating system problems
● Call tracking, case management, solution integration

Accomplishments

● Reduced help desk calls by developing end-user training and knowledge database
● Led migration for 3000+ client/server email accounts from HP Open Mail to MS Exchange.
● Developed data collection protocol for BLM Natural Resource Inventory.
● Mentored teammates on technical materials and procedures.
● Built relationships to quickly resolve business critical issues.

Certifications

Technical Certification for MS Network Support Program, 9/02
CCNA – Cisco Certified Network Associate, 8/02

Work History

Technical Support Engineer, ABC Technologies (Holt Services), 4/03–Present

E-mail Migration Specialist, ABC Technologies (Holt Services), 11/02–4/03

PC Technician, RBM (The Camco Group) 5/02–11/02

Protocols & Services
TCP/IP
DHCP
DNS
NetBEUI
Remote Access Service
WINS

Networking
Ethernet
Token Ring
Microsoft Networking

Customer Support Specialist, Centre Partners, 9/01–5/02
Recycle Technician, RBM (WasteNot Recycling) 2/01–9/01
Soil Scientist, Bureau of Land Management, 5/00–10/00

Education

ABC Institute Workshop – Goal Setting, Achievement,
Motivation, 1/01

BSc, Soil Science: Environmental Mgt. – London University,
12/00

Awards and Honours

ABC Shining Star Award for Outstanding Customer Service,
October '04

Outstanding Services to Technical Services Division, January '03

High Quality Customer Service Award, RBM Technical Support
March and April '02

Software development

James Sharpe
123 Anystreet
Anytown AT1 0BB
Tel: 020 8123 4567
james@anyaddress.co.uk

Summary
IS professional recognized for broad-based skills encompassing Web, hardware and software solutions. Move effortlessly through and adapt readily to ever changing technologies. Areas of expertise encompass: project management, team leadership, staff supervision, coding, design, testing, user training/support, troubleshooting, customer relations.

Technical Skills
Software: MS Office Suites, Quattro Pro, DacEasy, Act!, Premier, Avid Cinema, Authorware, Director, PhotoShop, CorelDraw, VoicePad, Naturally Speaking Impromptu, PowerPlay, Visio
Hardware: SCSI, RAID Systems, IDE, NIC's, video/audio network hubs, switches, and routers
Web/Internet: Netscape Commerce Server, MS IIS, HTML, CGI, ISAPI
Databases & Technologies: Dbase, Paradox, MS Access, MS SQL Server, Progress, DDE, OLE, OLE2, ActiveX, Automations Servers (in and out of process), Active Forms, DCOM, Memory Mapped Files, Compound Files, MS Transaction Server (version 1.0), NT Services, Named Pipes, Thunking, Multiheaded applications and libraries (Win32), WinSock, mail services, HTTP, FTP, NNTP, TCP, UDP, SMTP, POP3
Operating Systems/Services: MS DOS, MS Windows 3.11, 95, 98, NT Server/Workstation, UNIX, MS Exchange, MS SQL Server, WINS, RAS, DHCP, IIS
Programming Languages: Delphi, Pascal, Progress, C/C++, VB, Fortran, PowerBuilder, Perl, Assembly

Career Highlights
- Recruited to manage several major projects at Technical Services (TS):
  - Reconfigured entire IS department. Developed specifications for new servers for file sharing, Web and database. Redesigned network 100 Base T; installed T1; and enabled WINS, DHCP, Exchange Server, MS SQL Server and IIS.
  - Revamped networks, servers and Internet connections to resolve the weekly, sometimes daily, crashing of network.
  - Project manager for medical/Internet project that was designed to provide continuing education courses online.
  - Supervised two professionals in IS and Web development.
  - Wrote several interfaces for authorware, I.E. 4.0 and Exchange, and created Intranet as dynamic pages from MSQL database.

- Founded Holbrook Software, with sole responsibility for account development, project planning, staffing, and customer relations. Developed software solutions for several public agencies and private firms:
  - Created an employee scheduling software, married filing status software with yearly upgrades and conversion programme.
  - Developed a criminal history database, investigation and complaint software packages for South Gloucester and Somerset Police.
  - Developed a UCR (uniform criminal reporting) software package. Program enables small cities, villages, and towns to participate in computerized national UCR.
  - Created software to accommodate membership database, account histories, invoices, membership functions, bank deposits, reports, and rosters for the J&B Association.

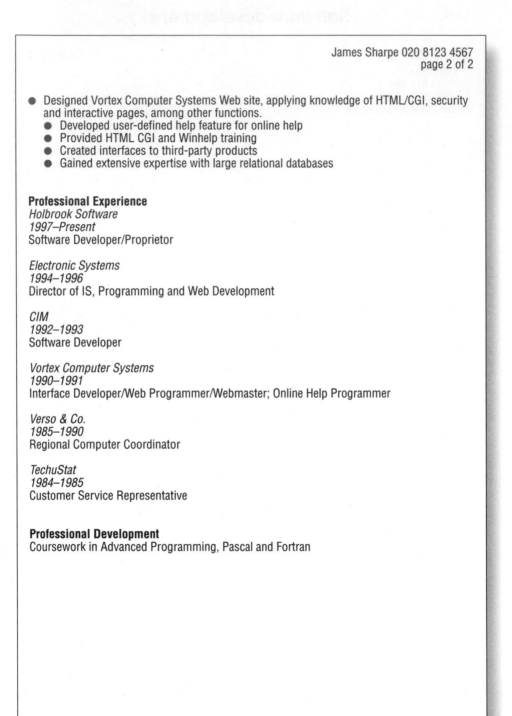

- Designed Vortex Computer Systems Web site, applying knowledge of HTML/CGI, security and interactive pages, among other functions.
  - Developed user-defined help feature for online help
  - Provided HTML CGI and Winhelp training
  - Created interfaces to third-party products
  - Gained extensive expertise with large relational databases

Professional Experience
Holbrook Software
1997–Present
Software Developer/Proprietor

Electronic Systems
1994–1996
Director of IS, Programming and Web Development

CIM
1992–1993
Software Developer

Vortex Computer Systems
1990–1991
Interface Developer/Web Programmer/Webmaster; Online Help Programmer

Verso & Co.
1985–1990
Regional Computer Coordinator

TechuStat
1984–1985
Customer Service Representative

Professional Development
Coursework in Advanced Programming, Pascal and Fortran

Systems and network manager

James Sharpe	Page 1 of 2

James Sharpe
123 Anystreet
Anytown AT1 0BB
Tel: 020 8123 4567
james@anyaddress.co.uk

Profile
- 15 years of management and hands-on background working in IT infrastructure.
- Experience with world-class banks and financial institutions in New York, London, Paris.
- Hold MBA in Banking and Finance.
- Chosen for the 2000 International Who's Who in Information Technology.

Areas of Expertise
network design ● systems management ● LAN administration ● strategic planning ● team formation and leadership ● budget preparation ● project planning and management ● presentation ● business writing ● resource management ● product and design research ● vendor interface and negotiation ● systems conversion ● computer operations ● systems implementation ● branch start-ups and automation ● disaster recovery ● system migrations ● data centre overhauls and moves ● applications support

Executive Development
Major Bank, London
Chief Executive and Manager of Network Operations   1998 to Present
Control £1 million budget and oversee five technicians in the design, implementation and support of company's WAN and LAN infrastructure. Handle heavy resource management and coordination with internal departments, vendors and network integration companies to define scopes of work, technical designs, product selection, required resources, schedules and price negotiation. Budget resources and prepare reports. Hire, schedule and review technicians.

Projects
AT&T frame relay and Cisco router implementation, TCP/IP address conversion, Compuserve RAS implementation, Cisco switched Ethernet 100mb/1 gb Catalyst implementation, HP Open View and Cisco Works implementation, MS DHCP and proxy server implementation. Managed project teams at remote sites to implement NT servers, routers, PC hardware upgrades, and Windows 95/NT images. Co-managed 1,100-user move.

A Major Investment Bank, London   1995 to 1998
Network Manager
Managed WAN daily support, hardware installation/configurations and network changes. Monitored/configured private frame relay voice and data network. Monitored ACC routes and NT servers. Performed Windows NT 3.51 server and workstation installations. Configured ACC routers, Adtran CSUs and Newbridge 3612 and 3606 multiplexors for remote site installations.

James Sharpe 020 8123 4567

A Large Multinational Bank, Paris   1992 to 1995
Network Operations Supervisor
   Managed all network and computer operations for the international hub site, reporting
   directly to the Technology Manager and supervising a team of technicians and computer
   operators. Supervised three direct reports, supported traders, reviewed/upgraded
   operations, handled troubleshooting, researched products and interfaced/negotiated with
   vendors.

   ● Completed full office start-up in Luxembourg in three months. Implemented LAN,
     voice, data, and video capabilities. Hired and trained computer operator to support
     local users. Implemented support procedures and documentation.
   ● Saved company over £50,000 annually: Migrated video conferencing from leased
     lines to ISDN, cleaned up multiplex or maintenance contracts, discovered
     overpayment on WAN lines. Set up a new process to review all invoices and pre-
     approved all purchases and communications costs before forwarding to
     Technology Manager.

Technology Expertise
Hardware: Cisco 7206/4700/25XX, Cisco PIX firewall, Cabletron MMAC+/Smart Switch
   6000's/MMAC8, Newbridge 46020/36XX, IDNX 20/12, CYLINK link encryptors, Paradyne
   CSUs, ACC routers, Northern Telecom Option 11, PictureTel 4000/M8000, VAX
   4000/6310/8000, HSC50, RA60/80/82/90 disk drives, MTI disks in DSSI architecture, HP
   9000 K100, Sun Ultra 10, HP Laserjet 3/4/5 and QMS laser printers, Dell/Digital/AST/IBM
   PC hardware, Intel/3Com NIC cards. Cabling knowledge includes category 3/5, IBM Type
   1, fibre optic multimode, v.35, x.21, RS232.
Software: SWIFT Alliance v3.0, IBIS, ST400, Montran (CHIPS), Reuters, Telerate, ADP
   Executive Quotes, IFSL Green Bar Viewer, Euroclear, Tracs, Soar, MS Project 95, VISIO,
   MS Word/Excel/PowerPoint, Lotus Notes v4.6, MS Mail, Ami-Pro, Lotus 1-2-3, DOS,
   Chameleon v4.6, Sybase v11, COBOL, Pascal, BASIC.
Protocols/Operating Systems: Cisco IOS version 11.x, TCP/IP, IPX, frame relay, EIGRP, OSPF,
   RIP, PPP, ISDN, SNMP, DHCP, WINS/DNS, Netbeui, NeBIOS, DECnet, LAT, VAX/VMS v5.5-
   2, Pathworks v4.1/5.0, Windows NT Server 3.51 and 4.0, Netware 3.12, HP-UX v10.2,
   Solaris v2.6.1, OS/400 v2.3.

Education and Professional Development
MBA in Banking and Finance, London University
BSc in Interdisciplinary Studies, The Polytechnical Institute
Computer Operations Diploma, Institute for Data Systems
Additional technology courses: Network Design and Performance, Advanced Cisco Router,
   Configuration, Microsoft Project 95. SYBASE SQL Server Administration, SYBASE Fast
   Track to SQL Server, Fundamentals of the HP UNIX System, Pathworks V5 Migration
   Planning, RDB Database Administration, Pathworks Tuning and Troubleshooting, PC
   Architecture and Troubleshooting.

Telecommunications/information systems management

TED SMOTHERS
1 Any Street, Anytown AX0 0AA
Home: 020 8123 4567   Mobile: 07850 515536   ted@smothers.com

Voice & Data Communications, Information Technology, Project/Budget Management, Strategic Planning

Expert in the design, development, and delivery of cost-effective, high-performance technology and communication solutions to meet challenging business demands. Extensive qualifications in all facets of projects from initial feasibility analysis and conceptual design through implementation, training, and enhancement. Excellent organizational, budget management, leadership, team building, negotiation, and project management qualifications.

Professional Experience

Food Systems International, Newbury   *1998–Present*
Achieved fast-track promotion through positions of increasing responsibility for multibillion pound International company with 30,000 employees worldwide.

Telecommunications Manager   *2001–Present*
Responsible for management of £15 million department budget. Fully accountable for overall strategy for telecommunications technology acquisition and integration, vendor selection and negotiation, usage forecasting, workload planning, project budgeting, and administration. Plan and direct implementation of emerging telecommunications solutions at all domestic locations consisting of 125 facilities. Provide direction regarding telecommunications technology to affiliates throughout the UK. Lead cross-functional project teams; supervise technical and administrative staff with 20 direct reports. Fully accountable for department's strategic vision and leadership. Representative achievements include:

- Directed £40 million annual MCI network conversion at 200 locations within six months, saving company £15 million over three years.
- Designed and managed implementation of network using Lucent and Octel at more than 100 locations in 12 months, realizing annual cost savings of £1 million.
- Served as technical project director for £12 million consolidation of North East headquarters with South West location.
- Facilitated move of corporate headquarters involving 3,000 employees over a four-day weekend.
- Implemented video conferencing technology at more than 60 sites.
- Built a four-digit dialling network for Food Systems locations within a four-month period.

Assistant Manager of Telecommunications   *1999–2001*

Management Trainee   *1998*

Education

BSc in Political Science, North West University
Professional Development/Continuing Education: Various Management Association workshops and courses; BCR technical/technical management courses.

Information systems audit and control

Alan was seeking a new position and was offered a managerial role overseeing disaster recovery and business continuity planning.

ALAN R GILLETTE

1 Any Street, Anytown AX0 0AA
020 8123 4567

SUMMARY

Master Electrician (VRQ Part P certification). Experienced in all types of electrical work – residential, commercial, industrial, electrical construction, and estimating. Six years management experience as a Foreman.

EXPERIENCE

XYZ Electrics. Master Electrician   *1999 to present*
Responsible for all sales, estimating, work scheduling, billing, ordering of parts and equipment, maintenance of inventories, and customer service. Projects have included complete wiring of a manufacturing business after relocation, new home construction, repair of equipment, building additions. Have worked as a contractor and subcontractor.

Industrial Light-Newport. Journeyman Electrician   *1999*
Foreman on medium-sized projects, with crews of 2 to 10. Scheduled the work, checked quality and productivity, provided layouts and supervision.

Prudhomme & Sons-Portsmouth. Journeyman Electrician   *1997*
Crew member on construction of the Portsmouth Sheraton.

Bechtel-Saudi Arabia. Journeyman Electrician   *1996*
Worked on a nuclear power plant (heavy industrial project), where safety and reliability were extremely important.

ABC-Newport. Journeyman Electrician   *1994 to 1995*
A variety of commercial and industrial projects (hospital, high-rise buildings, office-hotel complex).

TRAINING

XYZ Technical College, Newport
City & Guilds 2330
City & Guilds 2381/2391

PERSONAL

Willing to travel, relocate

References Available

Counsellor

Angel needed emphasis placed on educational goals, as well as demonstrating career advancement. This was effectively done in the Expertise section and the Education section showing her direction toward her doctorate.

Angel Roswell

1 Anystreet, Anytown AX0 0AA • Email: angel200620@athl.com • 020 8123 4567

Professional Profile

Highly motivated, versatile, and resourceful **professional** with a **BSc** in **Psychology** and currently in a **Master's** programme specializing in **Marriage & Family Counselling**. Over five years experience with children aged 2–6 in a disciplined, learning atmosphere combined with performing human resource duties, training, and counselling for teachers, co-workers and parents. Strong support experience in an office atmosphere with expertise in research and writing. Eager to excel, learn quickly, personable, and appreciated among peers.

Expertise includes:
● Highly effective writing skills.
● Strong research and reporting abilities.
● Experienced in budgeting, financial planning, fundraising, and donation solicitation.
● Naturally intuitive to children's needs with strong insight to unspoken needs.
● Strengths in listening, evaluation and counselling.
● Effective database management and marketing.
● Development of programmes/projects with effective implementation.
● Strong presentation skills, both written and verbal.
● Proven negotiation abilities.
● Proficient in assuring compliance with city, county, local and national government agencies.
● Able to accept responsibility and delegate where needed.
● Well-developed organizational skills.
● Personable and work well with all types of personalities.
● Loyal, driven, honest, and committed to a job well done.

Professional Experience

Associate Director • Educational Service • Southport • 2001–2006
Head Preschool Teacher (promoted)
Head Jr. Preschool Teacher (promoted)
Assistant Jr. Preschool Teacher (promoted)
Rapid upward progression in job responsibility from initial assistant, performing work as needed, to assuming Associate Director responsibilities involving the entire school, i.e., curriculum, teaching, training, counselling, supervising, providing assessments, budget planning, negotiations, parent involvement, marketing and fundraising.

Receptionist/Office Assistant • In Basket Business Services, Southport • 2000–2001
Receptionist for 10 companies along with answering multi-phone lines. Data entry, including invoicing, posting payables and receivables, and verification of statements. Variety of office duties.

Marketing Coordinator • Automated Machine Tool, Southport • 1999–2000
Telemarketing for strong sales leads. Relief receptionist. Maintained database, literature files and price books. Letter composition.

Certifications

Certified • City of Guilds (3049) level 3 NVQ

Education

Ongoing studies to qualify for **Doctorate Degree in Child Psychology** – *emphasis in* **Play Therapy**
Master's Degree – Marriage & Family Counselling • Southport University • *Degree expected 2008*
BSc • **Psychology** • Southport University • 2004

Mental health counsellor (entry-level)

Having acquired her Bachelor's degree, as well as in-depth voluntary experience, Jessica is seeking a full-time entry-level position within the mental health career field.

Jessica Devlin
1 Any Street, Anytown AX0 0AA
020 8123 4567 • 07850 515536 Mobile • jessdev@home.com

OBJECTIVE: Entry-level Mental Health Counselling position, such as Residential Counsellor, Mental Health Counsellor, Mental Health Associate, Clinical Case Manager, or Partial Care Counsellor.

EDUCATION
BSc Psychology/Professional Education May 2006
London University

Relevant Courses:

Introductory Psychology	Mental Illness	Developmental Psychology
Introductory Sociology	Psychodrama I	Educational Psychology
Physiological Psychology	Loss and Grieving	Sociology of the Family
Essential Helping Relations	Social Psychology	Field Experience I & II
Transcultural Health	Theory of Personality	Abnormal Psychology
Intro. Criminal Justice		

MENTAL HEALTH VOLUNTEER
- **Greenway Citizen's Advice**   2004–2005

Project co-ordinator for two Outreach Advice Projects, including implementation of Advice Helpline Website

- **Victim Support Greenway**

Counselling victims of crime with special training in Criminal Injuries Compensation Board applications, domestic violence, racial crime and child abuse cases.

EMPLOYMENT
Substitute Teacher, North Somerset   2006–present

- Teach all subjects as substitute teacher for primary and secondary schools, following lesson plans detailed by classroom teachers, as well as maintaining positive class atmosphere and discipline.

Hostess/Cocktail Waitress, Rusty Scupper, Bristol   2005–present

- Coordinate seating, efficiently and promptly, for popular city restaurant with seating for 500 indoors and outdoors. Seat 200 customers per 8-hour shift, while serving 1000 bar customers per 5-hour shift.
- Efficiently seat and serve group parties and banquets, such as four 2005 Christmas parties (75 customers each) in one day. Received recognition for top-notch customer service and positive attitude under stress.

- Entrusted with a £450 bankroll at beginning of each shift. Maintain 99+% 'count out' (cash reconciliation) accuracy for monies collected and disbursed daily.
- Chosen by management to promote upcoming shows and events via on-site and off-site marketing pieces and public relations appearances.

Administrative Assistant, XYZ Ltd, Taunton   Summer 2003

- Maintained orderly and productive environment in busy office with 6 staff. Effectively answered and transferred incoming phone calls on 8 lines, and scheduled 50–60 appointments daily.
- Word-processed, edited, and revised large volume of letters and documents weekly (20–25 documents, each 75–80 pages in length). Consistently completed assignments with short turnaround time (within 24 hours). Received live dictation, composed and sent correspondence and memos.

COMPUTER SKILLS
Windows 98, MS Office 2000 –Word, Excel, Access, PowerPoint, MS Outlook, PhotoShop, Internet Explorer

Clinical psychologist/social services professional

Veda's challenge was to present her wealth of qualifications in a neat, easy-to-read format.

Veda A Merritt

1 Any Street
Anytown AX0 0AA

Home: 020 8123 4567
Mobile: 07850 515536
vamerritt@netpro.com

CLINICAL PSYCHOLOGY & SOCIAL SERVICES • COMMUNITY OUTREACH

PROFILE
Versatile, dedicated Social Services Professional with solid clinical and administrative acumen. Committed team player and resourceful leader with proven ability to motivate and generate results through hands-on management and a sound knowledge base. Proactive community services advocate, continually seeking out new resources to aid patients.

EXPERTISE
- Counselling and therapy for individuals, couples and groups
- Identifying and matching resources to fit client/patient needs
- Teaching and facilitating workshops to train peers, subordinates and clients
- Managing cases, including writing and reviewing case notes, and auditing case files
- Networking to develop and sustain services, then propagating community awareness
- Relationship-building with patients of all ages, socioeconomic and cultural backgrounds
- Formulating, launching and managing programmes; developing new methods and procedures
- Directing Personnel operations, including payroll, grievance procedures, benefits administration and workers' compensation; enforcing EEO/Affirmative Action mandates

COMPUTER
Proficient in Mac & IB Platforms _ Lotus Notes _ QuickBooks _ MS Office Professional

EDUCATION
Master's Degree in Clinical Psychology – 2005
Kildare University
Master's in Business Administration – 2001
Metropolitan University
Bachelor of Arts in Management – 1996
University of the South

EXPERIENCE
Programme Manager   **2004–Present**
Comprehensive Family Services – Ipswich

- Provide counselling and therapy for individuals, couples, families and general groups.
- Team with social workers and other service providers to secure food, shelter, etc.
- Conduct Parenting Training classes. Supervise monitored on-site visits.
- Perform intake to assess mental history; refer to appropriate mental health agency. *To effectively deliver these services, I strive to gain clients' trust, assuage their fears, and get past the resentment and embarrassment that can ensue in these situations.*

EXPERIENCE
Veda A Merritt, Continued

- Facilitate multi-disciplinary case planning conferences. Manage staff.
- Conduct quarterly Community Networking meetings. *Built substantial network of service providers, which fortified our ability to provide resources and secure donations for clients' welfare.*

Programme Manager   2000–2004
Helping Hands, Ipswich

Managed 4 programmes: *Family Preservation_ Juvenile Mentoring_Healthy Start_Supervised Visits*
Provided in-home counselling and therapy/Assessed clients and patients/Conducted Parenting Training classes/Hired, trained and supervised staff.

Benefits Specialist   1997–2000
Partners in Health – Norfolk

- Managed company benefits of over £2 million annually.
- Managed five programmes. Tuition Reimbursement/Employee Transportation/Service Contracts/Workers' Early Return to Work/Retirement Plans.

Benefits Specialist/Workers' Compensation Case Manager   1993–1997
Downey Borough Council

- Increased employee benefits programme from standard plan to flexible benefits plan.
- Launched early Return-to-Work programme for employees out on sick leave.
- Expedited profit realization by implementing special training for new recruits.
- Maintained up-to-date EEO/Affirmative Action Programme for managers.

AFFILIATIONS

Supervised Visitation Network_Marriage & Family Therapists

PRESENTATIONS GIVEN

In-Services/Training: Child Abuse _ Mentoring _ Case Management _ How to Write Case Notes _ Suicide: When, Why & How to Report _ Working with Children's Social Workers

RECOGNITION

Awarded By:	In Appreciation For:
Home Connection...	Service and dedication to families
Children's Planning Council...	Extraordinary service and dedication to children
Dept of Children & Family Services...	Family preservation training
Diabetes Association...	Diabetes Walk-a-Thon Leadership (Team Captain)

Willing to relocate • Available weekends

Guidance counsellor

Sharon wanted to get into another district closer to her home, as she had a 1+ hour drive to work each day

SHARON WISE

1 Any Street, Anytown AX0 0AA • 020 8123 4567 – sharon_wise@hotmail.com

SCHOOL GUIDANCE COUNSELLOR

Dedicated primary and secondary school guidance counsellor, skilled at providing positive direction for students' academic, social, and emotional well-being. Work effectively with children with ADHD and with multicultural and diverse populations. Counselling Skills include:

Guidance Curriculum:	Classroom Guidance Lessons; Career Awareness; Conflict Resolution/Social Skills; Developmental Awareness
Individual Planning:	Student Assessments; Student Placement & Scheduling; New Student Transition; Academic & Career Advisement
Responsive Services:	Mental Health; Family & Teacher Consulting; Crisis Intervention & Grief Management; Psycho-Educational Support Groups
Systems Support:	Programme Evaluation; Programme Development & Coordination; Needs Assessment; Committee Participation

EDUCATION/CERTIFICATION

MA, *Teaching*, MARYGROVE COLLEGE
BA, *Teaching – Social Studies/French*, CITY UNIVERSITY

Certified – City & Guilds Counselling Skills
Certified – Social Studies & French
Certified – Higher Professional Diploma in Counselling – expected completion August 2008

PROFESSIONAL EXPERIENCE

HARTLAND COMMUNITY SCHOOL, Hartland   2005–2006
SCHOOL COUNSELLOR

Provide individual and small-group counselling sessions and large-group counselling presentations within classroom and guidance office environments for a school with 800 students. Participate in parent/teacher meetings to discuss and develop emotional and behavioural strategies for students with physical, mental, and emotional challenges.

- Developed 45-minute Bully-Proofing classes and presented them to each of 30 classes in the building.
- Wrote a monthly article for the school newsletter on a topic of relevance.
- Facilitated students participating in the Gifted & Talented programme.
- Held orientation for new students and their parents, providing them with a schedule of classes and showing them around the building.
- Created 30-minute Career Awareness/Exploration sessions so students would become exposed to various career options. Organized a Career Day, arranging for 40 speakers in various fields to talk with the students about their profession.
- Facilitated support groups dealing with social and coping skills, and conducted needs assessment and programme evaluation with staff and students.
- Designed a survey for students and teachers to evaluate the guidance programme.
- Hung a display of bully-proofing pledges with children earning hearts for 'acts of kindness.'

- Participated as a team member for the School Improvement Team (SCIT).
- Performed coordinator duties, planning and organizing initial structure mailings, assigning students to teachers, adhering to budgets, and scheduling classes.

HEADWAY COMMUNITY SCHOOL, Plymouth   2003–2005
GUEST TEACHER

Substituted in the middle school and high school, teaching most subjects, including special ed. Immediately tried to develop a rapport with students and engage in discussion of relevant topics. Facilitated the discussion to steer towards daily lesson plan. Discussion and debate kept students centred, entertained, and open to learning.

- Given long-term teaching assignment for students with disabilities. Taught maths, science and social studies in years 6–8 for a full term. There were 5–10 students in each of four classes, ages 11–13 – many students had ADHD. Wrote lesson plans, graded assignments and consulted with parents.

MARY HEATH COMMUNITY SCHOOL   1996–2003
FRENCH & SOCIAL STUDIES TEACHER

Taught five classes each day, with each class having between 30 and 35 students, engaging their curiosity and research abilities in structured classroom activities. Provided lectures, notes, study guides and projects for courses in History, Government, Economics, World Geography, Global Issues, and French.

- Devised an effective structure for parent communication.
- Gathered resources as supplemental materials to be used in conjunction with assigned texts to give students a richer experience.
- Assigned different subjects each year, showed flexibility in providing first-rate learning experience for each subject.
- Developed a system to track work and assignments while moving to different rooms for each class period.
- Provided students with practical experience, such as making menus and calendars in French.
- Member of School Improvement team and on the committee to improve student self-esteem.

PROFESSIONAL MEMBERSHIPS

- British Association for Counselling

RECENT CONFERENCE PARTICIPATION

Launching Career Awareness – Education Service Agency
Legal Issues for School Counsellors – Counsellors Association
Counselling Groups in Crisis – Association of Specialists in Group Work
A.D.H.D. in the New Millennium – Schools Association
Bully-Proofing Your School – Schools Association
The Human Spirit & Technology – Counselling Association
Understanding Attachment Disorders – Medical Education Service
Grief Counselling Skills – City University

Social worker

Tanya decided to pursue a job search in a large city when she realized that she was not reaching her potential while working the countryside.

Tanya S Richards

1 Any Street
Anytown AX0 0AA
020 8123 4567

STRENGTHS
- Funded college education by working full-time throughout full-time enrolment.
- Interact well with diverse populations.
- Take responsibility and work well without supervision.
- Eager to relocate.

CAREER EXPERIENCE

January 2005–Present
Community Psychosocial Services, Ruston
Qualified Mental Health Professional
- Provide mental health services to individuals with mental illness diagnosis.
- Complete psychosocial evaluations to determine appropriateness.
- Work with the psychiatrist assisting in completion of the psychiatric assessment.
- Provide individual, family, and group therapy as well as psychosocial skills training.
- Prepare care plans, charting, and other reports necessary to provide ongoing tracking of client progress.

January 2003–December 2004
Jobcentre Plus, Rygate
Intake Officer
- Scheduled clients for pre-employment programmes.
- Interviewed applicants and recorded information to determine job skills and training, income information, and programme eligibility.
- Reviewed all required documents from clients.
- Issued monthly stipend reimbursements to participants.
- Maintained records to provide a continuing history of pertinent action on each case.

January 1998–December 2002
City Hospital, West Layton
Resident Living Trainee
- Supervised mentally ill clients.
- Monitored progress on daily and monthly programme.
- Attended individual development training meetings to coordinate new programmes to help clients function independently.

EDUCATION
Metropolitan University
BA Social Welfare, 2002.

Substance abuse counsellor

Roy is a recovering substance abuser who has found his true calling in helping others overcome addiction.

ROY NASH

1 Any Street, Anytown AX0 0AA
020 8123 4567

FOCUS

To acquire field experience necessary to become an alcohol and drug rehabilitation counsellor.

RELEVANT QUALIFICATIONS

- Former alcohol and drug abuser now in recovery, having completed a rigorous rehabilitation programme without any recidivism for over 3 years.
- Avid supporter of others experiencing the nightmare of addiction; keenly sensitive to their feelings and needs to enable joining with clients in early stages of interaction.
- Confident facilitator; relate comfortably with diverse cultural and socio-economic populations in didactic sessions with groups of from 12 to over 40.
- Observant of clients' behaviours, with documentation of improvements or lack thereof, to assist authorities in planning appropriate actions upon their release from the 28-day programme.

EDUCATION

St. Jude's College, Ruxton
- Graduate of the Recovery Assistance Programme Training (RAPT), 2005
- Completed 270 educational hours towards CADC certification. Curriculum included: Addiction and Its Effects; The Recovery Process; Family Counselling; Individual Counselling; and Group Counselling.
- Passed written exam given by the International Certification Reciprocating Consortium (ICRC), 2005

PROFESSIONAL EXPERIENCE

Counsellor-in-Training at Straight and Narrow, a psycho-social 12-step rehabilitative agency in Newport (2005 to present).
- Conduct 1 1/2 hour didactic sessions to groups which include mentally ill chemical abusers (MICA), focusing on their recovery.
- Assist with the new client intake process, assessing and prioritizing service requirements.
- Orient prospective clients to the rehabilitative setting and the programmes available to them.
- Facilitate the adjustment of introductory groups on a daily basis, providing them with support and encouragement to stay with the programme.
- Schedule clients for art therapy and daily recreation, and coordinate their other activities.
- Ease clients' transition into didactic sessions by introducing deep breathing and relaxation techniques as a part of daily meditation preliminaries.

FORMER EMPLOYMENT

Bartender, Happy Days Lounge, Newport (1994–2004)
Server, Bartolucci's Ristorante, Newport (1992–1994)

VOLUNTEER ACTIVITIES

- Initiated support group for parents of drug addicted/alcohol dependent children and adolescents, working closely with the police department and the D.A.R.E. programme.

Paralegal

Jody needed to highlight her formal training as well as transferable experience
as she transitioned from law enforcement to paralegal work.

Jody Gilroy

1 Any Street, Anytown AX0 0AA
jgil@attol.com

PARALEGAL

Skilled office professional with exceptional interpersonal and communication skills. Highly organized and detail-oriented; efficiently manages time and projects with close attention to deadlines. Effective in stressful situations and able to successfully work with diverse populations. Persuasive and tenacious.

EXPERIENCE

- Drafting legal documents, affidavits, and preparing orders
- Conducting independent interviews and investigations without supervision
- Serving as liaison between solicitors, investigators, court clerks
- Researching case law using the library and Internet
- Proofreading for accuracy and consistency
- Opening and maintaining case files
- Proficient in Microsoft Office and scheduling applications

FORMAL TRAINING AND COURSEWORK IN CIVIL AND CRIMINAL LAW

Civil Litigation –	Drafting of pleadings, preparation of motions, discovery and pretrial data certificates and trial notebooks
Ethics –	Client confidences, conflicts of interest, unauthorized practice of law
Contracts –	Offers, acceptance, consideration, illegal contracts, third-party contracts, contractual capacity, remedies, Uniform Commercial Code, discharge of obligations, provision
Research –	Statutes, digest, case law, citators, encyclopedias, dictionaries, online databases
Torts –	Negligence, intentional torts, strict liability, personal injury litigation, settlements
Criminal Law –	Statutory and common law, criminal theory and interpretation of statutes
Public Law –	Business and economic regulation and ethical considerations

EDUCATION

Higher Certificate in Paralegal Studies – National Association of Licensed Paralegals

PROFESSIONAL DEVELOPMENT

- Leadership Training
- Administrative Plan, Policies, Procedures and Programmes
- Interviewing and Interrogation (Reid Technique)
- Conflict Management

WORK HISTORY

Paralegal, XYZ Legal Services 2003–2005
Communications Officer, XYZ Ltd 2002–2003
Paralegal Trainee, ABC Co. 2000–2001
Retail Manager, DEF Ltd 1996–2000
Management Trainee, DEF Ltd 1993–1996

Loss prevention management

Jerry's background in security for a large department store chain shows his fast-track progression to positions of increasing responsibility, which he used to move into a corporate loss prevention environment.

Jerry Zeliff

Home 020 8123 4567 Mobile 07850 515536 E-mail jerry_104@buzztalk.com

• **Loss Prevention Management** • **Industrial Security** • **Fraud Investigation** •

QUALIFICATIONS
- Expertise in investigation, analysis, and evaluation of internal and external theft cases gained through fast-track promotions over 8 years in retail security positions.
- Skilled trainer and motivator of loss prevention associates for a major retail organization.
- Experienced in collaborating with police and court authorities, as well as regional and corporate level investigators in matters leading to prosecution.
- Strength in timely and accurate tracking/preparation of investigative paperwork, which includes audits of shipping invoices, sales and inventory reports, and POS transactions involving underrings, cheque, credit card or refund fraud.

OPERATIONAL KNOWLEDGE
Equipment: Installation, testing and use of covert cameras, VCRs, two-way radios, alarm and fire systems, closed circuit TV, and Sensormatic devices.

Methods: Undercover investigation, observation towers, two-way mirrors, cash register monitoring, recognition of suspect shopper behaviour.

Related Matters: Trained in CPR and first response techniques. Basic PC literacy for database search, inventory reporting and word processing.

CAREER PROGRESSION

ABC DEPARTMENT STORES, 1999 to Present
Shortage Control Auditor, Company headquarters (since 2005)
- Implemented shortage awareness programme through audits of all stores and distribution centres to assure compliance to company's policies and procedures. Followed up on the matters of non-compliance.
- Through the audit process, identified areas where additional training was needed and instituted such.
- Resolved shortage related issues as they arose.
- Assisted in the development and monitoring of a high-tech security programme, designed to reduce shortages in selected stores with high occurrences.
- Participated in financial audits.
- Wrote and edited company policies and procedures, particularly in the area of inventory.
- Increased electronic communications with stores via computer and POS system.

Loss Prevention Manager, multistore operations (2003–2005)
- Held charge position for all internal and external investigations at store level for two locations.

…Continued

ABC DEPARTMENT STORES (Continued)

- Selected to fill position left vacant for 3 months. In less than 5 months, cleared up a paperwork backlog, reinforced procedures, then hired and trained new security staffs of 3 for each store.
- Instituted safety and security awareness programme throughout sales floors, fitting rooms and checkouts.
- Implemented £1 million budget for the security functions.

Loss Prevention Manager, Bristol (2002–2003)
- Applied and expanded security techniques for one of the largest stores in the chain, located in a busy mall.
- Communicated with other mall store security managers in efforts to apprehend shoplifters.
- Won 'Manager of the Quarter' award, out of over 25 other managers employed in this store.
- Promoted to manage neglected multistore security situation.

Loss Prevention Manager, new store opening, Bath (2001)
- Assigned to management team to oversee the installation and testing of all security systems at new locations.
- Screened, hired and trained new security personnel. Oriented all new hires for store opening. Implemented shoplifter detection incentive programme.

Loss Prevention Manager, single store, Burford (2000–2001)
- In first management assignment at store, trained staff of 3 in all store detective duties.

Manager Trainee, corporate headquarters (1999–2000)
- Intensive programme covering cash office, distribution centres, receiving, service desk, internal investigations, theft detection and statistical work.

VOLUNTEER WORK

TERRITORIAL ARMY RESERVE

EDUCATION

SIA Licensed Security Guard

Police officer/security operations

Originally from the US, Andrew has moved jobs a few times, so some short positions after his active-duty military time have been grouped together here. This is an interesting combination of law enforcement and medical background.

ANDREW LEXINGTON

1 Any Street
Anytown AX0 0AA

020 8123 4567 (H)
Lexington@yahoo.com

Career Focus

Law Enforcement, Security, or Force Protection Operations

Personal and Professional Value

International Police Officer, Liaison Coordinator, and Police Instructor, with 6 years experience in law enforcement and military medical operations with specific expertise in the following:

- Excellent Interpersonal Skills
- Superior Oral and Written Communications
- Intelligence Analyst
- Brief High Level Delegations
- Instructor and Trainer
- Tactical Operations Analyst
- Counterterrorism Activities
- Service to Kosovo and Operation Desert Storm

- Troubleshooter and Problem Solver
- Self-motivated
- Surveillance
- Tradecraft
- Marksman
- Liaison and Intelligence Sources
- Solve Crimes
- Surgical Technical

PROFESSIONAL EXPERIENCE

International Police Officer, Contracted through Brown & Root, Bosnia   2002 to Present
- Managed regular police duties from responding to murder and other crimes to handling neighbourhood disturbances. Work with interpreters and train local national police officers in managing crime scenes including surveillance, tradecraft, report writing, investigations, interviewing witnesses, and suspects.
- Conduct frequent liaison with local nationals and law enforcement agencies. Conduct hands-on training for new personnel.
- Promoted to a Primary Field Training Officer and conducted classroom training teaching local nationals how to develop and establish a working police department. Moved on as a SWAT trainer, responsible for working with the top officers in the field. Played an instrumental role in the development and foundation building of the Regional SWAT Team. Trained the special SWAT Team in lawful breaching of buildings, tactical entry methods, antiterrorism training, firearms instruction, team building, riot control, hostage extraction, vehicle extractions, explosives, etc.
- Utilized excellent mediation and interpersonal communication skills to bring the two groups together, solve problems, discuss issues, and form the multi-ethnic unit. Conducted constant liaison with local police and military forces to determine threat levels to ensure Force Protection
- Further promoted to Liaison Officer. Gather intelligence information from various source operations and prepare and deliver briefings to high-level decision makers. Act as a bridge between NATO and the United Nations to determine when to use police forces to diffuse public or military uprisings or other threats.
- Monitor intelligence data gathering and collection activities in the tactical operations centre. Gathered information culminating in the prosecution of seven bombings under terrorist activity.

ANDREW LEXINGTON

Police Officer, Baltimore, MD   **1998 to 2002**
- Patrolman working within inner city neighbourhoods. Responded to calls for service. Directed traffic at the scene of fires, investigated burglaries, or provided first aid as required to accident victims.
- Assisted other officers to secure crime or accident scenes, collect or protect evidence.
- Built relationships with local citizens mobilizing neighbourhoods to help fight crime.
- Investigated suspected crimes including murder, burglaries, domestic violence/disturbances, gang problems, suspicious activities, and unpaid parking tickets.
- Communicated effectively both orally speaking with citizens and responding to emergencies or diffusing problems at crime scenes/accidents, and in writing reports of investigation. Interviewed witnesses and suspects at the scene.

One-Year Assignments:

Sales Representative, American General Insurance Company   1997 to 1998
- Certified and Licensed Insurance Sales Representative for health, fire and life insurance.

Law Firm Runner, Baltimore, Mason and Associates, Baltimore, MD   1996 to 1997
- Acted as a liaison between the law firm and the court system. Filed legal paperwork with all courts: Federal, State, Municipal, Appeals, etc.

Operating Room Technician, Columbia Infirmary Surgical Unit, MD   1995 to 1996
- Assisted doctors during surgery in the operating room as a sterile member of the surgical team.

Army Medic, U.S. Army National Guard, Fort Meade, MD 1989 to present

Called to Active Duty for Operation Desert Storm and Operation Iraqi Freedom
- Received hands-on surgical training in various procedures for over 500 documented surgeries.
  Familiar with medical terminology, prescription medications and doses.
- Tasked to operate a medical clinic during the Persian Gulf War. Performed surgeries in combat.

EDUCATION

- Bachelor of Arts, Interdisciplinary Studies, University of Maryland, 2002
  Emphasis on Psychology, Sociology, and Criminal Justice

PROFESSIONAL DEVELOPMENT

- International Police Programmes – Police Assessment, Selection and Training Programme (Conflict, Analysis, Beretta M-9 pistol training, defensive tactics, baton and OC aerosol irritant and Officer Safety Defensive Mindset and Surveillance Detection)
- Problem Solving, Columbia Police Department
- Criminal Justice Seminar
- Emergency Vehicle Operator's Course
- Computerized Criminal Justice Training
- Police Academy, Elected Class Vice President (25 weeks)
- Operating Room Specialist and Certified Surgical Technical Course, U.S. Army Academy of Health Sciences, 1992 (4 months)

Received several awards for professionalism and exemplary performance in the military and police department
Supervised and organized the donation of over 7,000 hours of volunteer service to children's organizations as President of college fraternity. Received a National Award for Service

Security/operations management

James Sharpe
123 Anystreet ● Anytown AT1 0BB ● Tel: 020 8123 4567
james@anyaddress.co.uk

Career Profile
- Over 14 years of management and leadership experience in security operations and related functions with prominent hotels, retailers and security providers.
- Currently functions as Director of Security for a prestigious four star hotel, earning the highest performance ranking in the company in 1998. Have directed up to 200 officers and developed/managed £500,000+ budgets. Possess an extensive knowledge of security industry standards.
- Develop and lead effective and united teams, transforming fragmented factions into a cohesive alliance of professionals producing exceptional results and adhering to strict codes of conduct. Employ a dedicated hands-on management style that has dramatically increased effectiveness and reduced turnover.
- Certified in Security Management, Hospitality Law, Hotel Security Management, Disaster Preparedness and Emergency Response, Threat Management, Workplace Violence, and HSE Regulations. Member of the British Security Industry Association.

Areas of Expertise
- Security industry standards
- Budget creation and management
- Human Resources management functions
- Recruiting, training, and development
- Interviewing, selection, performance evaluations
- Departmental turnarounds
- Programme and procedures development
- Motivational team leadership
- Coaching, counselling and motivation

Career Development
Director of Security Operations, Four Star Hotel, Irvington   1997 to Present
- Manage all aspects of the security operation of this prestigious, top-rated 600,000 square foot luxury hotel with 300 rooms, a daily roster of 1,000 employees/guests, and 14 full-time security officers.
- Dramatically reversed poor performance history of key hotel departments, achieving ranking of first in the company in 1998
  - Decreased number of security-related incidents by 30%, the lowest in hotel's history.
  - Lowered workers' compensation injuries to 7 cases (of 300 workers), the smallest in the company's history.
  - Raised quality/efficiency while reducing overtime by 65%, the lowest rate in the department's history.
  - Instituted standards that did not allow a single successful safety or security litigation in five years.
  - Earned top ranking as company's best managed department.
  - Achieved lowest employee turnover rate in the entire company.

Produced these results by creating and implementing leading-edge programmes including… Innovative training, evaluation and TQM programmes that produced employee motivation, attention, interest, cooperation, and desired response… Standard operating procedures for crisis management, disaster prevention and recovery, risk management, emergency response, incident investigation, and report writing… Detailed investigation standards for all security and safety incidents, including policy violations, and guest or employee injuries.

Chief of Security, DeLuxe Hotel, Redcliff   1996 to 1997
Directed security operations of this three star national chain hotel with 200 guest rooms, 200 employees and 6 security officers, devising effective security policies and procedures, and budgeting and monitoring department's expenditures.
- Produced a 20% decrease in security-related incidents.
- Reduced employee turnover by 50%
Established new standard operating procedures. Developed and implemented emergency action plans. Contributed to creation of multiple departments' security and safety requirement training programmes. Cooperated closely with the Human Resources department on HSE, workers' compensation, and other industrial safety matters to ensure compliance.

Operations Manager, Redwood Security, Redfield   1993 to 1995
Managed over 200 plain clothes and uniform contract security officers in multiple facilities, including defence contractors and film studios. Developed and promoted a proactive culture of risk management and prevention. Promoted through the ranks from Field Officer to Operations Manager, the highest rank within the division.
- Implemented new rewards and recognition programmes that raised morale and provided continuous feedback.
- Frequently volunteered extended hours to meet clients' needs and critical project deadlines. Acted as client liaison to develop partnerships and strategic loss prevention and asset protection programmes. Oversaw Human Resources operations, including officer selection, field deployment, training, scheduling, inspections, evaluations and disciplinary actions. Established professional ties with local police authorities.

Loss Prevention Manager, J S Hoblins, Derby   1990 to 1993
Oversaw security staff and operations at this market retailer.
- Protected assets and reduced legal liability by creating ongoing prioritized loss prevention initiatives.
- Developed effective loss countermeasure strategies and prevention awareness training programmes.
- Conducted comprehensive internal audits and investigations for external/internal sources of loss and employee misconduct.
- Minimized accidents and injuries by managing effective safety programmes.

Technology Skills
- Proficient in Microsoft Word, Excel, IRIMS and PPM2000.
- PC proficient in Windows 98/95/3.1
- Extensive knowledge of computer-based, audio/visual and access control systems.

Education and Certification
BSc Political Science, University of the Midlands
Certifications:
- Security Management (Supervisor)
- Hospitality Law
- Hotel Security Management
- Disaster Preparedness and Emergency Response
- Threat Management and Workplace Violence
- HSE Regulations and Workplace Violence
- City & Guilds: Professional Guard parts 1 & 2

Security services sales

Jane Swift
123 Anystreet
Anytown AT1 0BB
Tel: 020 8123 4567
jane@anyaddress.co.uk

Professional Profile

Sales • Account Management • New Business Development Professional

Sales and Account Management Development professional with expert qualifications in identifying and capturing market opportunities to accelerate expansion, increase revenues and improve profit contributions in highly competitive industries. Outstanding record of achievement in complex account and contract negotiations.

Key Strengths:

- Account development/management
- Customer service/satisfaction
- Bilingual English/Spanish
- Customer needs assessment
- PC proficient
- Consultative/solutions sales
- New market development
- Account retention
- Presentation and negotiations skills

Professional Experience

Key Account Executive, 1996–Present
A&L Security Services, Largest privately held security company in the UK with annual sales of over £400 million.
   Recruited to start up and oversee the market development of contract security services in Northern England. Conduct in-depth client need assessments and develop technology-based security strategies to ensure maximum efficiency.

- Achieved consistent annual sales production in excess of £2.5 million
- Built territory from nowhere capturing 55% of the market share in region
- Expanded annual billable hours from 300 to more than 5,000, fostering a rapid growth in staffing from 30 to more than 300 employees in Raleigh branch
- Successfully negotiated and secured sales ranging from £300K to £1.2 million
- Earned several national and local awards for top sales performance, including the prestigious 'Salesperson of the Year' award

Account Executive/Loan Officer, 1998–1999
Equity Finance Ltd, UK's oldest finance company, a division of a Fortune 500 company.
   Generated and sold bill consolidation loans through telemarketing.

- Consistently exceeded monthly sales objectives
- Received national recognition as one of the Top 10 salespeople in the nation, and Number 1 salesperson in Raleigh branch.

Education
Bachelor of Arts, Business Administration/Finance, 2.1, 1997
University of Birmingham

Sales manager/office manager

Catherine M Sipowicz

1 Any Street, Anytown AX0 0AA • 020 8123 4567 • jcsipowicz2006@yahoo.com

---

SALES MANAGER – OFFICE MANAGER
Professional Sales Manager and Office Manager with over 10 years experience in all phases of the business cycle. Consistently exceed objectives and increase bottom-line profits for employers. A quick learner and an excellent communicator with an ability to perform well in a multi-tasking environment.

Extensive experience in the sales process from order entry through to customer service. Thrive in manufacturing and production arenas; a detail-oriented individual, friendly and personable, a self-starter with a willingness to work well as a member of a team.

Creative and skilled analyst with strong problem-solving skills offering outstanding systems expertise (conversions, upgrades, and training), excellent computer and internet skills.

Areas of Expertise:

- Office Management
- Project Management
- Customer Service
- Customer Sales Profiles
- Inventory Control

- Credit and Collections
- Problem Identification/Solutions
- Sales Management Support
- Commission Reporting
- Sales

PROFESSIONAL EXPERIENCE

XYZ Ltd – *Jersey (1993 to 2006)*
Sales Account Manager (2001–2006)

Responsible for maintaining £7 million of current business and coordinating all functions between the outside sales staff and the internal departments of the company.

- Directed and coordinated activities concerned with the sales organization including screening and evaluating new customers, performing credit authorizations, verifying client's sales history, and compiling monthly sales comparisons.
- Appointed as Sales Account Manager to handle a major supermarket chain buying £3 million of floral products, resulting in a 23% sales increase in the first year.
- Provided sales forecasts for holidays and special events which greatly increased the efficiency and accuracy of production schedules and purchasing requirements.
- Designed an innovative programme to evaluate effectiveness of new marketing campaigns. Hired and supervised a merchandiser to track the programme on a weekly basis.
- Developed an automated monthly sales comparison analysis with the IT department reducing the report generation time from 8 hours to 1 hour.

CATHERINE M SIPOWICZ

Office Manager (1996–2001)

Manage a multitude of tasks contributing to the daily operations of XYZ Ltd. Responsible for hiring, training, motivation and supervision of the telemarketing staff.

● Developed and implemented various systems for optimizing production resources and increasing efficiency. Designed Excel spreadsheets and standardized forms for use by all departments.
● Enhanced interdepartmental communications resulting in reduced production and billing errors.

Administrative Assistant (1993–1996)

Coordinated communications between sales and production. Performed credit checks, collections, and resolved price discrepancies. Responsible for inventory, price lists, and customer lists

● Project Manager for developing, implementing, and maintaining an inventory control system that used coding to correlate new orders with production scheduling.

<u>EDUCATION</u>

BA in Political Science, City University, 1993

Auto sales and service

Jonathan brought attention to his specific expertise of being able to locate 'hard-to-find parts' at the beginning of his CV and attractively displayed his skills balanced with well-placed graphic lines.

JONATHAN THOMPSON

1 Any Street, Anytown AX0 0AA   020 8123 4567

SALES/SERVICE • CAR AND TRUCK PARTS

Qualifications and Skills Summary

Over 20 years experience in the Car and Truck Parts industry specializing in locating the hard-to-find parts.

- Committed
- Dedicated
- Effective in fast-paced environment
- Efficient problem solver
- Even-tempered
- Excellent customer service
- Honest
- Learn and adapt quickly
- Persistent
- Personable

- Proficient under stress
- Reliable
- Resourceful
- Strong product knowledge
- Superb follow through
- TAMS Autolog and Triad Computer System
- Thorough
- Troubleshooter
- Trustworthy

History of Employment

Sales Counter • GO Garage Parts, Ltd • Portbury • *2003–2005*
Answered phones, received parts orders. Researched parts and supplied recommendations. Worked with shop equipment sales. Supplied customer service support often recommending specific tools for certain jobs. Looked up service bulletins on All Data and assisted technicians. Specialized in obtaining hard-to-find parts.

Parts Controller • Clark's Discount Honda Repair • Portbury • *1999–2002*
Received orders and ordered parts. Maintained inventory control. Wrote service orders for customers. Test-drove vehicles. Company had 6 bays.

Sales Counter • Ed's Auto Parts • Greenway • *1993–1998*
Looked up parts for walk-in and telephone customers. Received and processed orders from dealers and other shops. Troubleshoot and provide solutions for customers. Deliveries and some machine shop work.

Mechanic • Roy Farnam Supply • Greenway • *1983–1992*
Progressively promoted from initial position of **Stock Clerk/Delivery**
Mixed paint for custom colours. Worked extensively in machine shop. Operated overhead Broach cutter, performed valve jobs, installed valve guides and assembled two engines with excellent results.

Assistant Purchasing Clerk • Highways Department • Somerset • *1980–1982*
Purchased road repair supplies. Ordered parts for light to heavy trucks, Caterpillars, graders, and rock crusher.

Advertising sales (entry-level)

Melody J Courtney
1 Any Street, Anytown AX0 0AA

07850 515536 mobile   home 020 8123 4567

Strengths: Enthusiastic, creative, and hard-working media studies graduate with demonstrated successful sales experience. Reputation for providing excellent customer service resulting in increased sales and improved customer retention. Eager to translate solid classroom and work-placement experience in advertising sales into bottom-line revenues in the radio/television industry.

Education: BA in Media Studies, Metropolitan University, 2003.
Coursework Included advertising research and strategy, design and graphics, media planning, and sales and campaigns.

Final Year Project
- *Challenge:* Create an advertising campaign for the City Hospice Group.
- *Action:* As key member of a 6-person team, performed demographics survey, developed campaign strategies, created logo and slogan, authored and designed bilingual brochures, and created media kit within £250,000 budget.
- *Result:* After presenting project to 11-person panel, won first place out of 12 teams. The City Hospice Group implemented the slogan and several campaign strategies.

Work Placements
Advertising Sales Representative, AB Advertising, Truro   Sept.–Dec. 2002
- Solid print advertising to local businesses using cold calling techniques.

Production Assistant, XY Films Ltd.   Jan.–May 2002
- Assisted with production of 2 to 3 commercials a week. Accountable for delivering all technical equipment to the site and pre-production set up of lights, monitors, microphones, and cameras. Worked closely with sales department and producer, learning both the technical side of commercial production as well as sales and customer service issues.
- Handled pre-production and on-air tasks including studio set up, script delivery, operating cameras and soundboards.

Sales/Customer Service Experience
Sales/Waiting Staff, Great Brewpub, Truro
- Consistently generated additional revenues using thorough product knowledge and friendly sales technique to sell house specials and add-on items. Contender for the '£1,000 Night' sales award.

Host/Waiting Staff, Jack's Seafood, Falmouth
- Developed repeat business by providing excellent customer service in fast-paced environment.

Awards/Memberships
- Won Silver Medal, an annual award for college students, 2002
- Served as Co Director of Adwerks, developing ads for nonprofit organizations, 2001
- Member and committee chairperson of the Ad Society, a college professional organization, 2001–2003

International sales/marketing manager

Meghan had worked her way through a fast-track entry-level programme and was ready to strike out on her own with another company.

MEGHAN M ENGLAND

1 Any Street, Anytown AX0 0AA • 020 8123 4567

INTERNATIONAL SALES/MARKETING MANAGER
Strategic Planning/Staff Supervision & Training/Business Development

Highly accomplished and innovative marketing professional with key domestic and international experience in penetrating new markets, expanding existing accounts, and boosting profits. Fluent in English and Spanish. Results-oriented and visionary leader with proven success in new market identification, regional advertising, branding, and competitor analysis. Skilled in staff supervision and training, client relations, and strategic planning. Polished communication, presentation, negotiation, and problem-solving skills. Thrive in an intensely competitive, dynamic environment.

Core competencies include:

- Strategic Business Planning
- Budget Management
- Business Development/Planning
- Staff Training and Development
- Marketing Programme Design
- Market Identification
- Team Building and Leadership
- Account Relationship Management
- International Client Relations
- Key Networking Skills

PROFESSIONAL EXPERIENCE
SAP AMERICA/SAP CHILE/SOUTH AMERICA
Fast-track progression through the following key international marketing management positions:

South American Marketing Manager, **XYZ Latin America – London** (2003 to Present)
Direct and manage 360 degree company marketing programmes throughout Argentina, Bolivia, Brazil, Chile, Colombia, Mexico, Paraguay, Peru, Puerto Rico, Venezuela, Uruguay, and the Caribbean Islands for the third largest software company worldwide. Oversee all aspects of South American regional marketing operations with broad responsibility for strategic planning and the indirect supervision of a staff of four marketing managers and various partner PR/advertising agencies.

Initiate, develop, and nurture new leads to generate additional sales revenues; collaborate with sales representatives to turn over leads and establish key relationships. Accomplish marketing goals by launching comprehensive marketing, advertising, and branding plans. Manage PR marketing functions through press releases, executive interviews, press conferences, professional networking, and by creating an educational focus to allow greater company exposure. Ensure top-level customer satisfaction; collaborate with various outside agencies to administer and analyse customer surveys.

Develop and manage a £3 million marketing budget encompassing strategic industries such as banks, the public sector, and utility companies, as well as strategic solutions including customer relationship management, enterprise resource planning, supply chain management, and small to mid-sized businesses. Design and implement regional advertising/branding strategies, and analyse progress through brand tracking studies and competitive reports. Pioneer and manage key relationships with high-profile industry analyst firms. Interact with an outside global advertising agency to effectively leverage internationally syndicated relationship marketing campaigns. Serve as a company representative, liaison, and central point-of-contact for providing vital information, managing market research, and resolving issues at all levels.

Key Accomplishments
- Spearheaded and manage a highly effective electronic quarterly newsletter, resulting in increased communications among South American employees.
- Directed an extensive 8-month regional team project in successfully training and educating all South American marketing personnel on the newly implemented CRM system in the areas of budgeting/planning, campaign planning, preparation, execution/analysis, lead management, and reporting.
- Developed and initiated the first regional budget with the global marketing team.
- Pioneered the centralization of advertising, resulting in greater discounts and significant savings.
- Accomplished greater recognition for the company including the first, and many additional publications of the company president in regional magazine articles.

Marketing Manager, **XYZ CHILE – Santiago de Chile (2001 to 2003)**

Spearheaded, built, and launched the first marketing department for the company's Chilean subsidiary, with full responsibility for hiring, training, scheduling, supervising, mentoring, and evaluating marketing coordinator and marketing analyst staff members. Managed an £800,000 Enterprise Resource Planning marketing budget. Interacted directly with the sales team to implement marketing strategies and meet goals. Managed extensive market research and analysis functions by collaborating with a local agency to conduct focus group interviews in evaluating both company and competitor solutions. Involved in all aspects of production, public relations, sales, relationship building, and customer service.

Key Accomplishments:
- Created and implemented a lead generation programme, resulting in an increased amount of qualified leads for Account Executives and improved revenues due to shorter sales cycle.
- Built solid PR operations by developing and managing high-impact press strategies; concurrently continued to initiate key media relationships, conduct press conferences and executive interviews.

South American Coordinator, **XYZ LATIN AMERICA – London (1998 to 2001)**

Managed the international roll-out and training for the company's Sales and Marketing Information System. Travelled extensively to various international locations to oversee all implementation and training functions. Concentrated on providing a full range of support to Finance and Marketing Directors.

Spanish Teacher, **ABC CHEMICAL CORPORATION – Luton (1998)**
Taught Spanish to top-level corporate executives.

Education & Credentials

BA in International Studies
METROPOLITAN UNIVERSITY (1997)

Language Studies
Seville/Segovia, Spain (1997)

Comprehensive Spanish Language Studies
Adelaide, Australia (1996)

Additional Professional Training in Business and Communications

Private Pilot Licence with Instrument and commercial ratings

Excellent Professional References Available on Request

Database administration

Jackie enjoys most the database administration portion of her current job and will be targeting employers that will help her move from database marketing to database administration.

Jacqueline Alois

1 Any Street, Anytown AX0 0AA   020 8123 4567   jacqueline@alois.net

Database Management • Marketing Communications • E-mail Template Design

Profile

Sales and Marketing Support Professional with more than 14 years of experience in time-sensitive, fast-paced environments. Highly developed skills in oral and written communications, multitasking, attention to detail, and perseverance to completion. Keen insight into clients' perspectives, goals and target audiences. Proficient with various software programs including Word, Excel, Access and Goldmine.

Key strengths include:

- Database administration
- Market research
- Sales lead qualification
- Proactive problem solving
- Promotional copywriting

Internal/external customer service
Computer and procedural training
Project coordination
Relationship building
New account development

Professional Employment History

ABC COMMUNICATIONS LTD, CROYDON   2002–Present

Database Marketing Coordinator for trade-show design firm
- Assist the MD, Creative Director and sales force of 7 in developing targeted messages to promote company's services (trade-show display design and client training seminars). Contribute ideas in brainstorming sessions and translate concepts into persuasive written materials (brochures, Web pages, and e-mail templates).
- Generate leads through extensive phone contact, which has facilitated the closing of numerous sales by determining clients' interests and addressing their specific needs or concerns.
- Enter and update all pertinent information for up to 500 clients and prospects on Goldmine system; create profiles and periodically send electronically distributed promotional pieces to keep company in the forefront for future business.
- Initially train new sales consultants on data mining to their best advantage as well as empower them for success in prospecting and cold calling. Organize sales assignments to avoid duplication of efforts.
- Coordinate all pre- and post-sale details with various departments.
- Demonstrated versatility and talent in several areas; was retained on staff despite 2 company downsizings.

XYZ LTD, ORPINGTON   2000–2002
Sales Representative for graphic arts supply company
- Performed duties of sales liaison, assistant purchasing agent, and customer service representative.
- Streamlined department by automating the quote process and systematizing sales literature.

Education

County College, Diploma, Marketing Communications, 2000
Shelton Institute, Applied Writing and Database Administration courses, 2001

Sales and marketing director

Kevin J Bordon

1 Any Street
Anytown, Anycounty AX0 0AA
020 8123 4567
E-mail: kevBordon@aol.com

Summary of Qualifications

Increasing responsibilities in the following areas:

- National Sales Management
- Corporate Advertising
- Supervision of Employees
- Training and Motivation
- New Account/Business Development
- Contract Management

- Marketing Programmes
- Team and Relationship Building
- Performance Improvement
- Representative Liaison
- Purchasing/Inventory Control
- Vendor Relations

Profile

An accomplished sales and account management background, encompassing client relations and new business development...delivered presentations before FTSE 100 companies, manufacturers and distributors.

Planned and conducted networking, canvassing, lead generation and direct marketing campaigns, as well as trade show presentations...recruited, trained and supervised employees...developed rapport with senior management, department heads, vendors, clients and sales personnel.

Professional Experience

DX TUBE CORPORATION, Clifton   **2003–Present**

Director of Sales & Marketing

DX is the producer of welded pipe and welded tubing. Introduced a large customer base from the stainless steel industry to contract and continue as DX's clients in the welded pipe and tubing area of the business.

- Hired eight sales representatives to sell DX's products in different regions in the country.
- Developed new pricing strategies including rebates, freight considerations for inventory, business, and direct business to attract new accounts for long-term relationships.
- Personally covered local sales territories including Gloucester, Wiltshire, and North Devon.
- Ensured trust and service for new customers.
- Set up a sales group for sales training.
- Developed a new brochure and detailed chart for field sales presentations to enhance our company's communications.
- Created programmes for advertisements in various trade magazines and promotional vehicles that were successful in bringing in new enquiries regarding our products and ultimately new customers.
- Arranged outings for social events and served as liaison that designed new markets for growth opportunities.
- Defined markets and targeted the right customer populations for the sales force.

Professional Experience (continued)

AB TUBE, LTD, North Branch   **1988–2003**

Vice President of Sales   **1996–2002**
Sales Manager   **1988–1996**
Assumed full responsibility for all sales and marketing functions for this steel company. Played a key role in the organization's growth from £12 million to over £40 million in annual revenues, initiating and managing a series of business development strategies to increase activity from new and existing accounts.

Spearheaded programmes to target previously untapped markets, which included a campaign geared toward the beverage industry that produced £8 million in annual sales.

● Secured lucrative agreements with such industry giants as CDE Ltd and FG Oil, strengthening the company's overall competitive position.
● Built productive relationships with 10 independent representative agencies, instituting incentives, which heightened their efforts to promote the company's lines.
● Improved the performance of sales employees through effective training and motivation generating significant new business.
● Enhanced the company's image and visibility by launching aggressive advertising and marketing campaigns, which included ads in trade magazines, brochures and promotional items.
● Devised methods to facilitate more open communication between sales representatives and other departments in the company, including production, quality control and finance.

TUBE SALES, Canterbury   **1982–1988**

Purchasing & Inventory Control Coordinator

● Directed purchasing and inventory control activities for over £20 million of stainless steel tubing.
● Established a centralized purchasing system that generated substantial savings through more advantageous rates.

Education

City College, London
BA in Business

Affiliations

City Recreation Centre, Coach
Forest Gate Country Club Member

Additional Keywords: stainless steel industry, welded pipe, welded tubing, steel industry, management, business development, sales, manufacturing sales, vendor negotiations, advertising, marketing, manufacturing account management, sales management.

Sales executive

Mary Ann was a recent graduate looking for a job while she continued training as a performer.

MARY ANN BURROWS
1 Any Street • Anytown AX0 0AA • 020 8123 4567

Sales/Account Manager/Customer Service

Energetic and goal-focused sales professional with solid qualifications in large account management and customer relationship building/maintenance. Proven ability to develop new business and increase sales within established accounts and mature territories. Self-confident and poised in interactions across all business hierarchies; a persuasive communicator and assertive negotiator with strong deal-closing abilities. Excellent time management skills; computer literate. Areas of demonstrated value include:

- Sales Growth/Account Development
- Commercial Account Management
- Prospecting and Business Development
- Customer Liaison and Service
- Consultative Sales/Needs Assessment
- Territory Management and Growth

PROFESSIONAL EXPERIENCE
XYZ Ltd, Wolverhampton   1998–Present
SALES EXECUTIVE (2000–Present)
Promoted and challenged to revitalize a large metropolitan territory plagued by poor performance. Manage, service, and build existing accounts; develop new business, establishing both regional and national accounts. Serve as key liaison for all customers and work as the only sales representative in the company. Produce monthly reports for major national accounts.

Selected Results
- Reversed a history of stagnant sales; delivered consistent growth and built territory sales 22%, to £4.75 million annually, in less than 2 years.
- Surpassed quota by a minimum of 20% for 14 consecutive months.
- Personally deliver 95% of all sales generated for the company's main site.
- Prospected aggressively and presented products to key decision-makers during cold calls; opened more than 60 new commercial accounts.
- Improved account service and applied consultative sales techniques; grew sales in every established account a minimum of 15%.

MANAGER, Hartlepool Store (1998–2000)

MANAGER TRAINEE, Wolverhampton Store (1998)
Initially recruited as a management trainee and rapidly advanced to management of a retail location generating £4 million annually. Supervised and scheduled 12 employees. Budgeted and produced advertising, oversaw bookkeeping, and set/managed sales projections and growth objectives.

EDUCATION AND CREDENTIALS
BA, BUSINESS MANAGEMENT, 1998
Wilmington College, Newcastle

Additional Training
Building Sales Relationships, 2001
Problem Solving Skills, 2001

Professional & Community Associations
Member, Chamber of Commerce, 1999–Present
Member, Country Club and Women's Golf Association, 1999–Present
Youth Sports Coach and FIFA Certified Referee, 2002–Present

Senior account executive

Jane Swift   Page 1 of 2

123 Anystreet
Anytown AT1 0BB
Tel: 020 8123 4567
jane@anyaddress.co.uk

- 15+ years' experience building partnerships with leading corporations to develop consumer packaging, sales promotions, and merchandising to strengthen brand identity and awareness. In-depth understanding of technology, household products, personal care, drinks, and food categories.
- Account management capabilities enhanced by professional design, production, printing, and technical background. Formal design education and commitment to ongoing professional development.
- Adept in Macintosh and Windows applications for graphic design, desktop publishing, word processing, spreadsheets, e-mail, database management, Web site development and multimedia presentations.

Key Words

Consultative Sales	High-Impact Presentations
Customer Service	Problem Solving & Decision Making
Project Management	Sales Closing & Negotiating
Design Process	Team Building & Leadership

Achievements
- Generated nearly £1 million in annual sales for packaging design firm by winning key accounts and cultivating relationships.
- Won four Packaging Design Council (PDC) Gold Awards for package design in personal care and household appliances categories.
- Won account with major multinational corporation and developed packaging, promotional displays, trade, and consumer material. Facilitated the national redesign (60 product lines) in order to establish products as the technologically superior brand within the category.
- Collaborated on the national implementation of a 'company first' branding strategy. Key objective: to reinforce the brand name, weakened by a four-year trend of sub-branding. Brainstormed with marketing and creative executives to create a set of graphic standards to communicate the essence of the brand. Applied this branding system to the entire product line.
- Increased sales and distribution through development of innovative club-store packaging and promotions for a leading drinks supplier.
- Guided design and production of packaging and product launch materials for a 30-unit range of household products. Product was picked up nationally by ASCO and sales jumped 19% in an introductory period.
- Worked with a leading cereal maker to develop promotional back panel games, sweepstakes, and in-pack offers.
- Directed development of displays, brochures, and merchandising materials for Curtis Confectionery and Berry Farm Products (created through licensing agreement).
- Introduced multimedia capability to firm's new business presentations. Created Web site content, including a company tour, an interactive portfolio, and a creative access section – allowing clients online, confidential access to view work.

Career Chronology
Senior Account Executive – 1998–Present
Leading Package Design Firm, York
- Hired as a junior account executive to assist in all aspects of client services. Within seven months, promoted to account executive to develop new business in the consumer electronics category. Established key contacts with industry leaders through cold calling, direct marketing and client presentations. Consulted with clients to determine marketing objectives, packaging requirements and budgetary limitations. Directed numerous packaging, promotion, trade and consumer projects. Managed staff of five to implement the electronic design and production process.

Computer Graphics Artist – 1995–1998
Big Design Firm, York
- Worked with designers and art directors to take concepts through to highly refined computer based production. Trained members of the design and production department in the use of Adobe Illustrator. Set up a high-speed remote viewing network enabling select clients to simultaneously view design concepts.

Account Executive – 1991–1995
Freelance Placement Agency, York
- Instrumental in establishing a lucrative desktop publishing placement division. Identified and cultivated profitable markets. Managed and art directed freelancers and worked with clients through all project stages.

Graphic Designer – 1985–1991
ABC Marketing & Communications, York
- Accountable for all stages of the design and production of consumer packaging. Participated in beta testing of proprietary graphics software and various high-end peripherals, giving product reviews to manufacturers.

Education
BA Graphic Design, Industrial Design, Computer Graphics and Marketing – 1985
York University

Ongoing Professional Development
- Earned Certificate in Sales Promotion – St John's College
- Intensive seminars in Web site design, multimedia and advertising

Pharmaceutical rep

Jenny needed to translate 'sales' expertise gained in three years on a job most think of as far removed from selling. She was employed as a pharmaceutical rep in just 29 calendar days.

Jenny McClean

1 Any Street • Anytown AX0 0AA • 020 8123 4568 (Office) 020 8123 4567 (Home) • jamclean@hotmail.com

Summary of Qualifications
- Organized, efficient, and precise with strong communication and liaison skills
- Skilled in planning and execution of special projects during time-critical assignment
- Decisive and direct, yet flexible in responding to constantly changing assignments
- Able to coordinate multiple projects and meet deadlines under pressure
- Enthusiastic, creative and willing to assume increased responsibility
- Attention to details and strong follow-through

Special Skills
- Language – Fluent in Spanish
- Computer – UNIX, VMA, Lotus Notes, MS Office, Word Perfect, SPSS 8.0, ESRI
- Certified in radiation safety
- Experience with medical terminology
- Database development

Relevant Skills
Office Administration
- Collecting and recording statistical and confidential information
- Assembling and organizing bulk mailing and marketing materials
- Data entry, with exceptionally fast typing and related Office Administration activities
- Organization specialist, able to ensure smooth and efficient flow of functions
- Progressive experience in office management, scheduling, and support services, data analysis, and research collection

Customer Service
- Extremely sociable and able to put visitors at ease
- Excellent verbal and written communication skills
- Highly skilled at solving customer relations problems

Education
- MA in Public Administration, Metropolitan University
- BA, Sociology, University of the South

Relevant Professional Experience
DATA ANALYST
ABC Health Products, Havant

ADMINISTRATIVE CLERK
The Valley Healthcare Clinic, West Hants

GRADUATE ASSISTANT IN CONTINUING EDUCATION
Metropolitan University

SALES SUPERVISOR
XYZ Department Store, Plymouth

LAW CLERK
Patton & Page Law Firm, Plymouth

Property development

Michael had a background in law, and he desired to move into financial management/project management.

MICHAEL WILSON

1 Any Street, Anytown, AX0 0AA
Home: 020 8123 4567 Mobile: 07850 515536 E-mail: mwilson@ocean.net.com

OBJECTIVE
A position in PROPERTY DEVELOPMENT that will use strong analytical skills, knowledge of market-place trends and practices, and benefit from my legal background.

OVERVIEW
- Organized, take-charge professional with exceptional follow-through abilities and detail orientation; able to plan and oversee a full range of events from concept to successful conclusion.
- Demonstrated ability to efficiently prioritize a broad range of responsibilities in order to consistently meet deadlines.
- Dynamic negotiator; effective in achieving positive results.
- Demonstrated capability to anticipate and resolve problems swiftly and independently.
- Possess strong interpersonal skills; proven ability to develop and maintain sound business relationships with clients, anticipating their needs.
- Highly articulate, effective communicator, experienced presenter; possess excellent platform skills.
- Highly adept in using state-of-the-art software packages for industry-related functions, from data and finance management to CADD. Hands-on-experience with Argus and Project.

Demonstrated skills in:
- Research
- Urban Development
- Accounting
- Bankruptcy
- Tax Issues

- Mediation
- Legal Writing
- Analytical Writing
- Financial Analysis
- Small Business Development

- Mergers and Acquisitions
- Small Business Planning
- Corporate Finance
- Administrative System Design
- Foreclosure

PROFESSIONAL EXPERIENCE
May 2002–Present
SMITH & ASSOCIATES, Overland Park
Special Projects Consultant for well-respected communications consulting firm. Firm authored two critically acclaimed standards in the marketing/business field: *The New Positioning* and *The Power of Simplicity.*

- Perform directed Internet and other research in preparation for an upcoming book.
- Analyse research and draft description for inclusion in articles and future book.
- Specifically recruited for special projects on basis of past performance.

September 2001–Present
RIVERVIEW LTD, Overland Park
Assistant Manager for firm affiliated with the ABC Design Centre.

- Collaborate with decorative artist on projects in the £75K range, custom building business furniture, conference rooms, mahogany libraries, etc.
- Perform multitude of skilled operations from rough milling to fine detail finishing and veneer application.
- Assist in project estimates and sales proposals.

PROFESSIONAL EXPERIENCE (continued)

June 2000–December 2000
MATHEWS, WATERS & MILLS, Kirby
Paralegal

● Gained valuable experience in bankruptcy proceedings.

January 2000–May 2000
HENRY, MARGOLIS & WHITE, Lincoln
Paralegal

● Legal research and writing on legalities relating to general equity matters.

September 1999–December 1999
GIARDELA & ROSE, Lincoln
Paralegal

Summer 1999
SETTON, BIGGS & RUTTER, Overland Park
Clerk

EDUCATION

UNIVERSITY OF THE SOUTH
Higher Certificate in Paralegal Studies   2001

METROPOLITAN UNIVERSITY
BA, Political Science   1998

REFERENCES

Excellent references will be furnished on request.

Bank branch management

SCOTT E BOWMAN

1 Any Street, Anytown AX0 0AA • 020 8123 4567 •
bowman4765@hotmail.com

FINANCE – BANKING – Branch Management/Customer Service

Well-qualified and results-oriented **Finance and Banking** professional with experience and demonstrated accomplishments developing corporate growth, and financial performance. Skilled analyst with strong organizational and communications abilities, and proven leadership qualities. Broad-based understanding of financial needs at all levels of business including evaluating, analysing, and communicating financial data. Demonstrate broad-based strengths and accomplishments in:

Finance & Banking	Project Management	Teller Operations
Marketing Financial Services	Customer Service Relations	Loan/Account Origination
Team Management	Sales Management	Problem Solving
eBusiness Management	Communications	Continuing Education
Supervision/Leadership	Branch Management	Strategic Management

Recipient – Commerce Capital Markets Referral Award – July/August 2004

PROFESSIONAL EXPERIENCE

ABC BANK, Newport, 2004 to Present
CUSTOMER SERVICE REPRESENTATIVE (CSR)
Counsel clients in the selection of financial products in order to meet their financial planning and banking needs. Create and process client accounts providing excellent customer service. Sell and refer bank products based on specific sales focus (Commerce Capital Markets, Commerce National Insurance and Residential Mortgage). Identify prospective clients and develop and implement presentations for clients. Originate and process consumer and mortgage loan applications. Extensive knowledge of bank lending policies, practices, compliance, and underwriting criteria. Familiar with processing collateral loans, unsecured personal loans, asset-based loans, and mortgage-based loans. Process a myriad of loan documentation performing research activities when necessary.

Accomplishments
- Consistently met and exceeded sales quotas and standards by cross-selling and up-selling bank products and services.
- Increased branch loan production volume.
- Sold a variety of loans, created loan worksheets, and made recommendations to lenders upon request.
- Ensured that loan policies and procedures were followed in accordance with audit guidelines.

AUTOGRAPHS LTD, Manchester – 1999 to 2004
BUSINESS MANAGER
Established and currently manage Internet and mail order entertainment media business. Implemented strategic marketing programmes successfully retaining clients and achieving market position. Instituted pricing structure after conducting extensive marketing research utilizing industry resources. Explored marketing and advertising opportunities adding value to new initiatives. Tracked data and improved business operations accordingly.

Accomplishments
● Grew annual revenues to £30K.
● Authored inventory item descriptions and managed customer service relations.

EDUCATION/TRAINING
CITY UNIVERSITY, **BA – History and Politics**

ABC BANK COURSES
Finance, Supervision, Business Management, Consumer Lending, Customer Service, Loan
Products, Privacy Compliance, Loan Underwriting, BSA/AML, Foreign Assets Control, Bank
Secrecy, etc.

COMPUTER SKILLS
Microsoft Office, Lotus Notes, dBase, Basic, HTML

Financial services

Dara is seeking promotion and will use this CV internally.

Dara E Hanes

1 Any Street • Anytown, Any County AX0 0HA • 020 8123 4567 • daraehanes_10@aol.com

Professional Profile

Results-oriented financial services professional exemplified by a steady increase of responsibility.

Customer-satisfaction focused: Use verbal communication skills and superior product knowledge to perform benefits analysis and proactively recommend and implement solutions. **Results-motivated:** Deliver highly effective and energetic service and sales presentations culminating in exemplary results. **Team-oriented:** Apply negotiation and team building skills to coordinate the activity between internal departments required to meet client needs.

Education and Licences

MBA City University   **2003**

BA Political Science (International Business concentration) City University   **1997**

Diploma in Financial Planning
Pursuing CFP Designation

Professional Experience

ABC Financial, Dunstable	**August 1997–Present**
Institutional Liaison	**September 2003–Present**

- Create Time and Action plans geared toward the successful and timely implementation of all interdependent processes and compliance issues related to plan administration.
- Foster and maintain relationships with high priority institutions of £330,000,000 in assets and effectively retained 10 major institutional clients.
- Evaluate customer relationships and ensure that all recommendations and procedures are fully functional prior to their implementation.
- Monitor and proactively combat the administrative activities of competitors, resulting in the retention of 600 individual clients.
- Conduct sales and service meetings to determine best cost effective and efficient plan to implement.
- Assess and evaluate customer plan requirements by conducting needs assessments using service surveys.
- Advise institutions on changes or enhancements to administrative procedures and policies.
- Measure and manage internal procedures to identify and resolve service shortfalls.
- Coordinate communications between internal processing areas, ensuring proper plan implementation.
- Perform compliance testing and compute employer contributions.
- Develop strategies for implementing plan design changes.
- Interpret plan documents.

continued

Service Plus Representative   **August 2000–September 2003**

- Contributed to the development, implementation and control of specialized marketing campaigns targeted to individual customers.
- Monitored and combated the activities of competitors to influence individual customers.
- Conducted follow-up sales contacts resulting in increased annuity premium volume.
- Designed and implemented strategies to counter competitive tactics.
- Expanded new business from external rollovers and asset transfers.

Individual Telephone Consultant   **August 1997–August 2000**

- Promoted ABC Financial's products, services and investment performance relative to those of competitors.
- Calculated and recommended optimal combination of products needed to achieve retirement goals.
- Counselled individuals on a broad range of financial planning issues using superior product knowledge.
- Guided individuals in establishing financial goals.
- Proactively corrected misinformation.

Accounting and administrative assistant

Jean English

· ·

1 Any Street, Anytown AX0 0AA
Home 020 8123 4567
E-mail: jenglish@careerbrain.com

Accounting & Administrative Assistant
Accounts Payable and Receivable/Payroll/Computer Systems Expert

Organized and responsible Administrative & Accounting Assistant with more than 12 years of experience across diverse industries. Educated and energetic professional recognized as a quick learner with exceptional computer skills and the unique ability to manage several tasks in a stressful environment. Excellent communicator seeking a challenging position, using current skills and abilities, with the opportunity for professional growth.

- Accounts Payable/Receivable
- Payroll/Payroll Systems
- Employee Scheduling
- Purchasing/Lease Agreements

- Microsoft Windows, Excel, Word
- Daily Ledger/Bookkeeping
- Customer Service
- Database Development

PROFESSIONAL EXPERIENCE

Manager of Casino Administration/Analyst   2001–present
Casino Royale, Windsor
- Responsible for tracking, analysis and payment approval of all accounts payable for the department averaging £100,000 monthly.
- Created a computerized daily tracking system used by all managers and the casino President due to its flexibility and user friendliness.

Pit Manager   1999–2001
Casino Royale, Windsor
- Accepted the challenge to learn the scheduling system for the staff of 1,000 during a crisis, allowing payroll to resume uninterrupted for the entire casino.

Floor Supervisor   1997–1999
Casino Royale, Windsor
- After just one year as a dealer, was promoted to Floor Supervisor managing up to 300 dealers on a shift.

Agency Office Manager   1990–1997
Gulliver's Travel, Windsor
- Managed all day-to-day operations including accounts receivable, accounts payable, bookkeeping, payroll, budgets, employee training and customer service.

Travel Agent   1985–1990
Gulliver's Travel, Windsor

EDUCATION AND PROFESSIONAL CREDENTIALS

Computer Programmer Analyst, 3-year business programme including accounting
St. Clair College of Technology, 1986–1989

Microsoft Excel Advanced, *2001*   **Microsoft Access Advanced,** *2001*
Microsoft Excel Intermediate, *2000*   **Microsoft Access Intermediate,** *2000*
Microsoft Excel, *1994*   **Microsoft Word,** *1994*
St. Clair College of Technology

Financial consultant

Brian was laid off and was seeking a broader executive level finance role; he was offered a CFO position.

Brian Bachelor

1 Any Street, Anytown AX0 0AA
Mobile: 07850 515536 Home: 020 8123 4567
E-mail: bbac@aoz.com

OBJECTIVE: **Proprietary Trader/Hedge Fund Manager** position continuing a successful record of profit generation.

PROFILE:
- 12 years of high performance in financial investment. Past 10 years as a Market Maker on the floor of the Stock Exchange with a consistent, verifiable record of achievement in competitive and volatile environments. Traded futures, options, equities, bonds and derivatives.
- Licensed Broker Dealer.
- Demonstrated competencies in creative problem solving, decision making, negotiating and use of computer trading applications.
- Noted for options trading expertise, vision, initiative and ethics.

EXPERIENCE   **Market Maker**   1994–Present
XYZ Trading, London

- Earned over £10,000,000 in profits starting with £40,000 in equity. Reversed initial client investment within six months.
- Achieved strong and sustainable gains each year, regardless of market conditions, through a conservative trading approach.
- Acquired Lead Market Maker (one of three) designation for equity options traded on Microsoft and JDS Uniphase.
- Invested in and coached five novice traders securing a £500,000 return within three years.

Financial Consultant   1992–1994
ABC, London

- Cultivated and managed a base of 300+ clients (retail and institutions) with speculative investments, mutual funds, insurance, stocks, bonds, futures and options.
- Led the account development and service of a £24+ million portfolio in collaboration with management.
- Performed personal financial analysis including net worth, cash flow, income tax situation, investment portfolio analysis, insurance detail, retirement outlook and estate planning.

EDUCATION   **BA, Business Administration – Finance**   1992
London University

- Co-created an options trading computer program that funded 1.5 years of education.

Credit analyst

Sarah Jessica Ruth

1 Any Street, Anytown AX0 0AA
020 8123 4567 Home • Sarahjr@home.com

Branch Manager
Credit Analyst/Commercial Credit/Consumer Credit/Credit Administration/Credit Management/
Lending Office/Finance and Budgeting/Personnel Manager

Strong commitment to excellence. Dynamic presentation, communication, and marketing skills.
Distinguished performance encompassing a steady advancement of increasing accomplishments resulting in fast-track promotion and progressively responsible banking duties. Motivated,
results-oriented individual. Excellent planning, organizational, development and leadership
qualifications. High-impact negotiator, spokesperson, and client service manager.

Professional Experience
ABC Financial, Regional Credit Manager: Manage 30 employees covering North West region.
Analyse competitor programmes and develop marketing strategies for competitive market
positioning to increase market share. Communicate effectively with dealers to initiate, develop,
and maintain customer relationships and client satisfaction. Reporting, record keeping, and
documentation of business deals, self audits, and budget control. Manage and track funding
goals of credit analysts. Performance management of staff through effective training and
evaluations. Conduct regular staff meetings and communicate company policy and procedures.
Design, development, and Implementation of effective succession plan to reduce staff turnover.
(2001 present)

Regional Branch Manager: Managed 16 employees covering all of East Anglia. Regulated and
coordinated all aspects of branch operation to achieve volume and profit goals. Managed branch
operation within established guidelines and budget parameters. Scope of responsibilities
included lending, collections, marketing and sales, administration and personnel. Hired,
organized, trained, and evaluated personnel in all phases of branch operations. Motivated
production while organizing marketing activities and strategies in a changing market. Facilitated
monthly market, projection, and production reports for Senior and Regional Directors. Generated
quality customer service and ongoing customer loyalty. (2000–2001)

Assistant Manager: Evaluated and reviewed credit applications submitted by auto dealerships for
credit line and contract purchase in accordance with company policy. Supervised office staff to
ensure company policy and procedures. Performance management, training and evaluation of
personnel. (1997–2000)

NorthEast Bank, Loan Officer/Credit Analyst: Conducted all aspects of consumer and commercial
lending. Cultivated and maintained customer relationships through quality customer service.
Promoted from entry-level trainee to Associate Loan Officer to Loan Officer/Credit Analyst within
a 2-year period. Scope of responsibilities included cash flow, credit, financial statements, and
budget spreadsheet analysis. (1995–1997)

Education
BA Economics, University of London (1995)

Volunteer Work
UNICEF, RNIB

Credit and collections

James is a bank executive who wanted to relocate. This particular format showcased his credentials in a straightforward, results-driven manner.

JAMES HOFFMAN

1 Any Street, Anytown AX0 0AA   –   020 8123 4567

PROFESSIONAL OBJECTIVE

Opportunity with a Northampton-based financial services organization where expertise in commercial collections, credit administration, and financial analysis/structuring contributes to increased profits.

PROFILE

- Extensive general business experience in the financial services industry, with credentials in both line and staff positions. Areas of expertise:

  - credit/portfolio administration
  - asset structuring/restructuring
  - commercial collections
  - loan documentation
  - regulatory compliance

  - financial analysis
  - risk assessment/underwriting
  - problem asset resolution/loan work-outs
  - operations/information integration
  - lender liability issues

- Background in diverse environments ranging from major regional financial holding companies to large and small community banks.
- Driving force in the establishment of a newly chartered commercial bank in the Bristol area.
- Customer-focused professional whose philosophy is to 'do it right the first time.'
- Viewed by clients as an individual who is worthy of their trust, and who holds their best interests paramount.
- Effective at building sound internal/external relationships to support client and organizational goals.
- Actively involved in leadership roles focused on community development.

EDUCATION

MBA   **Financial Administration**
North West University, 1982

BA   **Business-Economics**
London University, 1980

Executive Professional Development Programmes:

- Management School for Corporate Bankers
- National Commercial Lending Schools
- Certified Commercial Lender
- Computer School for Executives
- Leadership and Lending

JAMES HOFFMAN   PAGE TWO

EXPERIENCE

ABC BANK, Preston   1998–Present
- Founder/Charter Director/Executive Vice President and Senior Lending/Compliance Officer.
- Established nine-member Board of Directors.

Key Accomplishments:
- Led efforts in generating £17.2 million.
- Grew bank into a profitable organization with £120 million in assets, while maintaining strong loan quality.
- Personally managed 70% of the bank's borrowing client base and 60% of £72 million in total loans outstanding.

XYZ, Teddington   1996–1998
- Senior Vice President, Leasing – Managed lease origination process for a national leasing company. Offerings included private label programme for five FTSE companies. Trained, supervised and developed new team members.

Key Accomplishment:
- Introduced commercial bank quality underwriting procedures to correct prior portfolio deficiencies for leases averaging £75,000 per transaction.

DEF BANK, Illminster   1989–1996
- Senior Lending Officer – Responsible for bank's credit administration and management of commercial, consumer, and residential lending. Chaired Loan and Community Reinvestment committees.

Key Accomplishments:
- Developed and implemented new credit culture, achieving an all-time bank record of 1.12% ROA, from a negative .67%.

GHI BANK, Chichester   1983–1986
- Commercial Lending Officer – Special Loan Division – Established and managed new loan workout activity to support the bank's domestic commercial lending group.

Key Accomplishment:
- Directed reduction of Internally classified credits and nonperforming assets by 70% each.

CIVIC AND PROFESSIONAL ACTIVITIES

- Board of Directors and Past Chair, Local Chamber of Commerce
- International Association of Bank Executives, Charter Member and Board of Directors
- Senior Board Member, National Banking Institute

Insurance claims specialist

Laura D Wenn   1 Any Street, Anytown AX0 0AA • 020 8123 4567 •
                                                              ldw56@yahoo.com

Career Profile
High-energy, cross-functional background as resourceful fast-track insurance claims specialist with an outstanding record of success in winning settlements and reducing claims payouts to acceptable and just amounts. Investigate, negotiate, and settle complex claims.

Areas of Expertise
Administration
- organized and effective performance in high-pressure environments
- presentation development and delivery
- word processing and spreadsheet development (type 60 words per minute)

- claims investigation with meticulous documentation
- heavy phones/switchboard
- skilled customer care
- Microsoft Office, Internet and intranet proficiency

Insurance Claims
- commercial and personal lines liability
- property damage, and bodily injury claims
- claimant, solicitor and litigation representation
- settlement and target value range setting
- medical and liability evaluation

- general liability, auto, homeowners, and products liability
- injury exposure values
- complex arbitration and mediation negotiation

Highlights
- Handle caseload of up to 230 pending commercial and personal claims. Establish contact within 24 hours, maintain impeccable documentation, and determine value of case based on liability/injury. Decide claims values up to £50,000. Negotiate/settle cases in mediation, arbitration, or litigation.
- Delivered a £15,000 saving to XYZ by obtaining a defence verdict on a case that a judge suggested XYZ 'buy out' for £15,000. Communicated with solicitors, evaluated liability/facts and determined feasibility for trial. Case went to trial and XYZ paid nothing but legal costs.
- Saved ABC £40,000 on complex £100,000 second-degree burn claim by determining case's suitability for mediation, and meeting with judge and plaintiff's solicitors. Case was settled for a fair £60,000 without incurring major legal costs for ABC.
- Promoted onto ABC fast-track after only one year; became the youngest adjuster in company history. Track record of positive mediation, arbitration, and litigation outcomes is equal to or better than that of more senior professionals.
- Possess outstanding administrative/organizational skills, superior presentation and negotiation abilities, a passion for excellence, and a contagious enthusiasm. Work well in independent or team environments. Tenacious, with the stamina needed to function in high-pressure environments.

Employment
XYZ Insurance Ltd, Claims Assessor   2001 to Present
ABC Claims Services
      Claims Specialist   2000 to 2001
      Loss Adjuster   1998 to 2000
      Claims Assistant   1997 to 1998

Education and Professional Development
CICCIA   ACII   CII Insurance Foundation Certificate

Industry Courses: Commercial General Liability, Claims Statements, Property Casualty Principles, Litigation Guidelines, Medical Terminology and Treatment, How to Handle Cases to Avoid Litigation, Accurate Reserving

Insurance executive

MATTHEW A SIMS

1 Any Street, Anytown AX0 0AA • 020 8123 4567 • masims@aol.com

Career Profile

- Over ten years background in ABC Insurance.
- Key player in the building of one of the nation's top ten insurers.
- Director and Core Management Team member of ABC Insurance. Recognized as an astute visionary, delivering fresh perspectives and keen assessments using intellect, judgement, and character. Known for making and upholding tough decisions.

Areas of Expertise

Management Skills and Insurance Experience:

- programme creation/strategic planning
- resource development
- multimillion-dollar budget creation
- budget management/cost controls
- corporate restructuring
- relationship and team building
- boardroom-level presentations

- loss development and analysis
- high-level claims analysis and resolution
- high exposure claims
- severe injury and multiple policy management
- complex litigation management
- medical profession liability policies
- reserving and settlement authority

Executive Highlights

Accelerated Growth
- During senior management tenure, helped to grow company from 3,000 to 7,500 policyholders, adding a wide range of clients. Growth exploded business and caused expansion of department from 15 to 50 employees.

Financial Analysis and Cost Improvement
- Handled complex financial analysis and legal cost containment. Reduced litigation costs by 15% to 20%. Streamlined claims-handling process by enabling claims examiners to handle larger caseloads through realignment of custodial tasks to clerical staff. Collaborated with company actuaries to interpret and act upon loss trends and developments.

Profit and Loss
- Developed highly accurate, multimillion dollar budgets. In addition, effective personal handling of reserving and settlement authority, legal cost containment, favourable trial results, and efficiency measures directly affected corporate bottom line.

New Systems and Technology
- Significantly reduced legal costs through research, development, and implementation of innovative automated legal processing and auditing programme.

Business Reorganization
- Following ABC's recent acquisition, collaborated as key member of transition team to develop and implement efficient reorganization plan to achieve efficiency gains.

Career Advancement
- Fast-tracked from claims representative to vice president in four years. Was handpicked, recruited, and mentored by CEO during ABC's initial period of accelerated growth.

Employment

ABC Insurance, Manchester

- Senior Vice President   2002 to present
- Vice President   1996 to 2001
- Claims Manager   1995 to 1996
- Claims Supervisor   1994 to 1995
- Claims Representative   1993 to 1994

Management Summary

- Report directly to the CEO and Board of Directors. Oversee two direct reports administering activities over 60 headquarters and branch staff members. Direct and manage claims reserves in excess of £900 million, handling reserving and settlement of individual claims of up to £1 million.
- Daily functions include £4 million budget development and management, staffing, cost control, appointment of legal counsel, policy creation, determination of complex coverage issues, high-exposure claims monitoring, and interface with re-insurers/excess insurers.

Significant Achievements

- Track record of wide-ranging contributions in systems development, cost containment, and claims management. Maintained severity at flat levels for the past five years, reduced litigation costs, and improved beneficial trial results. Fast-tracked from claims representative to Director in four years.

Professional Development

- UK Management Association continuing professional development courses include annual seminars on insurance issues, Accounting for Non-Financial Executives, Managing Conflict, Interpersonal Skills, Management of Reciprocals and Mutuals.

Education

BSc Biology, Metropolitan University

Communications

DEBRA JOY BISMARK

1 Any Street, Any Town AX0 0AA   020 8123 4567
E-MAIL: Bismark@ias.edu

SUMMARY OF QUALIFICATIONS

Communications and writing professional with expertise in areas including
- Research and Narrative Reports
- Newsletters and Feature Stories
- Grant Writing
- Academic Writing & Marketing
- Editorial Functions
- Public Relations
- Advertising & Promotional Writing
- Community Relations
- Proposals

WRITING
- Authored individualized newsletters for families of students with special needs
- Wrote detailed narrative reports citing student progress
- Wrote news stories, regular features for monthly newsletter with readership of 50,000 (Institute of Chemical Engineers, IChE)
- Wrote articles for student member magazine during six-year tenure as Communications Writer (IChE)
- Poetry published in *Without Halos*, *Worksheets*, *The Poet's Page*, and accepted into *Mediphors* and *Poet*
- Enjoy collaborating with colleagues to develop programmes and implement projects. Articulate ideas clearly and concisely

ACHIEVEMENTS
- Turned technical papers into crisp copy – Press releases received national recognition (IChE)
- Created and ran building code research business for York Architectural Support Services
- Designed brochure educating parents on early literacy
- Executive committee members wrote letters of appreciation for concept identifying a new engineering-in-schools campaign (Project VEGA, IChE)
- Won a company-wide logo competition (IChE)
- Created a proposal for a reading/writing clinic (South Somerset LEA)
- Trained and advised colleagues in strategies for supporting early reading and writing

TECHNICAL EXPERTISE
- Proofread and edited technical articles for a scientific journal (IChE)
- Computer literate with working knowledge of Microsoft Word, Desktop Publishing (Ventura), Access database training
- Capable Internet researcher

EMPLOYMENT HISTORY
2005–present Programme Assistant (part-time) THE INSTITUTE FOR ADVANCED STUDY, Somerset
2004–present Reading Tutor   SELF-EMPLOYED
2003–2004   Teacher   FRIENDS SCHOOL, DOVER
1990–2003   Teacher   SOUTH SOMERSET LEA
1992–1998   Communications Writer   THE INSTITUTE OF CHEMICAL ENGINEERS
1991–1992   Editorial Assistant   THE INSTITUTE OF CHEMICAL ENGINEERS
1989–1991   Researcher   ARCHITECTURAL SUPPORT SERVICES

EDUCATION
MA, Social Work   City University
Teacher training   City College of Education
BSc Psychology   City University

Publishing/marketing professional

SUZANNE A KENNEDY

1 Any Street
Any Town AX0 0AA
020 8123 4567

PROFESSIONAL: *A Norwich Publisher of trade and academic books*
EXPERIENCE: **DIRECTOR OF ADVERTISING AND PROMOTION (MARCH 2001–Present)**

Key responsibilities include: managing advertising/promotion department with staff of four; overseeing and actively engaging in all aspects of promotion, advertising, and publicity. I have established and am maintaining a 22-person national sales force and make seasonal visits to the UK's two largest book-store chains.

Active in negotiating special sales and acquiring new titles, and as liaison with domestic and foreign rights agents. In 2001 I travelled to the United States, visited several publishers, bought and sold rights.

Frequently arrange author appearances on television and radio. As a company spokesperson, I have been interviewed numerous times by newspapers, magazines, and radio stations.

ADVERTISING AND PROMOTION MANAGER (1999–2001)
Advertising and Direct Mail: Created, designed, and wrote copy for brochures, flyers, and display ads; created direct-mail campaigns; represented company at publisher's book exhibits.

Publicity: Wrote news releases, selected media, made follow-up calls, arranged author media appearances.

ASSISTANT EDITOR (1997–1999)
Responsibilities included reading authors' manuscripts, copyediting, proofreading; writing jacket copy, coordinating and writing copy for catalogues. Some editing and proofreading was done on a freelance basis.

ABC Advertising, ADVERTISING COPYWRITER (1995–1997)
Responsible for designing and writing copy for bimonthly catalogue and supplementary flyers. Created ads and brochures; wrote sales letters and edited and rewrote direct-mail pieces.

EDUCATION: Metropolitan University
Degree: BA (Hons) English, 1995

SKILLS: Word processing, working knowledge of typography, research proficiency.

REFERENCES: Will be provided on request.

Event planner

George wanted a job closer to home. Some of his past job titles did not fit with his career aspirations, and he wanted to focus on the specific skills needed for an Events Manager, so he used a functional style format.

George S Easton
1 Any Street, Anytown AX0 0AA
020 8123 4567

PROFILE SUMMARY
Meeting Planning • Conferences • International Events • Fundraising • Golf Tournaments

Creative professional with expertise in all aspects of successful event/programme planning, development, and management. Excel in managing multiple projects concurrently with strong detail, problem-solving and follow-through capabilities. Demonstrated ability to manage, motivate and build cohesive teams that achieve results. Sourced vendor, negotiated contracts and managed budgets. Superb written communications, interpersonal and organizational skills. First-class client relation and teaming skills. Proficient in Access, Excel, PowerPoint, Outlook, MS Project, Publisher, MeetingTrak and Corel WordPerfect.

PROFESSIONAL EXPERIENCE
Meeting Planning Management

Planned and coordinated government, association and private conferences, meetings, events and fundraising. Coordinated all conference activities, workshops, meetings, tours, and special events. Trained, directed, and supervised teams to accomplish goals. **Saved £72,000 on most recent meeting.**

- As Team Leader, coordinated 10–26 annual workshops for Association for Climate Change.
- Coordinated 2004 National Conference on Smoking and Health. (2,000 participants).
- Organized 6,000-participant national annual conferences.
- Coordinated Youth Education Conference Training for 200 third-world participants.
- Developed and supervised education sessions at ABC's 2001 National Convention.
- Directed ABC's National Seminar Series.

Meeting Coordination

As Team Leader, coordinated production, distribution, and grading of exam materials. Supervised registration and tracking of continuing education units. Negotiated hotel and vendor contracts. Prepared and administered budgets. Arranged all on-site logistics, including transportation, accommodation, meals, guest speakers and audiovisual support. **Consistently come under budget for each meeting planned.**

- Developed and maintained 5,000-person database.
- Developed, promoted and implemented ABC's National Certification Programme
- Managed logistics for a Regional Training Company

Fundraising

Team player in the development, promotion and implementation of membership and retention programmes for XYZ. Coordinated fundraising events. Supervised high-donor club fulfilment benefits. Provided updated donor reports.

- Coordinated 2 fundraising golf tournaments.

EVENTS MANAGEMENT EXPERIENCE
Conferences/Meetings/Programme Coordinator
1997–Present

- Association for Climate Change
- XYZ Training and Technical Assistance Project
- Children, Youth and Families Centre for Development
- UK Centre for Health Information
- National Library of Commercial Information
- Urban Development Association
- ABC National Seminar Series
- ABC 1998 and 1999 National Conventions and Exhibits

PROFESSIONAL EMPLOYMENT

XYZ SERVICES LTD   2003–Present
Senior Conference Specialist

DEF CONSULTING GROUP, Ascot   2000–2003
Logistics Manager
Senior Conference Coordinator

GHI CONSTRUCTION SPECIALISTS, Ascot   1979–1999
Assistant Coordinator of Education Programmes

NATIONAL ASSOCIATION FOR VOLUNTEERING, Walsall   1997
Assistant Director, Fundraising

EDUCATION & CERTIFICATIONS

Brownhills University
BSc Psychology, 1996

Certified Group Facilitator

PROFESSIONAL AFFILIATIONS

- Meeting Professionals International
- Logistical Committee
- Educational Retreat Committee
- Member Services Committee
- Community Outreach Committee
- Connected International Meeting Professionals Association (CIMPA)
- Special Olympics – Volunteer
- Hands On – Volunteer

Human resources manager

Jane E Barron

24 Old Stone Mill Drive
London AX0 0AA
020 8123 4567

Summary of Qualifications

Broad-based responsibilities in **Human Resource Management** including:

- Recruiting
- Training and Development
- Employee Relations Programme
- Office Management/Administration

- Counselling/Coaching
- Compensation
- Systems/Computerization

Profile

Known as a dedicated, results-oriented manager with the ability to build rapport at all levels…successful track record of motivating employees to obtain maximum performance and increase bottom-line profits for the company… developed internal training programmes that resulted in increased productivity and office innovation…experienced supervisor, multi-tasker…enjoy working in a fast-paced challenging environment.

Experience

ABC SERVICES LTD, Preston   2000–Present
Human Resources Manager
Responsible for all aspects of human resources for this nationwide mailing list company. Initially recruited for start-up operations and increased Human Resources functions to include responsibilities in three other satellite locations: Bristol, York and Cambridge.

Director/Human Resources
- Direct all programmes regarding employee relations, health, and welfare of the staff. Serve as a resource for new employees, counselling staff from executive levels to entry-level personnel. Travel to satellite locations to direct human resource functions.
- Serve as a coach and counsellor for personal and career transitions within the company. Attend various human resources seminars. Keep abreast of the latest legal and professional advances in the field.
- Direct all recruiting operations; create job descriptions and internal job postings. Initiate job offers. Monitor costs of classified advertising and employment agency usage.
- Create, implement, and enforce the policies and procedures for formal disciplinary actions and dismissals.
- Execute exit interviews and assist hiring managers with human resource functions in their respective departments.
- Computerized human resources office systems to enhance productivity and on-line database administration.

Training and Development
- Work with each department in developing specific training programmes required for each position. Assist in preparing training materials to support departmental needs.
- Develop and implement training programmes for general business functions including basic writing, stress management, and human relations.
- Prepare annual budgeting information regarding training programmes and present policy recommendations to the Director.

XYZ MARKET RESEARCH, Canterbury   1998–1999
Office Manager/Administrative Director
- As Office Manager, responsibilities included preparing departmental budgets and hiring and training of 10+ employees. Performed complete office purchasing for the facility.
- Implemented a customized computer database that monitored travel expenses for sales representatives and executives. The system tracked pertinent account data and human resource information. Prepared reports; interfaced with management regarding suggestions for budgeted versus actual expenses.
- Instituted new policies and procedures to guide the entire sales force regarding purchasing and administrative procedures.
- Coordinated a departmental move to a larger facility; worked closely with interior space planners and designers.

DEF SOLUTIONS, INC., Canterbury   1992–1998
Director of Human Resources
- Total responsibility for all activities relating to human resources including staff supervision, recruitment, training, personnel relations and goal setting.
- Analysed and procured appropriate insurance coverage for all areas of liability.
- Organized programmes, parties, and other company-wide events to encourage 'team' environment and a positive work atmosphere.

Business Administrator
- Initiated professional business practices and management to organize all aspects of office operations.
- Researched and recommended purchase of computers and appropriate software to meet financial and clerical needs.
- Trained other staff members in computer applications.
- Assumed responsibility for all accounting activities, including A/R, A/P, G/L, and P/R procedures.
- Analyzed cash flow for top management review.

Prior Employment

GHI SERVICES, Edmonton   1990–1992
Group Leader
Adjustment Analyst

JKL MANAGEMENT, Painswick   1989–1990
Assistant Supervisor

Education and Training

CITY UNIVERSITY, 1985 Courses in finance and commerce
Completed numerous corporate seminars in Management and Human Resources encompassing legal issues, recruitment, compensation, and administration. Member, Society of Human Resources Managers

Human resources

Joseph is someone with a psychology degree moving into Human Resources.

Joseph D Morten

1 Any Street, Anytown AX0 0AA • 020 8123 4567 (H) • 020 8123 4568 (Fax)
jmorten439@aol.com

Human Resources/Corporate Training
Supervision – Business Management – Employee Relations – Coaching

Energetic, reliable and adaptable professional with a solid understanding of human resources, business operations and various corporate environments. Proven abilities in creatively identifying methods for improving staff productivity and organizational behaviour. Recognized for ability to incorporate innovative management techniques to a multicultural workforce.

Results-oriented professional with excellent communication and interpersonal skills. Accurately perform challenging tasks with precision and attention to detail. Excel at organizing and setting up new procedures, troubleshooting and taking adverse situations and making them positive.

Competencies Include:
- Human Resources Management
- Operations Management
- Team building/Leadership
- Organization and Project Management
- Training and Development
- Staffing Requirements
- Problem Resolution
- Employee Relations

Professional Experience

ABC Waste Removal*, Preston (August 2000–September 2005)*

Administrator
ABC Waste Removal is the nation's largest full-service waste removal/disposal company
- Maintained and monitored multiple databases for more than 120 pieces of equipment in the company inventory.
- Generated accurate reports of budgets, repair costs, and personnel scheduling.
- Dramatically improved maintenance shop productivity through close budget monitoring.
- Served as a key link between management and mechanics, using excellent interpersonal and communications skills. Acknowledged for improving the overall flow of information throughout the organization.
- Initiated, planned, and managed the implementation of high-turn inventory management systems and procedures. The new inventory system was credited with improving the operation of a very high volume parts operation.
- Assumed a leadership role in the company by completely reorganizing the physical inventory process to assure greater accuracy and system integrity.
- Managed the successful integration of two new parts operations, turning a possible negative situation into a very positive one.

XYZ Video, *Coalport (March 1997–August 2000)*

Store Manager
Retail video rental and sales chain with over 600 outlets and 5,000 employees worldwide
- Managed all daily store operations including a staff of 5 employees. Responsible for recruitment, hiring, firing, training, and scheduling of all staff members.
- Ability to train and motivate staff to maximize productivity, and control costs with hands-on management and close monitoring of store budgets.
- Attained a 25% increase in sales over a 12-month period, leading all 45 stores in the district. The store ranked 40th in overall sales volume of the 600 stores in the company.
- Maintained a consistent Top 20 ranking for sales.
- Used excellent leadership, team building and communication skills to develop subordinates and encourage cooperation and responsibility. Ensured compliance with company HR programmes.
- Developed and implemented creative and aggressive promotional techniques that resulted in the store consistently exceeding its sales goals.

Education
BA – Psychology, NORTH WEST UNIVERSITY

Placement services

| Monica Jones | 1 Any Street | Anytown AX0 0AA | 020 8123 4567 |

QUALIFICATIONS SUMMARY
Human Resources Management
Programme Development, Recruitment, Training, Quality Process Management

EXPERIENCE
City College of Textiles and Science, London   1996 to Present

Director, Career Planning and Placement   2001 to Present
Liaison between college and industry, building international reputation through development of
the following support and services:

- Direct professional staff of three, semi-professional staff of 10 and £175,000 operating budget in providing comprehensive placement service for 3,000 undergraduate students and 250 MBA students.
- Develop network of corporate and government employers within Business, High Tech, Creative, and Science areas.
- Annually achieve 90% placement of graduates, and hundreds of graduates at management level.
- Market on-site recruiting programme resulting in over 200 companies visiting each season.
- Host VIP visits and receptions.
- Extensive travel includes organizing and supervising trade shows, attending conferences, visiting industry.
- Provide input for academic programme development through analysis of industry trends.
- Initiated seminar and workshop programme covering all aspects of career planning and search.
- Publish bi-monthly nationally circulated Job Opportunities Bulletin, Annual Placement and Salary Survey, CV Book, and Student Handbook on Placement.
- Supervise placements and summer job programmes for undergraduates.
- Directed software development and computerization of department, 1996.

Assistant Director, Placement Office   1996 to 2001

INVOLVEMENTS
- Selected for Task Force, evaluation for college accreditation, 2003.
- Visited/consulted with South African organizations on recruitment programme development, 2002.
- Member, College Placement Council.
- Past Chairman of Membership, Publicity and Office Training Committees.
- Published articles for trade journals, appear on media, conference speaker.
- Volunteer, AMS Arts Projects.
- Member, NIHA
- Member, City Community Project.
- Accomplished photographer, enjoy painting.

EDUCATION
CITY COLLEGE OF TEXTILES AND SCIENCE
1996 to 2001, Marketing/Management
Numerous Technical and Business Seminars
Executive Management Programme
Management Consultants, 2003

Trainer

Casandra lost her job. She wanted to move into a higher-level position for a better salary. She did not have a degree, so highlighting her skills helped employers get a quick overview of her many talents… and it worked!

Casandra B Jeeles

---

1 Any Street, Anytown AX0 0AA • 020 8123 4567 • casbjeeles@bxy.net

PROFESSIONAL OBJECTIVE

Training/Performance Development

PROFESSIONAL PROFILE

- Proven leadership and supervisory experience with ability to lead multiple projects/teams simultaneously.
- Outstanding project planning and project management skills, meeting tight time constraints/deadlines.
- Solutions-driven manager, mentor, and coach who relates well with all types of people at all levels.
- Strong organizational and analytical abilities applied to achieve desired goals, objectives and results.
- Unwavering commitment to excellence in building teams who are best of the best in serving others.
- Personal traits: professional; common sense; adaptability; focused; skilled trainer and team builder.

CORE COMPETENCIES

Passion for Customer Care Excellence:
- Instil a philosophy of immediate response to customer inquiries – no such thing as 'do it tomorrow.'
- Value each individual customer, exceeding expectations and paying diligent attention to small details.
- Act and serve with integrity and trust, essential ingredients for successful, long-lasting customer relations.
- Create an environment where customers are ecstatic with service, creating action-oriented advocates.

Motivating and Training:
- Analyse company culture and structure to pinpoint obstacles and create new pathways or adopt existing model to build an environment of solutions and forward movement.
- Recognize hidden solutions, already existing or external, through research, active listening, observation.
- Help personalize company vision and goals by implementing strategies to create ownership/advocates.
- Analyse and monitor sales figures and statistics to establish firm foundation for future growth.
- Identify the extraordinary among the team, systems, and practices and build upon strengths.

Team Building:
- *'My Job is to make the team successful'* – accomplished by coaching, nurturing, and stretching to reach beyond an individual's comfort zone to maximize personal/professional excellence.
- Discover talents/gifts of individual team members and build upon those to maximize results.
- Create an environment to link team members' strengths as the beginning of all endeavours.
- Capitalize on company structure, budgets, and timelines to build a 'let's do it' framework.

Managing and Supervising:
- Orchestrate a team, discover core values of individual members, and build consensus of goals.
- Analyse budgets and expenditures to align with company vision, mission and direction.
- Automate and systematize rote and mundane functions to improve operating efficiencies.

Solutions Oriented – Analysis to Action:
- Thrive on converting obstacles into opportunities by recognizing root cause and developing solutions.
- Structure work environment where fear, failure and blame are not responses and/or defences
- Incorporate active listening to unravel challenges and rebuild – be it systems, technology, or people.

Experience/Education
- Inside Sales/Assistant to Director – ABC Ltd., Heston, 2002–2006
- Senior Executive Club/Top Sales – XYZ Distribution Ltd, Midlands, 1994–2002
- Various administrative roles, Heston, 1989–1994
- Numerous leadership, management, and customer relations courses – company sponsored, 1986–2006

Operations/human resources manager

Jason needed to move from seasonal work with national
fairs into a more traditional management career.

JASON CHAMBERS
123 Main Street • London AX0 0AA
Home: 020 8123 4567 • Mobile: 07850 515536 • jchambers@chambers.com

---

Management Professional
Operations/Human Resources/Labour Relations/Staff Development

---

Dedicated organizational manager with track record of assuming positions of increased accountability. Background includes experience in industrial food service (world exposition food service management), restaurants, and catering. Proven leadership skills – able to recruit, retain, develop, and motivate employees to new levels of productivity. Communicate successfully and productively to any and all types of people. Excellent problem solver. Strong team orientation. Accomplished public speaker.

Core competencies include:

Verbal/Written Communications   Performance Evaluations   Prospective Employee Interviews
Relationship Building/Facilitation Promotional Programmes Interpersonal Skills
Programme Development   Policy Creation   Contract Negotiations

Particular Expertise in Boosting Profitability by Maximizing Sales and Reducing Costs

Employment History

XYZ Exposition Services, Corby   1989–2006
Leading provider of food service logistics and restaurant operations for world fairs and expositions.

Director of Personnel and Human Resources/General Operations Manager
● 2005 French National Fair Exposition-Paris, France
● 2001 World Fair Exposition-Biel, Switzerland

Accountable for all phases of personnel management – hiring, staff development, evaluation, promotion, and separations. Created general employee contracts and work policy manuals. Controlled labour costs by optimizing staffing requirements according to customer visitations and by monitoring break times, clock-in/out accuracy, and on-the-clock productivity. Developed and monitored customer service systems. Created working relationships with government officials in European Union. Procured visas for core team members. Secured expo accreditation passes for all company employees.

Directed activities of all managers and assistant managers in supervision of multiple locations (8 in France, 10 in Switzerland) and up to 280 food service and facilities maintenance personnel. Also oversaw one beverage director to ensure full stocking and successful operating of all restaurants, bars, and food concessions. Reported directly to CEO.

Selected Contributions (French National Fair)
● Initiated full-scale recruitment of host-country hotel school interns. Secured a group of motivated general employees who were paid 20% less by law.

JASON CHAMBERS
Page 2 of 3

- Cut additional labour costs from 27% to 20%, significantly increasing net profit to investors. Company grossed £8.5 million in 6 months of operation.
- Streamlined staffing needs by reengineering food service stations allowing employees to multi-task.
- Discovered thousands of pounds overpaid by auditing every pay slip for inaccuracies.
- Increased sales in Mexican food concession. Designed innovative ticket system to reduce queueing. Simultaneously eliminated loss of impatient customer sales and boosted service capacity.
- Successfully interpreted and complied with all host country labour laws and regulations. Faced comprehensive labour policy audit by host country's top labour official. Passed with flying colours.

Selected Contributions (World Fair, Switzerland)
- Streamlined staffing needs by designing employee multi-task and partnership system.
- Discovered and broke multiple-employee theft ring at two separate concessions.
- Played key role in company meeting exposition revenue goals (grossed £11.25 million in 6 months with only 9 concessions) by facilitating open and productive communication with management-level and general employees.
- Became conversant with Swiss labour laws, culture, and practices. Resulted in productive, lasting international business relationships.

Operations Consultant
- 2008 Canadian National Fair Exposition-Vancouver, B.C., Canada* preparation in progress
- 1995 World Exposition-Osaka, Japan
- 1989 World Exposition-Lisbon, Portugal

Participated in formulation of management structure, labour policies, employee handbook, management and employee training handbook, and operating guidelines in preparation for expo.

GOURMET FOODS LTD, Birmingham   1998–1999, 2002–2004, 2006

General Manager
Monitor customer service levels, employee performance, and labour costs. Track and evaluate daily sales. Responsible for prospective employee interviewing and hiring. Teach and facilitate communication skills. Supervised up to 50, including concession managers, counter staff, cooks, and cashiers for 4 locations.

Selected Accomplishments
- Launched innovative ongoing promotions.

  ✔ Police and fire service discount programme
  ✔ Home-meal and catering menu programme
  ✔ 'Daily Special' programme

- Improved customer service levels by retraining employees in the following areas: quick/personal attention to customers, cleaning without turning backs to customers, and interpersonal communication skills.

JASON CHAMBERS
Page 3 of 3

ABC GYM – Accrington   1989–1992

Sales Representative/Personal Trainer
Performed membership sales. Helped customers achieve fitness goals.

DEF PIZZA – Cambridge   1986–1988

Assistant Operations Manager
Promoted from positions on counter/delivery to oversee operations of 4 stores. Supervised roughly 70, including store managers, counter staff, cooks, delivery personnel, cashiers and dishwashers. Ensured store cleanliness, product availability and timely delivery, and customer satisfaction.

Computer Skills/Foreign Languages

Internet (Netscape Navigator, Internet Explorer)
E-Mail (Outlook, Outlook Express)
MS Word, Excel

Beginning Conversational French

Inventory manager/store manager

DAN DOLAN
1 Anystreet, Anytown AX0 0AA • (H) 020 8123 4567 • 07850 515536 (M)

INVENTORY MANAGER/STORE MANAGER

Operations – Sales – Business Management

Delivered strong and sustainable revenue and profit gains in highly competitive markets

Empowering manager with multiple responsibilities and the ability to direct a large staff. Focus group efforts; counsel, mentor, and train employees. Experience in directing new store openings and store remodelling projects. Proven ability to perform multiple tasks at once with special attention to detail.

Consistently meet and/or exceed corporate goals and operational deadlines. Respond well in high-pressure managerial situations calling for excellent organizational skills and interpersonal communication skills.

A problem solver with strong leadership ability and an in-depth understanding of profitable business operations across many disciplines. Known for successful implementation strategies with a high commitment to excellence.

Professional strengths include:

- **Inventory Control**
- **Store Operations**
- **Customer Service**
- **New Store Startups**
- **Troubleshooting/Problem Solving**
- **Leadership/Mentoring**
- **Employee Staffing and Scheduling**
- **Shrinkage Control**
- **Productivity Improvements**
- **Payroll Forecasting**
- **Logistics**
- **Team Building and Training**

BUSINESS EXPERIENCE

ABC LTD   2001–Present

ABC LTD, Luton   2003–Present

Operations Executive
- Use a strong strategic planning management style to supervise a staff of 125.
- Responsible for the operations and flow of all merchandise from warehouse to sales floor. Annual sales of the store total £40 million.
- Direct the staffing and daily operations of 6 managers and their teams.
- Selected by ABC as one of 4 Senior Managers of the 'New Store Team'. Participated in start up of the Luton store in March 2003.

Dan Dolan   Page Two

ABC LTD (Continued)
- The Luton store was in the top 10% of all ABC stores nationwide for operational excellence in 2005.
- Selected as Risk Assessment Manager for the district for last 2 years.
- Selected for the High Level Management team for the district.
- Completed the interview process and on the list to be the ABC's next new store manager.
- Chosen as District Trainer, Mentoring 5 additional Flow Executives at other stores.

ABC LTD, Manchester   2001–2003
Sales Executive/Logistics Executive

- Hired as Logistics Executive responsible for all stock into the store.
- Promoted from Logistics Executive to Sales Executive with responsibility for sales and sales floor management.

OFFICE DEPOT   1997–2001

OFFICE DEPOT, Liverpool   2000–2001
Store Manager

- Responsible for all facets of daily business functions and operations for the entire store. Store revenues grew to exceed £5 million.
- Responsible for staff of 40, including scheduling, sales quotas, performance reviews, daily staff duty assignments, and employee training.
- Implemented and maintained store policy and procedures as directed by company standards.
- Using a passionate execution style and strategic planning, the Liverpool store developed into a top performer in the region.

OFFICE DEPOT, Bridgend   1999–2000
Sales Manager

- Increased sales by 20% in first year as Sales Manager.
- Increased gross margin by 32% through an increase in extended warranty sales of 17%.
- The store was the winner in a companywide contest for having the highest warranty sales to overall sales ratio.

OFFICE DEPOT, Preston   1997–1999
Operations Manager

- In charge of all incoming stock, staff scheduling, and inventory rotation.
- During first year as Operations Manager, shrinkage decreased from 3.2% to .32%.

EDUCATION

North West University
BSc Environmental Economics – 1997

Purchasing director

Peter's CV was shortened from a four-page CV which listed 30+ bullets outlining responsibilities for each job, and no impact/achievements/value

PETER M RABBIT
1 Any Street, • Anytown AX0 0AA
(H) 020 8123 4567 • (M) 07850 835516
ptrbt@aol.com

PURCHASING DIRECTOR
SENIOR PROJECT MANAGER
SENIOR OPERATIONS MANAGER

Professional Summary

Driven operations leader offers extensive hands-on experience and a consistent track record in **exceeding goals** for large-scale domestic and international capital projects, **fostering growth** and **delivering strong and sustainable gains**. A self-starter with a proven ability to conceptualize and implement **innovative solutions**. **Technologically competent**, past achievements demonstrate a clear ability to use new, **cutting edge technologies** as a means of updating processes/systems. **Highly effective leadership and motivating skills** support the development of cohesive teams in the collaborative achievement of strategic goals. **Extensive experience** partnering with influential business leaders within successful organizations.

CORE COMPETENCIES

Business Planning	Financial Analysis	Quality Assurance
Business Process Re-engineering	Influencing Skills	ERP/MRP
Contracts Administration	Negotiation Skills	Supplier/Vendor Management
Cost Containment	Logistics Management	Systems Implementation
Efficiency Improvement	Project Management	Warehouse Management

Selected Achievements

- Initiated the development of a **first-ever computerized purchasing/inventory system** for the ABC Company resulting in substantial reductions on labour and material costs; these improvements resulted in a request for support in the implementation of the system from the UK-based Newspaper. Subsequently consulted on the second successful implementation.
- **Reduced operating costs by £500,000 per year** by outsourcing an 'in-house' printing department.
- Provided comprehensive capital procurement services for the **£800 million construction and start up of two large daily newspaper printing press facilities**.
- **Significantly increased waste recycling revenues by £545,000 per year** through successful negotiations with individual recycling firms.
- Directed an **operating budget of over £180 million** during construction and operations of the **Famous World Exhibition**.
- Initiated the development and implementation of a **first-ever budget tracking and reporting system in support of a £90 million capital project**; this system accelerated the project's successful completion – **90 days ahead of schedule and £1 million under budget**.
- Shortly after assuming responsibility for Security operations, **reduced in-house theft, drug and alcohol abuse by 99%, while reducing costs by £100,000 per year**.

Relevant Experience

Independent Consulting   2005 to Present
- **Sourced and introduced a comprehensive, cutting-edge finance management software solution**, which enabled a £5 million business to more effectively manage sales, inventory and distribution.

- Established warehouse management procedures, facilitating highly effective **inventory planning and control** practices; **trained and coached warehouse staff**.
- Established the foundation for a **fully integrated logistics management function** consolidating inventory, warehousing and distribution.

ABC, Manager, Procurement & Security   **1991 to 2005**
*Hired as Assistant Manager of Purchasing. Quickly demonstrated **aggressive turnaround management capability**, resulting in **significant increases in responsibility** – Fleet, Security, Facilities, and £40 million in newsprint inventories.*

- Established clear processes and procedures, and **centralized purchasing and inventory management** via first-ever electronic system in the newspaper system, **reducing costs by £500,000/year**.
- Introduced new technologies resulting in **increased efficiencies and cost-savings**; technologies included fax services and colour scanning, which increased turnaround in ad presentation and makeup and **saved £125,000/year**.
- **Reduced annual operating costs by £500,000/year through offshore purchasing and vendor partnerships.**
- Successfully **sourced national and international vendors, negotiated and administered contracts** and executed **procurement strategies** on several large-scale capital projects: Development of a new £60 million facility; £97 million development project for implementation of new printing processes.
- **Directed international sourcing and managed logistics**, which included customs documentation and inspections.
- Served as **Project Manager in the design of a waste management system**, providing detailed specifications and managing project activities; **generated a significant increase in revenue**.
- **Overhauled the Security function** – outsourcing, modernizing equipment, establishing and training contract staff on new procedures and roles; significantly reduced costs, and nearly eliminated all incidences of theft.
- **Initiated and implemented the 'pay in advance' system** – now used internationally among all newspapers – which contributed to a significant increase in revenue.
- **Revamped First Aid and Safety programme, and implemented Assassination Protection Programme**.
- Managed sale of assets from old facilities, building deconstruction, and **seamless relocation of 900 employees**.

WORLD EXHIBITION, Manager, Site Operations Procurement   **1987 to 1991**
World Exhibition's 6-month World Fair exhibition is orchestrated and attended by over 70 countries, each with its own on-site pavilion. Managed comprehensive procurement services for construction and start up of operations. Held signatory responsibility for all purchases, and spearheaded profitable vendor partnerships.

- **Hired and established a procurement team and introduced new technology**, which facilitated shared procurement activities throughout liquidation and site deconstruction.
- **Orchestrated first-ever buyback contracts** for heavy equipment and machinery used by the Exhibition, regaining a full 50% of the initial purchase price; negotiated and received free maintenance, providing additional cost savings; **negotiated service contracts** for site equipment and operations.
- **Demonstrated creative problem-solving skills**, which enhanced operations ability to provide ongoing entertainment, while significantly reducing operating costs.

Peter M Rabbit, page 2.

PAPER COMPANY, Project Budget Controller/Buyer   **1984 to 1987**
Provided project support for a £90 Million operations implementation.

- Led the development of an innovative financial tracking and control system.
- Controlled spending and ensured consistent use of the system, enabling a perfectly balanced budget.
- Identified an opportunity to apply for a tax break, saving an additional £600,000 at project's end.

Previous Experience

BIGWIG COMPANY, Project Expeditor, 1982–1984
CHEMICAL COMPANY A, Project Buyer, 1981–1982
CHEMICAL COMPANY B, Project Buyer/Expeditor, 1979–1981
BIG COMPANY, Materials Supervisor, 1978–1979

Technologies

Accpac, Crystal Report Builder, Dun & Bradstreet, EDI, Microsoft Office, Purchase Soft, RAL, Visio

Professional Development

Newspaper Purchasing Association
Society for Industrial Security
Business/Marketing Management Diploma

Purchasing manager

MARC M KELLEY

1 Any Street   020 8123 4567
Anytown AX0 0AA   Email@email.com

Results-oriented **FINANCE PROFESSIONAL**. Consistently successful in controlling costs and improving net profitability while continuing to support critical operations. Background includes procurement responsibility of up to £5 million annually. Excellent communicator with a good attitude and sense of humour. Tenacious negotiation with keen vendor management skills. Strong research and analysis, organization, and decision-making abilities. PC proficient with Word, Excel, and MainSaver.

CAREER SUMMARY

Purchasing/Maintenance Assistant, ABC Ltd., Hambourne, 1997–present
Progressed from Purchasing Assistant to Maintenance Assistant. Selected by upper management to train as Assistant Plant Operator.

- Conducted and oversaw all procurement operations – requisitions, purchase orders, price negotiation, receiving, delivery verification. Commodities consisted of chemicals, hardware, consumables, office supplies, and maintenance equipment.
- Prepared weekly and monthly reports of pounds committed and delivery status. Ensured inventory was current and needs were met. Performed preventive maintenance and assisted mechanic with machinery repairs.

Subcontract Administrator, Huge Aircraft Company, Bristol, 1987–1996

- Administered yearly government subcontract purchases of £1+ million. Solicited bids, negotiated prices, awarded jobs. Interfaced with representatives of many different organizations. Coordinated with Engineering, Programme, Quality, Price, and Cost Analysis staff through completion.

Received High Achiever Award for saving over £100,000 annually.

Purchasing Manager, XYZ Ltd., Manchester, 1984–1986

- Procured electronic components of purchases in excess of £5 million annually, including price negotiation, and delivery. Ensured compliance with applicable Government Procurement Regulations.

Buyer, Huge Aircraft Company, Bristol, 1980–1984

- Placed purchase orders for computer and test equipment, electronic hardware, optics, and other commodities.

Received Superior Performance Award for outstanding attitude and work performance.

EDUCATION/ADDITIONAL TRAINING

BA, General Business Administration, University of London
CPR/First Aid Certification – Licensed Forklift Driver
Continuing Education includes Teaming Techniques, Negotiation Skills, and other relevant classes.

Management consultant

James Sharpe
123 Anystreet ● Anytown AT1 0BB
Phone: 020 8123 4567 ● james@anyaddress.co.uk

Professional Profile

A seasoned, highly motivated senior executive with a successful track record in international operations and project management. Recognized for exceptional problem solving and motivational skills as well as the ability to **negotiate, deal, and close successfully across cultural barriers**. Extensive experience in management consulting in diverse industries, ranging from unit construction and mining/drilling operations to industrial equipment procurement, sales and distribution. **Bilingual with extensive international experience**, including Africa, the Middle East, South Asia, and Western Europe.

Areas of Impact

- International Conflict Resolution
- Operation and Project Management
- Global Emergency Planning
- Worldwide Corporate Security
- New Business Development
- International Public Relations
- Risk Assessment
- International Law
- Recruitment/Training

Career Highlights

- Successfully providing diplomatic, risk management and crisis resolution services to a broad range of blue chip companies, Ambassadors, Heads of State, cabinet ministers, and senior government officials, UK and foreign.
- Successfully negotiated, on behalf of OCL Oil, with an East African government to resolve a cross-cultural crisis and avoid closure of a £1 billion distribution facility.
- Developed and implemented logistics and training programmes involving several thousand UK and foreign personnel and a £40 million annual budget. Effectively achieved all objectives with budget savings of 12%.
- Directed Smith & Jones Trucks Ltd, and Haulage International in the successful negotiation of more than £15 million of capital equipment sales to a West African government.
- Conducted numerous feasibility studies and risk assessments, both political and economic forecasts, for a variety of projects including gold, platinum and diamond mining, nuclear energy development, port, railroad and packaging facilities.

Employment History

International Affairs Consultant
Professional Services Provided to: Whitway International, Vella Properties International, OCL Oil, OACH Petroleum, Haulage International, Smith & Jones Trucks Ltd, Flight Airlines, Technology Co Ltd, M3C International Ltd, National Telecommunications Co Ltd, OX Technologies

National Security Agency
Near East and Africa Referent   Chief of Station ... Chief of Operations ... Chief of Branch, Counterterrorism ... Deputy/Chief of Station.

Education

Doctorate, *International Law*, University of London
Master of Arts, *History*, University of the South
Bachelor of Arts, *History*, New College, Oxbridge

Traffic control (shipping and receiving)

DAPHNE TREEMONT

1 Any Street
Anytown AX0 0AA

dtreemont@email.com
Home 020 8123 4567
Mobile 07850 515536

SUMMARY OF QUALIFICATIONS
- Extensive, large volume *Traffic Control*, *Shipping & Receiving* knowledge; strong leadership abilities.
- Solid record of promotions based on performance. Insightful commitment to positive communication.
- Willing to take on new challenges within demanding deadlines using progressive, results-oriented performance style.
- Strong time management and interpersonal skills. Extremely organized.
- Self-motivated, adaptable, loyal team player. Impeccable work ethic.
- Competent blueprint reading capabilities. Computer literate – proficient with spreadsheets.

EXPERIENCE
ABC EXTRUSION, Division of General Corporation, Greenwich   1995 to 2003
Manufacturer of machinery for the rubber and plastic industry. Company name changed several times due to new ownership. Retained as a valuable employee through each transfer.

- **Traffic Control Manager** – Facilitated all shipments of large machinery and spare parts. Coordinated all paperwork and documentation including Bill of Lading, Certificate of Origin and Customs documents. Entered applicable data into computer system.
- **Receiving Manager** – Handled all receiving and stockroom department responsibilities. Identified, tagged and located parts in stock area. Retrieved components and piece parts for assembly floor personnel. Skilled using Federal Express Powership & Pitney Bowes shipping equipment.
- **Receiving** – Supported all receiving department functions. Identified, verified and received parts optimizing the computerized database.
- **Stockroom** – Stocked parts; recorded and catalogued items in database. Assisted in retrieving parts for assembly floor work orders.
- **Shipping** – Prepared and arranged UPS shipments and packing of parts. Operated UPS equipment documenting size, weight and type of cargo. Typed Bills of Lading and Customs forms. Recorded all shipping data.
- **Data Entry** – Logged all new parts and stockroom locations into database.
- **Expediter** – Identified, traced and accelerated parts in process to the next manufacturing operation. Directed finished parts to appropriate assembly areas. Tracked and updated shortage lists.
- **Licensed** – to operate overhead crane, forklift and overhead lifts.

HOMETOWN MARKET, Greenwich   1978 to 1995
Produce Market

- **Owner/Manager** – Directed and oversaw daily store operations. Supervised up to ten employees. Facilitated operational performance of store, implemented all phases of management functions inclusive of inventory, presentations, display, advertising, customer and employee relations, all accounting/bookkeeping, payroll and receivables. Generated and maintained reports, spreadsheets and mailing lists of over 10,000 people.

CONTINUING EDUCATION
- Blueprint Reading Certification
- Crane Operation
- Forklift Operation
- Accounting I, II

References Available Upon Request

Vice president of operations

Jane Swift	Page 1 of 2

123 Anystreet
Anytown AT1 0BB
Tel: 020 8123 4567
jane@anyaddress.co.uk

SUMMARY OF QUALIFICATIONS

Vice President of Operations, Manufacturing, for US subsidiary. 20+ years' experience in the creative leadership of multisite manufacturing operations to improve productivity, quality and efficiency. Facilitated significant cost savings through expertise in:

- Operations Systems
- Strategic Planning
- Cost Management
- Facilities Design
- Offshore Production

- Manufacturing Process
- Quality Control
- Supplier Partnership
- Human Resources/Labour Relations
- Compliance

PROFESSIONAL EXPERIENCE

ABC Automotive Products, Houston, Texas   *1992–2002*
    A national leader in the manufacturing of automotive water pumps with annual sales of £380 million and 1,500 employees.
        Director of Operations

- Managed the company's two plants in Texas and Mexico. Directly supervised two plant managers, a materials manager, advanced manufacturing systems manager, distribution manager, manager for special projects, and training and a Quality Control Division.
- Initiated and secured ISO9002 certification in two plants on the first application.
- Reorganized preventive maintenance schedules that decreased scrap rates by 50% and virtually eliminated rework rates.
- Orchestrated teamwork and communication between marketing and production to ensure customers received precise delivery dates and improved quality.
- Guided efforts with a major supplier to turn around its sub-quality standards. Avoided a change to the competition's vendors that could have been costly. Result: vendor achieved ISO9000 certification and is now rated top in field.

A1 Heating plc   *1982–1992*
    A residential and industrial water heater manufacturing company.
        Director of Operations, Leeds   1988–1992
        Plant Manager, Glasgow   1984–1988
        Manufacturing Manager, Leeds   1982–1984

- Instituted a quality control system that resulted in highest product quality in industry. Responded to suspicions from customers and suppliers about quality of product by arranging for decision-makers to see plant in operation.
- Reduced accident rate 200% and turnover rate (from 12% to 3% per month in four years) in Leeds by implementing unilateral training programmes (eg, skills, teamwork, supervisory).

- Negotiated commitments from vendors to ensure JIT system.
- Established a 5,000 sq. ft. distribution centre to improve service to mid-continent customers.
- Prevented theft of valuable copper shipments by working with police.
- Selected by senior management to solve problems on Glasgow site which resulted in opening on schedule.
- Improved Leeds plant operations efficiencies as a result of executing a comprehensive study. In four years increased output significantly and profits by 200% by optimizing space, decreasing product damage during production and consolidating shipments.
- Oversaw Glasgow plant closing and transfer to modern facilities. Responsibilities included identification of most economical way to equip new plant, comprehensive study on disposal of buildings, and employee transition management. Production levels remained stable and efforts led to promotion to Director of Operations.

Hillside Water Products plc, Darlington   *1977–1982*
   Manufacturing Engineer

EDUCATION
MBA, School of Management, University of the North
BSc (Hons) 2.1, Mechanical Engineering, University of the North

ONGOING PROFESSIONAL DEVELOPMENT
- Strategic Planning Seminar, South West University Executive Programme
- Leadership at the Peak, Centre for Creative Leadership
- World Class Manufacturing & Process Capability Studies
- Human Resources Seminar, The Manufacturing Association
- The Employee Team Concept, The Centre for Productivity

Emerging technologies executive

Louis Edward
1 Any Street • Anytown AX0 0AA • 020 8123 4567 • louis@email.com

Emerging Technologies Globalization Executive
Deal Maker/Market & Product Strategist/Business Developer/Negotiator

Results-driven and innovative Telecommunications Industry Executive with a 20+ year successful track record driving revenue growth and winning market share primarily in turnaround, start-up and high growth situations. Consistently deliver strong and sustainable revenue gains through combined expertise in Strategic Business Planning, Product Management, Market Strategy, Contract Negotiations, and Customer Relationship Management. Recognized for exceptional ability to assess business unit capabilities, identify and implement appropriate business and produce re-engineering measures thus assuring bottom line growth. Rare ability to establish the organization's vision, develop 'C' level relationships and negotiate the deals that guarantee success.

Key Accomplishments

- 'C' level relationship builder with a track record personally negotiating contracts with companies such as Xerox, Lockheed, Martin, ABC Bank, Morgan Stanley, EDS, Visa, Oracle, Microsoft, Nottel, Boeing, Nordstrom and The Gap.
- Consistent track record developing contracts and terms that used company capabilities and met customer needs, including the first pre-paid international contract. This allowed the company to accelerate into the international market achieving £1+ billion in revenue. This approach became the industry standard.
- Turn around an under-performing business unit lacking leadership by redesigning and motivating the sales and services teams, successfully recovering 60% of the lost accounts and adding new business to increase revenues to £5+ million annually in the first 12 months.
- Conceived and coordinated the global account management process; identified customer needs and product capabilities, spearheaded product and service level agreement changes to win the first global contract. Not only did this grow market share from 7% to 100% and revenue from £330,000 to £6 million per month, it set new industry standards in global business practices.
- Revitalized a product offering by identifying and implementing an International Reseller channel, re-engineering the existing product through the addition of a conversion process adding packaging enhancements and aligning a service/support structure extending the product life by 2 years and capturing a potential revenue of £10 million annually.
- Within 45 days, conceived and implemented a National Accounts Programme, establishing pricing model, sales organization structure and customer service delivery format, successfully increasing revenue from £12 million to £27 million per month. This programme became the standard for the entire company.
- Led the company's new technologies market development (VPN, Web Hosting, co-locating Internet) securing sales in excess of £15 million within 6 months.

Employment Summary

Software Company, Ltd   **2004–Present**
Director, Business Development and Alliances, London

Recruited to drive the product development process and expand market reach through the implementation of an international reseller channel and strategic business alliances.

Louis Edwards page 2
Ph: 020 8123 4567

- Negotiated contracts with Fuji Xerox, Xeros, Accenture and Lockheed Martin capturing £10 million in potential revenue.
- Managed the re-negotiation of two existing alliances that will net the company at least £2 million over the next 12 months.
- Established a new technology relationship with Open Text extending the company's reach in the Life Sciences Market.

International Telecom, Ltd   **1997–2004**
Regional Director National Accounts, Newbury

Recruited to develop a major account programme and subsequently developed a national account programme. Responsibilities included full P&L, £20 million operational budget and more than 250 personnel.

- During a 15-company acquisition period, including the XYZ acquisition (the largest in Telecom history), consistently exceeded all business objectives.
- Managed the best corporate A/R and bad debt levels, achieved outstanding customer retention level of 94% and managed corporation's lowest employee turnover rate of 10%.
- Developed and implemented a National Account Programme expanding revenues within the first year from £180 million to £260 million and achieved Top Regional Director award for outstanding revenue increase.
- Averaged a 21% annual internal revenue growth and was selected to the Gold Award Club from 1998 through 2003 by continually identifying new business opportunities and establishing the right teams, resources and support to grow the organization and meet the customer's expectations.

ABC Telecom, Inc.   **1995–1997**
Executive Director – Global Ltd, Cambridge

Promoted to manage the UK team of 139 sales and support staff, 5 direct reports and to oversee 35 national accounts.

- Managed and negotiated £750 million in contracts with 'C' level players including BOA, Visa, Microsoft, The Gap, Sun, Apple, Oracle, AMD and Nordstrom. Grew market share from less than 15% to 48% in two years.
- Averaged 122% of revenue target every year.

ABC Telecom, Ltd   **1992–1995**
Branch Manager, Cambridge

Recruited to grow and manage XYZ Bank account, successfully leading a team of 39 cross-functional members.

- Grew annual sales and revenue from £3.6 million to £80 million within two years, attaining 100% market share.
- Spearheaded largest commercial sale in ABC history, valued at £400 million, successfully converting the entire XYZ Bank network to ABC in less than 6 months while maintaining 100% customer satisfaction.

Louis Edwards page 3
Ph: 020 8123 4567

BS&S   1986–1992
Field District Manager, Swindon

● Consistently exceeded quota, averaging 112% and made Gold Award Club every year while in sales/sales management position.
● As staff member for XYZ Information Systems, was responsible for revenue and issues for all national accounts, approximately 200 accounts, achieving 109% of the revenue quota.

DEF   1983–1986
National Account Manager, DEF Headquarters, York

● Negotiated and implemented the largest government equipment contract, valued at £20 million.
● Named to Management Development Programme (top 2% of all management personnel), recognized for superior executive and leadership potential.

Education

Bachelor of Arts, York University

Career Development: Intensive 18-week account management and product training seminar

Senior international marketing and business development executive

Jane Swift
123 Anystreet
Anytown AT1 0BB
Tel: 020 8123 4567
jane@anyaddress.co.uk

Expertise in Product Development • Commercialization and Global Market Expansion
Telecoms • Consumer Electronics • Sports & Leisure Industries

Dynamic management career leading turnaround and high-growth organizations through unprecedented profitability and explosive market growth worldwide. Combine extensive strategic planning, competitive positioning, life cycle management, channel management and product development/management qualifications with strong general management, P&L management, organizational development, workforce management, and multicultural communication skills, MBA; multilingual – fluent German, English, Italian, intermediate Japanese.

PROFESSIONAL EXPERIENCE

Major Electronics Company, Dusseldorf, Germany   1995 to 2003
The second largest electronics company worldwide ranking #15 in the Forbes International 800 ratings.

Marketing Director
Executive Board Member recruited to design marketing strategies and implement systems/processes to lead a worldwide marketing function as part of the business group's aggressive turnaround programme.

Accountable for a £250 million marketing budget. Oversee worldwide marketing operations including business strategy and benchmarking, technology strategy, market research, consumer marketing, regional marketing, Europe, Asia, USA, marketing communications, new media including Internet, intranet, and extranet, and business-to-consumer e-commerce. Manage a staff of 77 through 10 direct reports.

● Led the marketing initiatives for a successful launch of two mobile phone product lines transitioning losses of £200 million in 97/98 to profits of £30 million in 98/99 and doubling world market share to approximately 8%.
● Delivered a 5-point improvement in brand awareness, and 50% relevant set improvement for mobile and cordless phones throughout China and Europe.
● Introduced a worldwide marketing communications spending performance initiative slashing communication costs by £10 million.
● Identified and initiated business development strategies and technology vehicles instrumental in developing international marketing partnerships and equity investments.
● Established a price/value-based market analysis instrument together with the market research and consumer marketing groups to develop pricing accuracy generating revenue increases exceeding £20 million.
● Directed e-commerce marketing initiatives leading to the development of 7 operational online stores in 5 European countries generating 4 million contacts with CAGR of 20% per week, followed by development of a virtual Customer Care Centre.
● Conceived and initiated PR strategies for a new product launch generating over 130 million contracts within a few months.

● Led improvements in competitive market intelligence through enhancements to statistical reports and customer satisfaction surveys.

ELECTRONICS COMPANY, Bonn, Germany   1990–1995
A leading European high-end TV, audio and consumer electronics company.

Marketing Director
Joined this privately held company to improve product life cycle management and channel marketing initiatives. Oversaw budget administration, strategic planning and market research, international communications, training and product management. Directed a staff of 21.

● Instituted a series of channel management and segmentation improvements to correct market planning and positioning initiatives and reduce price erosion throughout retail distribution channels.
● Led development of product definition, life cycle management and market launch strategies positioning company as the value-based market leader of high-end TV sets in Germany with market share exceeding 14%.

ABC BICYCLE COMPANY, Berlin, Germany   1986–1990
A global leading automotive, motorcycle and bicycle component equipment manufacturer.

Director of Marketing International
Led transition from an engineering-driven traditional gear hub manufacturer to a market-oriented competitor in the sport and leisure industry. Reported to Divisional Director.

● Established a marketing department, devised strategies for over 1,000 items within 6 product lines, delivered a profit for the first time in 8 years, and boosted new product sales ratios from 10% to 40%.
● Headed up a special internal R&D unit and restructuring project leading to the creation of marketing-driven product development teams. Replaced 15% of R&D personnel, established R&D controls, reduced R&D costs by £500,000, and earned a £30,000 project completion bonus.

ABC AUTOMOTIVE, Wolfsburg, Germany   1983–1986
Leading automotive and home appliance manufacturer.

Product Group Manager
Oversaw European product management and marketing initiatives for the £500 million Electronic Division/Successfully introduced brands in France, Italy and the UK.

EDUCATION

MBA, University of London
Diplôme d'enseignement Supérieur Européen de Management, Centre d'Etudes Européennes Supérieures de Management (CESEM), France,
Diplom-Betriebswirt (FH), Business Administration, Europäisches Studienprogramm für Betriebswirschaft (ESB)

WORK EXPERIENCE PLACEMENTS

Country Chamber of Commerce, Osaka, Japan, Exchange Scholarship, counselled German and Japanese firms in all aspects of business for their respective countries. Kornwestheim Club Vertrieb GmbH, Kornwestheim, Germany, marketing concepts in direct sales.

Senior management executive

Jane Swift   Page 1 of 2

123 Anystreet
Anytown AB1 0BB
Tel: 020 8123 4567
jane@anyaddress.co.uk

New Business Development • Strategic Partnerships • Product Marketing

Accomplished Senior Executive with a strong affinity for technology and a keen business sense for the application of emerging products to add value and expand markets. Proven talent for identifying core business needs and translating into technical deliverables. Launched and managed cutting-edge Internet programmes and services to win new customers, generate revenue gains and increase brand value.

Unique combination of technical and business/sales experience. Articulate and persuasive in explaining the benefits of e-commerce technologies and how they add value, differentiate offerings, and increase customer retention. Highly self-motivated, enthusiastic and profit oriented.

Expertise in Internet services, emerging payment products,
secure electronic commerce, smart card technology, and Java.

AREAS OF QUALIFICATION
Business

- Sales & Marketing
- Strategic Initiatives
- Project Management
- Business & Technical Requirements
- Contract Negotiations

- Business Development
- Business Planning
- Strategic Partnerships
- Revenue Generation
- Relationship Management

Technical
- Electronic Commerce
- Key Management
- Firewalls
- Stored Value
- Internet & Network Security
- Authorization, Clearing, Settlement

- Encryption Technology
- Public Key Infrastructure
- Smart Cards
- Digital Certificates
- Complex Financial Systems
- Dual and Single Message

PROFESSIONAL EXPERIENCE
ABC Credit Card, High Green   *2002 to Present*
E-COMMERCE AND SMART CARD CONSULTANT

- Developed strategic e-commerce marketing plans for large and small merchants involving Web purchases and retail transactions using a multifunctional, microcontroller smart card for both secure Internet online commerce and point-of-sale offline commerce.

- Combined multiple software products for Internet and non-Internet applications: home banking, stored value, digital certificates, key management, rewards & loyalty programme, PCS/GSM cell phone, and contactless microcontroller with RF communications without direct POS contact.
- Consulted on business and technical requirements to define new e-commerce products and essential deliverables for ABC Credit Card, values at £2.5 MM, supported and enhancing Internet transactions.
- Analysed systems relating to the point of sale environment in the physical world and at the merchant server via the Internet for real-time authorization, clearing and settlement.
- Managed projects including the requirements management system for electronic commerce products affecting core systems; authorization, clearing and settlement. Provided expertise about business and technical issues regarding SET and the Credit Card Payment Gateway Service.

Communications Technology Ltd, Heybrook Park   *1997 to 2002*
MANAGER OF WESTERN REGION CHANNEL PARTNER PROGRAMME

- Developed and maintained business relationships with large blue chip customers and partners that use or resell client-server software for applications and contracts involving e-commerce and smart card technology for a variety of Internet/intranet products: home banking, EDI, stored value, digital certificates, key management, perimeter defence with proxy firewalls, secure remote access.
- Negotiated an exclusive contract with one of the largest government and commercial contractors in the industry, projected to generate £2–4 million over a 24–36 month period. Contract includes secure remote access, telecommuting, secure health care applications.

Antava Ltd, Heybrook Park   *1993 to 1997*
SENIOR SOFTWARE ENGINEER/SOFTWARE INSTRUCTOR

- Designed new programs and trained software engineers in object-oriented analysis and design using UML Solutions that were implemented in C++ in a UNIX environment.
- Managed a software engineering group of 53 individuals. Developed in-house program that saved over £150,000 in training costs for state-of-the-art communications system software development.
- Received Peer Award for outstanding performance; earned a performance evaluation rating of 4.2/5.0.
- Developed and maintained C and C++ communication software in a UNIX environment.
- Created curriculum and course materials that reduced overall training costs by more than £150,000. Coordinated and presented software training programmes.

EDUCATION

- BSc Electrical Engineering, University of London. Emphasis: software engineering
- Top Secret Security Clearance with Polygraph

Senior personnel manager

Jane Swift
123 Anystreet
Anytown AT1 0BB
Tel: 020 8123 4567
jane@anyaddress.co.uk
Page 1 of 2

PROFILE

A well-organized, disciplined individual used to working calmly, effectively and efficiently under pressure. A first-rate communicator, both orally and in writing. An outgoing personality with excellent interpersonal skills who enjoys working with a wide range of people. Self-motivated with the skill and determination to succeed.

STRENGTHS

Recruitment and Selection • Employee Development • Employee Relations • Employee Services • Motivation and Reward • Human Resources Planning

EXPERIENCE
Montgomery Bank plc

SENIOR PERSONNEL MANAGER   1998–Present

PERSONNEL MANAGER   1995–1998

Covered all aspects of Human Resources Management from recruitment to redundancy.
● Held a senior management position in an organization employing over eight hundred staff
● Managed, organized and developed a team of six personnel managers and twenty support staff to cover all aspects of personnel management
● Developed excellent communication and motivational skills encouraging staff to achieve their objectives
● Successfully implemented an Appraisal Scheme for Head Office staff and for personnel in thirty-five branches across the UK
● Recruited specialist staff for all departments
● Introduced new and rigorous absenteeism review procedures which led to a 25% annual reduction in absentee levels
● Developed excellent working relations with the Staff Association greatly facilitating successful negotiations on matters of pay and conditions
● Negotiated new working practices as new services introduced, resulting in a 15% increase in production with a staff reduction of 2% through natural wastage
● Resolved serious disciplinary matters not dealt with at line-manager level

SENIOR PERSONNEL ASSISTANT (EMPLOYEE SERVICES)   1992–1995

● Authorized all staff borrowing from the bank
● Authorized personal loans and overdrafts up to £50,000.
● Stood in for the Personnel Manager in their absence.
● Acted as a point of contact for staff on all account issues for managers and staff throughout the organization

PAYROLL CLERK   1989–1992

- Updated and maintained employee records
- Achieved weekly and monthly payroll deadlines
- Provided payroll assistance to bank staff
- Handled all payroll procedures, including PAYE, SMP and SSP
- Used both manual and computerized systems

EDUCATION AND TRAINING

Diploma in Personnel Management
CIPD Professional Qualification Scheme – Core Management; Core Personnel and
Development
CLAIT

MEMBERSHIP OF PROFESSIONAL BODIES

Licentiate Member of the Chartered Institute of Personnel and Development (FCIPD)
Currently studying to become Graduate Member

Senior sales and marketing manager

JAMES SHARPE
123 Anystreet   •   Anytown AT1 0BB
Tel: 020 8123 4567
james@anyaddress.co.uk
Page 1 of 2

Top-producing sales and marketing professional with nine years of management experience in world-class organizations. Consistently successful in developing new markets, penetrating new territories, identifying and capturing new business, and managing large-scale events for blue chip companies worldwide. Goal-driven manager committed to developing outcomes mutually benefiting the company and the client. Excellent qualifications in building corporate relationships with industry leaders.

Areas of expertise include:

- New Account Development
- Key Account Management
- Client Needs Assessment
- Contract Negotiations
- Competitive/Strategic Planning

- Large Scale Meeting/Event Planning
- Catering Planning/Management
- Co-Marketing Partnerships
- Relationship Management
- Customer Service/Satisfaction

PROFESSIONAL EXPERIENCE

E&R LEISURE, Hilverside   1999 to 2003
Senior Sales Manager
Joined company to lead market entry/penetration initiatives throughout the Northeast Region of the UK for this privately-held exclusive leisure complex with 800 suites, a 60,000 sq. ft. conference centre, and a full range of guest amenities. Managed business growth among blue chip corporate accounts and national association accounts.

- Developed and maintained relationships with corporate meeting planners of major accounts including FCS, TS&H, Chanteclere, Niki Portman, S&G, Kentland, Glentrich and others to develop custom-tailored business meeting packages.
- Worked closely with corporate planners throughout all phases of strategic and tactical planning, coordination, and execution of major events to ensure superior service and guest relations.
- Captured national association accounts including National Cancer Society, Heart Association, The Law Society and Chartered Institute of Psychologists.
- Sold and orchestrated multiyear bookings to numerous associations and corporate accounts.

Achievements

- Built territory and increased revenues from £1 million to over £7 million within first-year.
- Achieved 157% of annual booking goals (2,500 room nights per month).

ALDEBURGH HOUSE, Aldeburg   1996 to 1999
Catering Sales Manager
Challenged to develop new markets and products for visiting multicultural groups.

- Identified target market, initiated contact with prospects, developed proposals, and forged major account relationships.
- Worked closely with corporate planners at DeLa Mere, FTA, Foresham, Newsline, and others to create unique and extravagant parties and events ranging up to £2 million per event.
- Sold, planned and coordinated catered group events for corporate accounts and private parties ranging from 2 to 19,000 guests.
- Developed comprehensive strategic and tactical plans for every phase of event including logistics, transportation, food and beverage, entertainment and gifts to create a memorable occasion.

- Oversaw scheduled events and served as troubleshooter and liaison between staff, event managers and corporate clients to resolve issues and ensure guest satisfaction and loyalty.
- Compiled planning, tracking and forecasting reports using proprietary computer system.

Achievements
- Achieved 130% of Catering Sales & Service Team Goals, 1999.
- Consistently exceeded individual annual sales goals.

INTERNATIONAL HOTEL, Southgate   1988 to 1996
Fast track promotions through a series of increasingly responsible positions based on business growth and improved sales revenue for this high-volume airport property.
Sales Manager-North (1995 to 1996)
Sales Manager-South (1992 to 1995)
Associate Director of Catering (1988 to 1992)
Catering Manager (1988)
- Created innovative guest packages for corporate accounts locally and nationally for this first-rate property with 300 rooms, a 12,000 sq. ft. conference centre and several guest services facilities.
- Developed corporate and professional relationships throughout the industry and coordinated with other properties to accommodate extremely large groups.
- Identified target accounts and consistently developed new business driving increased revenues.
- Promoted property through trade show and convention participation, including public speaking engagements for large groups.
- Planned and coordinated exclusive large-scale intimate client events for the affluent.

Achievement
- Achieved 131% of sales goals throughout the Northern Region, 1996

CHINESE COURT RESTAURANT, Midvale   1986 to 1988
Catering/Sales Manager
Successfully sold Chinese themed parties to international wholesale and corporate convention groups.

EDUCATION
Diploma in Marketing – Institute of Marketing
Diploma in Multinational Business Operations – Institute of Marketing
Diploma, Certificat de Langue Française, Institut Catholique De Paris, 1986 (Study Abroad Programme)

PROFESSIONAL DEVELOPMENT
Sales Training:
International Hotel, BEST programmes (Building Effective Sales Techniques), Top Achiever Sales, Travel Management Companies, Best Practices

Designation
Certified Meeting Professional (CMP)

Affiliations
Meeting Planners International, Member
Society of Association Executives, Member

Senior technology executive

James Sharpe   Page 1 of 2
123 Anystreet
Anytown AT1 0BB
Tel: 020 8123 4567
james@anyaddress.co.uk

Accomplished Management Executive with 15+ years of experience and a verifiable record of delivering enhanced productivity, streamlined operations and improved financial performance. Natural leader with strong entrepreneurial spirit and a special talent for transitioning strategy into action and achievement. Highly effective team building and motivational skills.

Multifunctional expertise includes:

- Corporate Information Technology
- Staffing & Management Development
- Quality & Productivity Improvement
- Marketing Strategy & Management

- Strategic & Business Planning
- Customer Service & Satisfaction
- Operations Management
- Team Building & Leadership

PROFESSIONAL EXPERIENCE

InterTech Group plc   1995–Present
CHIEF INFORMATION OFFICER (1995–Present)
CHAIRMAN, Martins Systems (InterTech subsidiary) (2000–Present)
> Appointed to these dual senior-level positions and challenged to create and execute technology strategy for InterTech and subsidiaries of the £700 million Information Services Group. Concurrently provide executive oversight for the development and deployment of software products/services and MIS solutions for Martins Systems, affiliate offices, and 3,900 independent agents.

> Provide leadership for a team of 200 management and support personnel. Administer a £16 million annual budget. Scope of accountabilities is expansive and includes planning and strategy, operations management, human resource affairs, customer service, marketing, management reporting, and communications.

Key Management Achievements
- Built the complete corporate technology infrastructure from the ground up. Developed technology strategies and tactical plans mapped to align with corporate goals.
- Served as a member of the corporate Leadership Council. Defined corporate vision; developed business plans, created strategies and establish tactical goals for all business units.
- Established a high-performance management staff and created a team-based work atmosphere that promotes cooperation to achieve common corporate objectives. Instituted a series of initiatives that substantially improved communications between staff and management.
- Developed and integrated programmes to maximize productive and efficient use of technology throughout the corporation. Instituted 'user champions' to serve as technical experts within each business unit, launched executive 'boot camps' to train management in aggressive computer use, and built responsive help centres for technical support.
- Spearheaded creation and implementation of a customer information and marketing team responsible for developing an award-winning marketing programme, promotions, direct-mail campaigns, and demonstrations and tours.
- Created innovative processes using product specialists for management of sales leads and distributor networks, resolution of customer escalated issues, and provision of work-flow and engineering consulting for company offices and agents.

James Sharpe 020 8123 4567
page 2 of 2

Key Technical Achievements
- Led implementation of client/server software suite that won the industry's 1999 and 1998 Title Tech Discovery Award for best and most innovative title industry software.
- Spearheaded development of numerous technical infrastructure projects, including the corporate Internet presence, corporate intranet, Web hosting solutions for independent agents, and electronic commerce solutions for offices, agents and service providers in the property management industry.
- Orchestrated development of an award-winning marketing programme, Power Tools for the Modern World, that won the local and district awards for best overall marketing programme.
- Guided development and implementation of a title industry software suite installed in 400 systems throughout the distributor network. Designed and deployed training programmes to ensure high quality service levels.
- Managed creation of an Electronic Underwriting Manual that was selected as best policies and procedures implementation in the National Awards competition, 1996.
- Led design and implementation of a 1,200-user corporate WAN, a centralized help desk, a 2000-user corporate e-mail system, and a comprehensive training centre for desktop applications.

CHIEF EXECUTIVE, InterTech (1991–1995)
Promoted to manage all operations for this subsidiary. Took over leadership for a staff of 25 and recruited/built to 90+ personnel. Oversaw all management reporting, finances, marketing, product delivery, and closing services.

Key Management Achievements
- Delivered profits throughout a severe recession.
- Maintained a consistent 15% market share despite a tripling in the local competition.
- Achieved standing in the top 15% in profitability and revenues across all company offices nationwide.
- Created and deployed a marketing programme including a series of 20 seminars; built strong industry relationships and established a reputation as the area's premier experts.
- Pioneered innovative marketing strategies to reach new markets and build a network of industry professionals.

COMMERCIAL SALES (1988–1991)
Hired to develop and manage a commercial closing division. Achieved the highest market share of commercial closings in the local market.

EDUCATION
MBA, University of the West (1988)
Bachelor of Arts, Business, University of the West (1982)

PROFESSIONAL ACTIVITIES
Frequent Lecturer, Technology Conferences, 1998–Present
Member, Systems Committee, Technical Association, 1997–Present
Member, 'Technology 2000' Planning Committee, 1997–Present

Senior technology executive

Jane Swift
123 Anystreet
Anytown AT1 0BB
Tel: 020 8123 4567
jane@anyaddress.co.uk

SENIOR TECHNOLOGY EXECUTIVE
Project Management • Multimedia Communications & Production • MIS Management

Exceptionally creative management executive uniquely qualified for a digital media technical production position by a distinctive blend of hands-on technical, project management and advertising/communications experience. Offer a background that spans broadcast, radio and print media; fully fluent and proficient in interactive and Internet technologies and tools.

Proven leader with a strength for identifying talent, building and motivating creative teams that work cooperatively to achieve goals. Highly articulate with excellent interpersonal skills and a sincere passion for blending communications with technology. Capabilities include:

- Project Planning & Management
- Account Management & Client Relations
- Multimedia Communications & Production
- Information Systems & Networking
- Conceptual & Creative Design

- Work Plans, Budgets & Resource Planning
- Department Management
- Interactive/Internet Technologies
- Technology Needs Assessment & Solutions
- Team Building & Leadership

PROFESSIONAL EXPERIENCE
LTR Investments, Inc., St Mary's   1989–Present
DIRECTOR OF MIS (2000–Present)
ASSISTANT DIRECTOR OF IT/CORPORATE COMMUNICATIONS (1995–2000)
CORPORATE COMMUNICATIONS OFFICER (1992–1995)
ASSOCIATE (1989–1992)
Advanced rapidly through a series of increasingly responsible positions with this UK based, European investment group. Initially hired to manage market research projects, advanced to plan and execute corporate communications projects, and in 1992, assumed responsibility for spearheading the introduction of emerging technologies to automate the entire company.

Current scope of responsibility is expansive and focuses on strategic planning, implementation and administration of all information systems and technology. Lead technical staff members, manage budgets, select and oversee vendors, define business requirements, and produce deliverables through formal project plans. Manage systems configuration and maintenance, troubleshoot problems, plan and direct upgrades, and test operations to ensure optimum systems functionality and availability.

Technical Contributions
- Pioneered the company's computerization from the ground floor; led the installation and integration of a state-of-the-art and highly secure network involving 50+ workstations running on 6 LANs interconnected by V-LAN switching technology.
- Defined requirements; planned and accelerated the implementation of advanced technology solutions, deployed on a calculated timeframe, to meet the short- and long-term needs of the organization.
- Orchestrated the introduction of sophisticated applications and multimedia technology to streamline workflow processes, expand presentation capabilities and keep pace with the competition.
- Administered the life cycle of multiple projects from initial systems/network planning and technology acquisition through installation, training and operation. Saved hundreds of thousands in consulting fees by managing IS and telecommunication issues in-house.

Business Contributions
- Created and produced high-impact multimedia presentations to communicate the value and benefits of individual investment projects to top-level company executives. Tailored presentations to appeal to highly sophisticated, multicultural audiences.
- Assembled and directed exceptionally well qualified project teams from diverse creative disciplines; collaborated with and guided photographers, videographers, copywriters, script writers, graphic designers and artists to produce innovative presentations and special events.
- Performed market research and analyses to determine risks and feasibility of multiple investment projects valued at up to £150 million. Developed and recommended tactical plans to transform vision into achievement.

Broadcast, Print and Radio Advertising & Production   (1974–1988)
DIRECTOR OF ADVERTISING, Blackwell Advertising Associates   (1986–1988)
ADVERTISING ACCOUNT EXECUTIVE, Vividian Press (1987) / Rainbow Advertising (1984–1986) / M&K Advertising (1983–1984) / Wells Publishing (1982–1983) / Image Advertising (1974–1982)
WRITER/PRODUCER, Radio Programming, Southern Counties Radio (1971)

Early career involved a series of progressive creative and account management positions spanning all advertising media: multimedia, television, radio and print. Worked directly with clients to assess complex and often obscure needs, conceptualized and developed advertising campaigns to communicate the desired message in an influential manner.

Achievement Highlights
- Designed, wrote, produced and launched advertising campaigns that consistently positioned clients with a competitive distinction. Developed a reputation for ability to accurately intuit and interpret clients' desires and produce deliverables that achieved results.
- Hand-selected and led creative teams consisting of graphic designers, artists, musicians, talent, cartoonists, animators, videographers, photographers, and other freelancers and third-party creative services to develop and produce multimillion pound advertising campaigns.
- Won accolades for the creation, production and launch of a 4-colour fractional-page advertisement that generated the greatest response in the history of the publication. Honoured with a featured personal profile recognizing achievements.
- Developed and applied a unique style and advertising philosophy that accounted for the nuances of human psychology and used innovative, intelligent, and sometimes startling techniques to capture attention and influence the target market.

EDUCATION & TRAINING
HND Media Studies, Irvington College
Continuing education in Marketing Research and Broadcast Production, 1984–1986
Northern College of Arts

TECHNICAL QUALIFICATIONS
Innate technical abilities and interest in emerging technologies and digital communications. Trained and fully versed in all aspects of network design, implementation, installation and maintenance. Advanced skill in the installation, configuration, customization and troubleshooting of software suites and applications, hardware and peripherals within the Windows environment (3.x, 95, 98, NT 3.5, NT 3.51, NT 4). Proficient with most Web development, multimedia, word processing, spreadsheet, graphic/presentation and database tools and applications.

Administrative assistant

Intent on working for a multinational company, Lillian needed to communicate her skills in a way that would stand out from the competition.

Lillian V DiFrancesa
1 Any Street, Anytown AX0 0AA
020 8123 4567 • Lilli3evee@mydomain.com

Career Profile

Administrative assistant with strong organizational and interpersonal skills, able to multitask a variety of responsibilities and challenges.

Related Skills

- Types 65 wpm
- Transcription
- MS Excel
- Purchasing

- Planning and Scheduling
- MS Word
- Written Communication
- Customer Service

- Internet Research
- Filing
- Telephone Reception
- Interdepartmental Coordination

Selected Achievements

- Handled 30-50 daily incoming calls on a six-line telephone system, offered a customer-friendly greeting, and promptly routed calls to proper party among 65 employees
- Scheduled weekly meetings for all employee levels and their clients, greeted and escorted visitors to staff members' offices, and provided hospitality service (food and beverage) as requested by staff.
- Composed and distributed interoffice memorandums via electronic, voice and traditional paper means, increasing delivery and receipt of important information, and preserving the confidentiality of sensitive data.
- Assembled media kits for marketing and public relations department, saving approximately £35,000 in additional labour costs.
- Scheduled 15–20 monthly client and internal meetings for both on-site and off-site locations, ensuring housing, catering and materials.
- Coordinated domestic and international travel arrangements for ten senior-level executives on a weekly basis using Internet travel sites that saved company an average of £100–£200 per round-trip airfare ticket.
- Established confidential electronic filing system for all correspondence and incoming faxes, creating a history for staff and eliminating excess paper and chance of exposing sensitive data to unauthorized personnel.
- Dispatched three messengers on bank runs and special assignments as requested by management, coordinating trips to ensure that multiple stops were made each time. This saved the company approximately £25.00 per messenger per day in excess travel expenses.
- Sorted and distributed mail for 65 employees.
- Ordered office supplies through the Internet, taking advantage of online savings and using electronic means to ensure accuracy and distribution of supplies to employees. This logging process helped improve the accuracy of inter-department charge backs.

Employment History

Administrative Assistant, ABC Associates, Easton	1993–2007
Secretary/Receptionist Logic Systems and Solutions, York	1984–1993

Education

City Community College, OND Business Administration

Receptionist

With this CV, Keisha had no trouble finding another job after her last employer moved away.

Keisha A Jackson

---

1 Any Street • Anytown AX0 0AA • 020 8123 4567

PROFILE

Responsible and dedicated office professional with 15 years of experience in heavy-volume environments. Cooperative team player who enjoys working with people and using direct telephone contact. Detail-oriented, thorough and accurate in taking and relaying information. Well-organized to handle a variety of assignments and follow through from start to finish. Strong work ethic, with eagerness to learn and willingness to contribute toward meeting a company's goals.

- Visitor reception
- Multi-line phone system operations
- Data entry and retrieval (Word and Excel)
- Customer relations
- Sales department support

- Account maintenance/reconciliation
- Order processing and invoicing
- Research and resolution of problems
- Regular and express mail distribution
- Office supplies and forms inventory

WORK HISTORY

ABC LTD, Chingford   1998–2007
Personal and commercial insurance company

Receptionist

- Represented the prestigious image of this company in a high profile position requiring public contact with important clients in the sports and entertainment field as well as various other industries.
- Entrusted with opening the office daily and handling confidential material.
- Operated 24-line Premiere 6000 phone system, routing calls/faxes appropriately, and relaying messages accurately. Saved managers' time by screening unwanted calls.
- Reorganized shipping room to run more efficiently and operated automated labelling/tracking system (Powership), processing 5 to 50 outgoing packages daily.
- Ensured prompt delivery of express packages.
- Took initiative to update insurance certificates on computer.
- Participated in hiring a new assistant and trained her in company procedures.

XYZ LTD, Chingford   1994–1997
Nation's largest distributor of speciality paper

Telephone Account Coordinator (Customer Service Representative)

- As one of 80 employees in a busy call centre averaging 200 incoming calls per hour, handled the ordering process, billing, and issuing credits or rebills to ensure accurate account records.
- Consistently achieved excellent scores in the mid-90s on monitored activities.
- Provided support to sales representatives all over the country.

- For four months in 1996, assisted the product director, creative director, and sales director, providing them with daily sales activity reports and analyses, pricing updates, and sales strategy presentations for company's two divisions.
- Processed invoices and deliveries for international shipments.

DEF VENDING COMPANY, Chingford   1992–1994
Distributor of confectionery items sold in vending machines

Customer Service Representative

- Worked in a team of six, processing telephone orders from individuals and retailers, including four house accounts. Resolved invoice discrepancies.
- Offered information on promotions and discounts, which encouraged larger orders.

THE PLAYHOUSE, Chingford   1987–1997

Director of nursery

- While raising a family, owned and operated a full-service nursery for preschool children.
- Administered all aspects of the business (invoicing, accounts payable, accounts receivable, and maintaining client files).

Office support professional

Janet is a longtime (15 years) worker within the veterinary field who successfully moved into an administrative assistant's job in a medical office. She sent out one CV and got the job.

Janet Cooper
020 8123 4567 • jcooper@email.com
1 Any Street • Anytown AX0 0AA

EXPERTISE

Records Management

Customer Liaison

Front Office Operations
Workflow Planning/
Scheduling

Troubleshooting/Problem
Solving

Inventory Control

COMPUTER SKILLS

● Microsoft Word

● Cornerstone Proprietary
Contact Management
Software

TRAINING

● Annual training for
receptionists
and managers

OFFICE SUPPORT PROFESSIONAL
Receptionist... Clerk ... Administrative Assistant

Top-performing office assistant with a reputation for professionalism, integrity, creativity, resourcefulness, and competence. Superior communication and listening skills. Strong client focus, with attention to detail and excellent follow through.

SELECTED CONTRIBUTIONS

● Redesigned administrative processes to streamline functions, eliminate redundancy, and expedite workflow. Initiated the conversion from manual processes to a fully computerized office. Implemented the automated HR Payroll Programme.
● Improved customer service by developing a new client survey, soliciting feedback to quickly resolve client complaints and ensure top-quality service and satisfaction.
● Launched an employee-of-the-month incentive programme to build unity and promote outstanding customer service.

PROFESSIONAL EXPERIENCE

Practice Manager – 1993 to 2006
Receptionist – 1992 to 1993
COMPLETE ANIMAL HOSPITAL, Torquay
(Veterinary clinic comprised of 6 doctors, 10 technicians, and 7 receptionists with annual revenues of £1.4 million)
Oversaw scheduling, managed inventory, and trained receptionists. Accountable for financial reports including daily deposits, monthly invoicing and collections.

Receptionist – 1990 to 1992
WILLS & SMITH, Torquay
(One-doctor veterinary clinic, 2 technicians, 2 receptionists)
Professional and cheerful first point of contact. Broad-based experience in answering multiple telephone lines, scheduling appointments, and filling prescriptions.

RELATED EXPERIENCE
Administrative Assistant
ABC BUSINESS SYSTEMS, Torquay

Administrative Assistant
OSTEOPATHIC SCHOOL OF MEDICINE
Exeter

Office assistant (initial CV)

After interviewing Barbara, it became clear that she had done more than her CV reflected. Aside from her initial CV being poorly formatted, it lacked focus, an interesting summary, and a content-rich presentation of her experience

---

BARBARA WINSTON
1 Any Street, Anytown AX0 0AA
020 8123 4567

OBJECTIVE

TO OBTAIN AN OFFICE ASSISTANT POSITION, ENABLING ME TO USE MY SKILLS AND DEVELOP CAREER PROGRESSION.

SKILLS

WORD PERFECT 5.0 AND 6.0
LOTUS 123
MICROSOFT WINDOWS 98
KEYBOARDING
DICTAPHONE, OFFICE PROCEDURES
KNOWLEDGE OF BUSINESS AND ORAL COMMUNICATIONS
MEDICAL FORMATS
WORK HISTORY

12/01 to Present

CITY UNIVERSITY, BRENTWOOD
LIBRARY ASSISTANT

ORGANIZING CIRCULATION DESK. ATTENTION TO DETAIL, EDITING, DATA ENTRY, XEROXING, FAXING, FILING, ASSISTING STUDENTS WITH RESEARCH, ADMINISTERING TESTS.

3/99 to 6/00

BRENTWOOD EDUCATION AUTHORITY, BRENTWOOD
TEACHING ASSISTANT

ASSISTED TEACHERS WITH SPECIAL EDUCATION STUDENTS, COMPUTER LAB, LUNCH ROOM MONITOR, PERFORMED DUTIES IN PUBLICATIONS DEPARTMENT, CLERICAL DUTIES SUCH AS COLLATING, HAND INSERTING AND PROOF READING.

EDUCATION

10/97

SECRETARIAL SCHOOL
MORRISTOWN
Certificate in Information Processing

1/85

ABC TRAINING SCHOOL
BRENTWOOD
Certificate in Information Handling

EXCELLENT REFERENCES AVAILABLE UPON REQUEST

Office assistant (revised CV)

The result of this before and after CV is dramatic in many ways., It has gone from a confusing document to a personal marketing tool that clearly expresses Barbara's objective. Most importantly, the experience section is very detailed and interesting to read compared to before.

BARBARA WINSTON
1 Any Street, Anytown AX0 0AA • 020 8123 4567 • BWinston@aol.com

Seeking a position in the capacity of **OFFICE SUPPORT ASSISTANT** within a general business or medical office environment, bringing the following experience, skills, and attributes:

• • • • •

Extensive experience working in general public, educational, and medical office settings. Interface well with others at all levels including patrons, patients, professionals, children, and students. Caring and hardworking with excellent interpersonal communication, customer service, and office support skills.
Windows 98/DOS, MS Word, Dictaphone, CRT data entry, basic Internet skills, and medical terminology.

Work Experience

Library Assistant, City University, Brentwood   12/00–Present
Provided diversified information services and research assistance to the general public and student populations

- Assisted patrons in obtaining a broad selection of books, periodicals, audio-visuals, and other materials.
- Catalogued library materials, prepared bibliographies, indexes, guides, and search aids.
- Performed multifaceted general office support, and administered academic placement tests.

Teaching Assistant/Office Assistant, Brentwood Education Authority, Brentwood 3/96–6/00
Assigned to the Publications Department, Computer Laboratory Special Education Resource Room

- Assisted teachers with diversified clerical support in areas of document proofreading, duplication, collating and distribution, classroom management, student monitoring, and miscellaneous assignments.
- Easily established rapport with students, and interfaced well with parents and school-wide faculty members.

Nursing Assistant, Our Lady of Consolation, West Islip   6/90–1/96
Physical Therapy Assistant, Mother Cabrini Nursing Home, Dobbs Ferry   3/85–6/90

Held the following combined responsibilities at Our Lady of Consolation and Mother Cabrini Nursing Home:
- Obtained vital signs and followed up with timely and accurate medical records-keeping procedures.
- Interfaced extensively with patients, staff personnel, orthopaedic surgeons, and neurologists.

- Observed and reported changes in patients' conditions and other matters of concern.
- Performed ambulatory therapeutic treatments such as range of motion, gait training, and whirlpool baths.
- Transported patients to and from the hospital for emergency care and scheduled tests.
- Ensured the proper use of equipment and medical devices such as wheelchairs, braces, and splinters.
- Assisted patients with personal hygiene, grooming, meals, and other needs requiring immediate attention.
- Maintained sanitary, neatness and safety conditions of rooms in compliance with mandatory regulations.

Education

Certificate, Information Processing, 1997
SECRETARIAL SCHOOL, Morristown

Certificate, Information Handling, 1985
ABC TRAINING SCHOOL, Brentwood

Customer service specialist

Brenda Forman
1 Any Street
Anytown AX0 0AA   Home: 020 8123 4567

CUSTOMER SERVICE PROFESSIONAL

SENIOR CUSTOMER SPECIALIST • INVOICING • CREDIT

Shipping and Dispatching • Inventory Control

Top-performing customer service specialist with more than 20 years experience in diverse environments. Outstanding reputation for keeping and maintaining excellent customer service standards. Experienced in working with high volume calls and answering intricate enquiries.

Train and observe other customer service staff. Take pride in order processing accuracy and efficiency; receive excellent customer feedback. Punctual in meeting deadlines. Interact with the MD of my present company on a daily basis. Known to go the 'extra mile' for customers and colleagues. Dedicated, efficient, task-oriented employee.

Perform the functions of Order Processing Specialist, Diversified Account Specialist, and Crediting/Invoice Specialist. Skilled planner with the ability to analyse client needs and achieve objectives. Professional strengths include:

- Customer Service
- Shipping Receiving
- Manufacturing Processes
- Troubleshooting Accounts
- Leadership/Supervision
- Sales Force Support
- Accounts Receivable
- Inventory Control Functions

- Pricing/Quoting Customers
- Prooocsing Orders
- Expediting Deliveries
- Tracking
- Special Attention Order Entry
- Customer Service Observations
- Invoicing
- Written Reports

BUSINESS EXPERIENCE

ABC, Canterbury   2000–Present

Senior Customer Service Assistant and Trainer
Team Leader

- Currently serve as a Team Leader for this fine art and supplies manufacturer. Responsible for training and observation of other customer service employees. Lead customer service meetings and prepare written reports of findings.
- Replace supervisor in her absence.
- Ensure that discounts are applied correctly, and credits are entered in a timely fashion.
- Work with orders from start to completion. Interact daily with Daler-Rowner sales force and district manager.
- Handle customer requests. Take orders via fax, place on our system, send to purchasing, then send to warehouse, edit order, invoice, print, and send to customers.

BRENDA FORMAN PAGE TWO

- Process all orders from Wal-Mart, our largest customer, through an EDI system.
- Work with Internet order processing systems including Microsoft Orbit program, Navision Financial Program, Trading Partners, Retail Link, Microsoft Word, and Excel.
- Attend trade shows and handle special orders in the field. Work with export customers.
- Print back order reports on a weekly basis. Work with potential new clients and their sales representatives regarding administrative work.
- Process numerous orders per day including 500–1,000 lines. Write reports in Microsoft Excel and word.
- Responsible for the issuance of all return authorization numbers. Research credits and input information into our system.

XYZ INDUSTRIES, Canterbury   **1991–2000**

Shipping/Receiving Coordinator
Customer Service Representative

- Responsible for a wide range of shipping/receiving and customer service functions. Handled an extremely high call volume. Processed orders, answered customer inquiries, tracking inbound/outbound shipments; expedited deliveries and set up delivery schedules. Prepared shipments and participated in cycle counting and quarterly inventories.
- Attended trade shows and expedited special attention orders.
- Coordinated with and supported sales representatives in the field. Performed cash receipt reconciliations and resolved customer complaints, disputes or discrepancies.
- Received Employer of the Month Award out of 300 people.

DEF LIFE INSURANCE, Maidstone   **1989–1991**

Customer Service Representative

- Responsible for pricing/quoting customers, answering phone enquiries, processing orders, and expediting deliveries along with troubleshooting accounts.

CHILDCRAFT, Maidstone   **1988–1989**

Customer Service Assistant

- Duties similar to above. Position required ability to work in a high-pressure/fast-paced environment.

GHI LTD., Birmingham   **1985–1988**

Shipping/Receiving Coordinator/Accounts Receivable Clerk

Letters of Recommendation and References upon Request

Customer service professional

Anne's CV states several benefits she would bring to a position in an insurance office

Anne Granger

1 Any Street
Anytown, AX0 0AA

020 8123 4567
agranger@fastmail.com

PROFILE

Customer service professional, skilled in problem solving and responsive to needs of clients, co-workers and management. Poised, resourceful and adaptable to any office environment. Organizational ability to handle multiple priorities and meet deadline schedules. Attentive to detail, with sharp awareness of omissions/inaccuracies, and prompt to take corrective action. A self-starter and quick study, eager to assume increasing levels of responsibility.

OFFICE SKILLS

Professional phone manner; data entry and word processing; updating/maintenance of files and records; composition of routine correspondence.

EMPLOYMENT HISTORY

CUSTOMER SERVICE ASSISTANT
ABC Insurance, Cheltenham   *(2002–2007)*
Hired as a data entry operator and advanced to customer service position in less than a year. Took over problem desk, which had been inadequately handled by 2 previous employees. Worked closely with underwriters, answering client enquiries by phone or mail. Analysed complex situations affecting insurance coverage. Recognized opportunities to increase sales and advised clients when coverage was lacking in specific policy areas.

Key Accomplishments: During major restructuring of company resulting in 70% staff reduction, assumed more than triple the normal account responsibility, from 450 to over 1,500, while still in training. Simultaneously studied for insurance licensing course; passed exam on first try, with score of 95.

APPLICATIONS SCREENER
XYZ Insurance, Cheltenham   *(2000–2002)*
(Applications processing centre for Mutual Surety Corporation)
Screened homeowners' new lines of business applications, verifying coverage. Filled in whenever needed for switchboard, typing, and clerical assignments.

CHILD CARE RESPONSIBILITIES   (1993–2000)

CENSUS TAKER
UK Census Bureau, Cheltenham   *(1993)*
Visited individuals who had not filled out census forms properly. Worked in a multi-ethnic territory, overcoming language barriers and mistrust. Clarified discrepancies and ensured accuracy and completeness of reported information.

ADMINISTRATIVE CLERK
DEF Insurance Company, Middleton   *(1991–1993)*
Started as receptionist and promoted shortly thereafter to handle various clerical assignments. Prepared paperwork for file with arbitration board. Kept ledgers up to date for auditors' review.

EDUCATION

City College – Diploma in Business Administration   (1989–1991)
Completed 12-week basic course in Property and Casualty, Insurance Law, and Health Insurance (2003)

Retail manager

Scott needed a CV that would highlight his strong retail and store management experience.

SCOTT KELLY
1 Any Street
Anytown AX0 0AA

020 8123 4567
ScottKelly3@hotmail.com

RETAIL – SALES & MANAGEMENT

Successful retail manager with over 14 years experience in Sales, Purchasing/Buying, Customer Service, Inventory Management/Merchandising, Staff Recruitment and Supervision. Proven ability to increase sales revenue and improve profitability through effective sales consultation, merchandising, purchasing, and inventory management. Demonstrate a high level of motivation and enthusiasm in all aspects of work.

- **Record of improving sales, successfully introducing new products, and growing customer-base.** Expanded business for large volume – wine speciality –liquor establishment.
- **Excellent leadership skills** – can communicate effectively with employees and motivate them to perform at their best. Can set direction for the team. Hands-on approach to training.
- **Established record of dependability and company loyalty.**
- **Experience in both general merchandising and speciality retail sales.** Extensive knowledge of the wine industry including suppliers, distributors, and consumers; extensive product knowledge.

PROFESSIONAL EXPERIENCE

Manager (General Operations), ABC Stores, Woburn   1996–present

Direct the daily operation of a high-volume liquor/wine speciality store, servicing over 1,000 customers per week. Manage staff of 15 in the areas of sales and customer service, cash management, budgeting, sales forecasting, employee relations, merchandising, promotions, and security.

- Steadily increased revenues through strong focus on customer service, excellent merchandising, and teamwork.
- Attracted new clientele to store through the development of a full-service wine department. Expanded product line, increased sales and special-order purchasing by implementing specialized sales methods, such as promotional wine-tasting events.
- Established strong reputation as leader for extensive wine inventories at competitive pricing, including regularly stocked hard-to-find selections.
- Trained staff in selling through increased product knowledge and food and wine pairing.
- Participated regularly in trade tasting, shows, and vintner dinners.

Manager (Stock and Display), DEF Department Stores, Oxford   1994–1995

Managed a staff of 12 in a large, national general merchandise store. Marketed and sold products; developed merchandise and promotional displays; maintained stock levels.

- Increased profits through effective displays and merchandising.
- Improved operations through effectively supervising daily staff assignments.

Stock/Inventory Manager, XYZ Gifts, Oxford   1992–1994

Managed purchasing and supervised sales staff for a high-traffic speciality gift store.

- Expanded customer base by offering a wide range of attractive product displays and creating a welcoming atmosphere that increased the comfort level of patrons.
- Supervised staff of three, ensuring quality of store display and product inventory levels.

Additional experience includes entry-level inventory/shipping–receiving position at City University (1990–1982).

Store manager

James Sharpe
123 Anystreet
Anytown AT1 0BB
Tel: 020 8123 4567
james@anyaddress.co.uk

WORK EXPERIENCE

Manager, A National Kitchen Utensil Retailer. 2000–Present
Manage daily operations of a £2-million annual business. Staff of 12 people. Responsible for increasing sales and profitability and decreasing expenses.

Increased gross margin by 25% and net contribution by 105% on a 3% sales increase.

Senior Assistant Buyer, Turner's, Brent Green. 1996–2000
Controlled purchasing – profitability reports, weekly three-month estimate of sales, stocks, and markdown items. Planned and negotiated sales promotions, advertising and special purchases.

Coordinated training and teamwork with managers and merchants in the 22 stores.

Increased department sales 18% more than the Division's increase.

Assistant Buyer. Assisted selection and distribution of merchandise. Managed all buying office functions while learning to plan sales and control stocks. Created weekly, monthly and seasonal financial plans.

Developed all systems to support the growth of the branch from a £1-million volume to a £4-million annual volume.

Buyer/Manager, Green Gifts. 1993–1996

Bought merchandise for two different gift stores. Directed daily store operations and sales. Directed merchandise presentation, inventory control and customer service. Scheduled and supervised a 7-person staff.

Increased sales volume 22% more than corporate projection.

Manager, Webb & Grant. 1990–1993

Directed daily store operations. Analysed trends in fashion, merchandise and consumer needs. Planned effective marketing strategy, displays, advertising and an employee sales programme.

Increased annual net sales volume by 33%.

EDUCATION   Institute of Purchasing and Supply: Diploma in Purchasing and Supply.

Visual merchandising specialist

Jane Swift
123 Anystreet
Anytown AT1 0BB
Tel: 020 8123 4567
jane@anyaddress.co.uk

With fifteen years' experience in Visual Merchandising Management, I have successfully:

- Coordinated all Visual Merchandising in Nairn's third-most-profitable store.
- Supervised visual aspects of a successful £1.5 million store renovation with responsibility for new fixtures and merchandising.
- Conducted seminar in Visual Merchandising for all new department managers in Nairn's Eastern region.
- Used innovative image control techniques that contributed to a new high-fashion store's becoming the volume leader for its entire chain in one year.

RECENT ACCOMPLISHMENTS
Visual Merchandising Manager of a Nairn's store with a £20 million sales volume, I coordinated fixtures, merchandising, and seasonal changes for all twelve departments, along with responsibility for overall store image.

- Analysed stock levels to determine new fixture needs, prepared requirement reports and coordinated on-time deliveries of all fixtures.
- Reporting directly to the Director of Corporate Visual Merchandising, I supervised five Visual Merchandising Managers brought in from other stores to assist in the project.
- Interfaced with construction personnel while directing movement of departments under construction.
- Guiding all Department Managers through renovation and construction, I familiarized them with new fixtures and applicable merchandising techniques.

EARLIER ACCOMPLISHMENTS
As District Display Director for Daisy Chain, a 100-store speciality women's ready-to-wear chain, I developed fashion awareness, coordinated displays, and trained staff, including new District Display Directors throughout the country. Reporting directly to the Corporate Display Director, I was:

- Given responsibility for image control at the company's new flagship store in Oxford Street, where fashion image was crucial. My innovative merchandising and display techniques contributed to this store's becoming the number-one-volume store for the entire company by its first anniversary.

- Recognized for my planning, organizing and coordinating abilities, I was involved in several new store openings throughout the UK and Europe.

As Display Coordinator/Visual Merchandising Manager with IMAGE Ltd, I progressed to having a five-store responsibility. Developing my functional skills, I was promoted to Visual Display troubleshooter for the region.

EMPLOYMENT
NAIRN's 2000–Present
DAISY CHAIN 1986–2000
IMAGE 1982–1986

EDUCATION
A graduate of Harpdale College, with a speciality in Fashion Design, I have also completed intensive course work in Architectural Technology which has significantly contributed to my expertise in store renovation and floor plan know-how. Course work in photography has rounded out my background.

PERSONAL
Interests include fashion design and construction, sketching, and free-hand drawing.

Merchandise buyer

The use of a title and keywords list allows the reader to see exactly what Mary's objective is and the scope of her skills in relation to the position of interest. Notice the keywords are very specific rather than general attributes.

Mary J Sanders

1 Any Street • Anytown AX0 0AA • 020 8123 4567

Assistant Buyer

Skilled in areas of:

- Wholesale/Retail Buying
- Product Merchandising
- Inventory Replenishment
- Product Distribution and Tracking
- Sales Analysis & Reporting
- Regional Marketing Campaigns
- Information Systems
- Vendor Relations
- Order Management

Professional Experience

Merchandise Buying/Coordination

- Report directly to ABC's Director of Sales, providing support in areas of commodities buying and merchandising activities that reach annual sales volumes of £3 million for the division.
- Collaborate with multiple buyers to facilitate the marketing efforts of new products, and development of promotional calendars, product launches, and employee incentive programmes.
- Maintain open lines of communication between manufacturers, sales teams, vendors, and warehousing personnel to expedite product orders, distribution, and problem resolutions.
- Reported directly to the Senior Buyer of XYZ Bedding in charge of day-to-day retail merchandise buying and merchandising activities impacting bedding sales across 37 Northeast locations.
- Successfully trained 45+ XYZ employees on a complex LAN database management system.

Sale Tracking, Analysis and Reporting

- Perform ABC's weekly sales analysis activities on regional/local transactions, achieving a recovery of £1,800,000 from 2001 to 2007 resulting from identification and resolution of accounting discrepancies.
- Develop sales books reflecting product lines, monthly promotions, discounted items, order forms and transparencies used by sales teams and personnel throughout 26 store locations.
- Formulate price breakdowns and track sales levels to determine product volume adjustments, replenishments and allocations with a demonstrated proficiency in internal networking systems.
- Researched, compiled, and recorded XYZ's historical data to develop innovative sales strategies through close examination of inventory and product availability, pricing, and store promotions.

Work History

Assistant Buyer/Sales Analyst   7/00–Present
ABC LTD., York

Assistant Buyer/Merchandise Coordinator   4/96–7/00
XYZ BEDDING, York

Education

BA (Hons), Business Management, 1996
UNIVERSITY OF YORK

Sommelier

Angelica's CV was tricked out to look like a menu.

Angelica Merceau
1 Any Street, Anytown AX0 0AA
Phone: 020 8123 4567 Email: wineangel@yahoo.com

Sommelier Extraordinaire

Piedmonts Cheltenham
Master Sommelier, September 2001 – Present

- Expertise in all aspects of wine, including regions of the world and their products, grape varietals, fortified wines, methods of distillation, international wine law, cigar production, and proper storage and handling.
- Manage wine inventory averaging over 12,000 bottles, worth £1,550,000.
- Supervise and personally train staff of 25 sommeliers and wine stewards in pairing wines with cuisine, presentation of wine, brandies, and liqueurs, and selection, preparation, and placement of glassware.
- Coordinate all wine-tasting events, and varietal seminars.
- Handle all client enquiries and complaints.

Bordeaux Steak House, York
Sommelier, May 1999 – January 2001
Lead Wine Steward, December 1997 – May 1999

- Supervise and train staff of wine stewards in all aspects of wine presentation, pairing with cuisine, and glassware selection and placement.
- Choose appropriate cuisine and wine pairings, assist clients in selection of wines, brandies, liqueurs, cigars, properly present and decant wines, and select and place stemware.

Education, Certifications and Professional Development:

- City Catering College
NVQ2 Food and Drink Service
- Institute of Master Sommeliers
Master Sommelier, 2001
- International Sommelier Guild
* Sommelier Diploma Programme 1999
* Wine Fundamentals Certificate, Level II, 1999
* Wine Fundamentals Certificate, Level I, 1998
- Sommelier Society

Varietal Courses:
* Cabernet Sauvignon, 1999
* Sauvignon Blanc, 1999
* Chardonnay, 1999
* Merlot, 1999
* Sangiovese, 1999
* Syrah, 1998
* Pinot Noir, 1998
* Riesling, 1998

Professional Memberships
- Association de la Sommellerie Internationale (ASI)
Member, 2001 – Present
- *The Sommelier Society*
Member, 1999 – Present

Restaurant server

Valerie uses an 'Outstanding Achievement & Recommendations' section to bring attention to her strengths, and she has done a nice job in identifying the type of restaurants in which she has gained experience.

Valerie W Butler
Any Street • Anytown AX0 0AA
07850 515536 mobile • home 020 8123 4567

SERVER

Professional Profile

Energetic and highly motivated **Food Server** with extensive experience in the food service industry. Expertise lies in working with the fine dining restaurant, providing top-quality service, and maintaining a professional demeanour. Solid knowledge of the restaurant business with strengths in excellent customer service, food and wine recommendations.

Get along well with management, co-workers and customers. Well-developed communication skills, known as a caring and intuitive 'people person', with an upbeat and positive attitude. Highly flexible, honest, and punctual, with the ability to stay calm and focused in stressful situations. Committed to a job well done and a long-term career.

Outstanding Achievements and Recommendations

- Served notable VIP clientele including clients associated with Elmdale Charitable Trust.
- History of repeat and new customers requesting my service as their waitress.
- Known for creating an atmosphere of enjoyment and pleasure for the customer.

'…Valerie was warm, friendly, kind and very efficient.
We didn't feel rushed – she handled our requests and
we appreciated her genuine "May I please you" attitude…'

Related Work History

Waitress • Banquets • Heathman Lodge • Maidenhead • *2005–present*
Seasonal cuisine.

Banquets • Dolce Skamania Lodge • Stevenage • *2004–2005*
Casual to fine dining restaurant.

Waitress • Hidden House • Stevenage • *1996–2004*
Exclusive fine dining restaurant.

Waitress • Falls Lodge Restaurant • Stevenage • *1995–1996*
Historic Gorge Falls restaurant serving authentic local cuisine.

Waitress • The XYZ Restaurant • Oxford • *1 year*
World renowned award-wining fine dining restaurant.

Steamfitter

Fred had experience in highly specialized jobs. His expertise and training were attractively emphasized with graphic lines.

Fred G Jamisen
1 Any Street • Anytown AX0 0AA
020 8123 4567

Steamfitter

Professional Profile

Highly skilled, conscientious, and precise **Steamfitter** with over 6 years experience and 10,000+ hours of training in all aspects of Steamfitting. Familiar with all required codes, appropriate use of equipment, steamfitting techniques, safety standards, and proper procedures to prevent injuries. Proficient in reviewing plans, blueprints and specifications for steamfitting projects with proven ability to provide expert recommendations. Well-developed troubleshooting skills with accurate and precise repairs. Experienced EMT willing to volunteer EMT services on the job. Excellent communication skills, personable, trustworthy, adaptable, and committed to a long-term career.

Expertise and Training Includes:

- Air Conditioning and Refrigeration Systems and Equipment
- Boilers
- Commercial and Industrial
- Conduit Flex, Duct and Controls
- Electrical and Electronic Contracting
- HVAC, Air Conditioning and Refrigeration
- Instrumentation
- Outdoor Installations
- Overhead and Underground
- Process Systems and Equipment
- Steam and Heating Systems and Equipment
- Troubleshooting and Maintenance
- Welding Processes including Orbital Welder Arc 207
- Wire Pulling, Wiring Devices, Removal and Finish

Licences

Pressure Vessel and Boiler Licence Class V
United Association of Steamfitters

Employment History

Steamfitter • United Association of Steamfitters • Portsmouth • 6 years
Assignment to various companies and projects as needed.

Paper Machine Operator • ABC Ltd • Westover • 11 years
previously owned by XYZ Paper Company
EMT (Emergency Medical Technician) • Served as volunteer EMT for the paper mill.

Sales Representative • DEF Bottling Company • Portsmouth • 8 years • Beverage sales.

Military

Specialist E-4 – Nuclear Missile Technician • Honourable Discharge • 1979

Education

BA (Hons) Humanities
City College and North West Community College

Automotive service manager

TOM PARSONS

1 Any Street Anytown AX0 0AA • 020 8123 4567 • E-mail: dtjpar@aol.com

Automotive Service Manager

Twenty-three years successful customer service management experience within the automotive industry; proven track record meeting challenges and creatively solving a myriad of problems. Extensive knowledge of automotive warranty policies and procedures. Decisive hands-on manager with an interactive management style able to lead several service teams and administrative staff. Ability to motivate employees' performance levels and develop rapport with diverse audiences; excellent employee relations. Developed excellent product and service knowledge throughout career. Computer literate with experience of Microsoft Office. Broad-based responsibilities and knowledge include:

- Customer Service
- Problem Solving
- Leadership, Supervision and Training
- Service Repair Analysis
- Safety and Quality Control
- Warranty Expertise

- Product Knowledge
- Conflict Resolution
- Team Building
- Service Accounting (Expenses/Revenues)
- Technical Knowledge/Efficiency
- Operational Policies and Procedures

PROFESSIONAL EXPERIENCE
XYZ & ABC, Keasby – 1992 to Present
Service Manager

- Direct reports include 35 staff (Service Advisers, Service Teams, Cashiers, Receptionists, and Detailers).
- Manage XYZ and ABC Service Departments while supervising service advisers and administrating client issues; ensure customer satisfaction.
- Solve product issues for both departments while working with company representatives and senior management.
- Improve department productivity and solve warranty issues when necessary.
- Monitor departmental budget taking correct actions when required.
- Oversee the development and implementation of new ABC franchise, and obtain required certification for service department.
- Achieve 2.2 hours per service order ratio for each customer.
- Eliminate expense and waste while reducing employee time-schedule loss.
- Perform repair order analysis, and monitor team efficiency improving shop use and work in process ratios.
- Analyse monthly owner first reports for XYZ, and communicate findings with staff.

Stanhope XYZ, Stanhope – 1987 to 1992
Service Manager

- Direct reports included 13 staff (Service Advisers, Service Teams, Cashiers and Detailers)
- Oversaw entire Service Department ensuring complete customer satisfaction.
- Communicated with XYZ Service Representatives regarding product issues and warranty concerns.
- Improved departmental productivity implementing several new programmes.
- Conducted repair order and service department analysis.

Tom Parsons
Page 2 of 2

- Substantially increased service revenues and volume by 60% during first fiscal year.
- Maintained warranty expenses within manufacturers' guidelines.
- Transferred to another location to manage larger department.

HAYNES XYZ, Haynes – 1982 to 1987
Service Consultant

- Handled and wrote over 20+ customer service orders per day.
- Sold service and maintenance plans to clients.
- Coordinated service orders with technical staff ensuring quality control through entire service process.
- Prepared final accounting of orders.
- Implemented first nationwide service team model for dealerships.
- Moved to new organization after company purchase.

Heavy equipment driver

Trevor was interested in driving heavy equipment in the Middle East.

TREVOR BLACK
1 Any Street, Anytown AX0 0AA
020 8123 4567 (h) + 07850 515536 (m)

+ DRIVER/HEAVY EQUIPMENT +

PROFILE

- Skilled driver with Class A Commercial Driver's Licence (CDL), Expires 1/1/09.
- Over two million miles driving commercial vehicles loaded with general or refrigerated freight.
- Superior driving/safety/inspection record and on-time delivery.
- Excellent health and physical condition.
- Mechanically inclined and maintenance minded.
- Customer-service oriented; personable with instructional communication skills.

VEHICLE EXPERTISE

Several tractor/trailer rigs including refrigerated vans	32 years
National 2003 Flatbed Trailer	3 years
2006 2T Ford F550 with Jerr-Dan Bed, Hydraulic Winch, Diesel	1 year
2004 35T Pete Wrecker with Nomar Bed, Hydraulic Winch, Diesel	3 years
Racetrack road graders and water trucks	13 years

TRUCKING EXPERIENCE

Driver, ABC RECOVERY, Birmingham   2003 – present
Clean up heavy equipment wreck sites and transport vehicle remains to ABC storage facility. In addition to using wrecker with hydraulic winch, use refrigerated vans, trailers, flatbed trailers, and Jaws of Life, as situation requires. Interface with customers and insurance providers. Maintain daily log and paperwork. Worked dispatch and accepted management responsibilities as needed.

- Receive consistent raises due to outstanding performance.
- Underwent police background check to secure driver's position.

Driver, DEF TRANSPORT, Birmingham   2000–2001
Leased refrigerated lorry to haul produce and meat products throughout UK. Worked 12–14 hour days; maintained daily logs and trip sheets; and hired own loaders (lumpers) at docks.

Owner/Driver, XYZ HAULAGE, Birmingham   1993–2000
Leased out transport during summers to clients that included GHI Transportation, JKL Haulage, and MNO Transport. Drove during winters.

OTHER EMPLOYMENT

Promoter, City Speedway (summers)	2002–2003
Manager/Promoter, Plains Speedway (summers)	1990–2002
Auctioneer, Birmingham Area	1996–2002

Material handler

Glenda used her 'Outstanding Accomplishments & Achievements'
section to bring strong focus to her capabilities.

Glenda Pension

1 Any Street, Anytown AX0 0AA
Email: pen333333@attbi.com • 020 8123 4567

Material Handler

Professional Profile
Energetic, highly motivated, and organized Material Handler with extensive experience in
purchasing, inventory control, and shipping/receiving. Strong liaison and negotiator for
improving product delivery and lowering expenses. Well developed tracking and research
abilities. Outstanding communication skills. Personable, independent, and committed to
producing top-quality work. Positive and upbeat attitude; get along well with co-workers and
management. Thoroughly enjoy a challenge and committed to a long-term career.

Experience Includes

• Accuracy	• Import	• Order Pulling	• Quality Assurance
• Customer Service	• Inventory Control	• Ordering	• Receiving
• Dedication	• Liaison	• Organization	• Shipping
• Export	• Negotiator	• Purchasing	• Tracking

Outstanding Accomplishments and Achievements

- Advocated to get certification through Quality Control to achieve IAA approval on specific
  products.
- Secured credit, due to my personal reputation, for a company in receivership.
- Negotiated effective contracts to obtain product shipment with little or no shipping
  charges.
- Recaptured thousands of pounds in warranty monies for company.
- Developed and implemented inventory tracking system.
- Reorganized and set up efficient stock room.

Professional Experience

Enlargement Printer • ABC Ltd • Portsmouth • 2003–2007
Temporary Associate • Manpower • Portsmouth • 2002–2003
Inbound Auditor/Quality Control • DEF Sportswear • Portsmouth • 2001–2002
Warehouse Tech/Quality Control • GHI Ltd • Portsmouth • 1999–2001
Records Clerk • JKL Airlines • Slough • 1998
Purchasing Agent • MNO Air Express Ltd • Gatwick • 1996–1998
Japan Airlines Liaison for Inventory Management by PQR Airlines
PQR Airlines • Gatwick • 1994–1996
Purchasing Manager/Warranty Administrator/Inventory Control
STU Airlines – Slough • 1991–1994

Education and Training

Various classes offered by HSE and Japan Airlines
Hazardous Materials Training • 1995

Personal driver

John needed to refocus his background as a driver to effectively target a position as a personal driver/chauffeur at a large, local corporate headquarters facility.

John Collins

1 Any Street, Anytown AX0 0AA • myemail@myemail.com • 020 8123 4567

PERSONAL DRIVER/CHAUFFEUR
TRANSPORTATION • DOT REGULATIONS • MAINTENANCE • CLIENT RELATIONS

Accomplished and dedicated Driver/Transportation Specialist with a proven track-record of increasing efficiency, quality, and customer satisfaction. Skilled in all aspects of vehicle maintenance, DOT regulatory compliance, driving operations, expense management, client relations, and customer service within startup and high growth organizations. Results-oriented and driven professional with a solid work ethic and dedication to excellence. Professional communication, negotiation, conflict resolution, problem-solving, and technical/troubleshooting skills.

Core Competencies

- Professional Driver
- Expense Management
- Client Relations
- Chauffeur
- DOT Regulatory Compliance
- Customer Satisfaction
- Transportation Specialist
- Customer Service
- Vehicle Maintenance

Professional Experience

ABC – Farmington   2001 to Present

Full Service Driver
Manage a wide range of full-service transportation and customer service functions including collecting payments and delivering products.

Oversee routine vehicle maintenance and process all Department of Transport (DOT) regulations paperwork. Serve as an account manager with full responsibility for tracking and maintaining customer/order records and facilitating communications between owner/manager clients, sales, and company management. Collaborate with technical and maintenance personnel to arrange machine repairs, replacements, and new placements for services. Service machines and troubleshoot technical onboard computer problems. Operate forklifts to load and unload equipment. Train new employees in onboard computer operations and correct procedures/techniques.

Key Achievements:

- Recognized by the company for achieving a four-year safe driving record; received a letter of commendation.
- Played a key role in the suggestion and implementation of having off calls regulated instead of automated to significantly increase quality and customer satisfaction.
- Promoted to account management responsibilities due to dedication and profession-alism.

XYZ – Missenden   1999 to 2001

Driver
Ensured correct products were delivered to the proper business locations and managed all aspects of vehicle safety and maintenance.

Recruited to manage daily transportation, warehousing, order-taking, and customer service/client relations functions to ensure top-level service. Effectively learned warehouse layout to increase efficiency and operated forklifts to load and unload trucks. Assisted in unloading products at each stop and provided direct customer service to resolve issues at all levels. Managed petty cash receipts/reports and compiled/delivered all required paperwork.

Key Achievements:

● Recipient of a letter of commendation for 'Excellence in Customer Service.'

EDUCATION

Diploma: Business Studies • City College

Property management (joint CV)

Pamela and Katherine needed a combined CV for their Team Managers application. This format was highly effective.

Pamela Heshe	**Katherine Heshe**

1 Any Street

Anytown AX0 0AA

020 8123 4567

Property Managers

PROFESSIONAL PROFILE

- Highly motivated, dynamic and energetic with over 30 combined years experience successfully working with diverse personalities.
- Experienced management and maintenance of various houses and flats.
- Possess strong organizational skills and effective paper processing techniques.
- Expert bookkeeping abilities.
- Skills include: Minor repairs, simple plumbing, light electrical, painting, garden maintenance, landscaping, strong maintenance and clean-up experience.
- Effective in pre-qualifying new lease applicants and collecting rents in a timely fashion.
- Personable, loyal, honest, committed, creative, able to maintain property impeccably, and get along well with tenants and management.
- Computer literate.

Pamela Heshe

EMPLOYMENT HISTORY

Sales Consultant • Plymouth • *1993–2007*
• ABC & Co. • Plymouth • *2002–2007*
• XYZ Ltd. • Dartmouth
• PQR Stores • Dartmouth • *1999–2002*
• NOP Ltd. • Plymouth • *1994–1998*

EDUCATION

South West Community College
A levels – English and History

Graduate
BA (Hons) History
South West University

Katherine Heshe

EMPLOYMENT HISTORY

Account Manager/Administrative Assistant
• National ABC Ltd. • *2003–2004*
Willington

Bookkeeper • *2001–2003*
• DEF International
Willington

Bookkeeper • *1979–2000*
• GHI Ltd. Plymouth

Clerical Assistant • *1974–1978*
• JKL Ltd., Plymouth

EDUCATION

Bookkeeping & Accounting • *1979*
South West Community College

Fitness trainer

Anna has a great start in her career as a fitness trainer with super client results that are detailed in her CV making it an action-packed, results-oriented document.

Anna Mead 1 Any Street, Anytown AX0 0AA • 020 8123 4567 • fitness77@sbcglobal.net

Physical Fitness Specialist

DIPLOMA IN KINESIOLOGY
December 2004
Metropolitan College

PROGRAMMES DEVELOPED
- Volleyball League
for health club members
- Women's Self Defence
- 'Silver Hearts'
group exercise class for mature members over sixty years of age.
- 'HealthPlex Holiday Challenge'
- 'Suit Up for Summer'
- Personalized exercise programmes for clients
- 'Tiny Mites'
gymnastics for preschool
- 'Gymnastic All-Stars Cheerleading Programme'

GROUP EXERCISE CLASSES
- Yoga for Fitness
- Muscle Pump
- Rock Bottoms
- Aquafit

Proficient in the use of PC and Macintosh computers.

Motivated and driven

FITNESS SPECIALIST
brings eighteen months of ENERGETIC professional training experience to health and wellness programmes yielding enthusiasm, commitment and results.

SELECTED ACHIEVEMENTS
- Develop strong and strategic weightlifting programme for male clients.
- Implement customized fitness programme for group and individual clients.
- Manage personal training programme, results and profiles for 13 clients.

PROFESSIONAL CERTIFICATIONS

• IDEA Personal Trainer • YogaFit Certified Instructor
• CPR and First Aid • Advanced Personal Trainer Diploma
• Studio Professional

PROFESSIONAL PHYSICAL FITNESS EXPERIENCE
EXERCISE PHYSIOLOGIST

• **Develop, produce and implement** internal and external marketing plans.
• **Instruct and create** programmes for Cardiac Rehabilitation Phase III members.
• **Organize** Fitness Team and Health Assessment Testing schedules.
• **Exceed expectations** and **deliver excellent customer service.**

PERSONAL TRAINER

• **Develop** personalized exercise programmes for each client.
• **Monitor** the transition and progressions of each client into new, more effective exercises.
• Prepare exercise prescriptions.

FITNESS INSTRUCTOR

• **Instruct** various Group Fitness and Yoga classes.
• **Conduct research** on the latest trends and newest exercises.

GYMNASTICS COACH

Advanced Personal Trainer Diploma

CLIENT PROFILES

Profile: Female, age 33 – Stay-at-home mother
Goal: Lose weight and get in shape after birth of baby.
Results: Within 4 months, weight: 147 to 128 lbs; body fat: 30.8% to 18.9%

Profile: Senior male, age 57 – Retired
Goal: Exercise to maintain and get the benefits for his heart.
Results: Developed regulated fitness programme to reach target heart rate.

Profile: Female, age 40 – Professional
Goal: Lose weight (100 lbs.) and get in shape.
Results: Lost 12 lbs. and 14 inches in a six-week period.

PROFESSIONAL EXPERIENCE

ABC HEALTHPLEX – Richmond, **January 2005 – Present**
DEF GYMNASTICS – Richmond, **2001 – 2004**
GHI GYMNASTICS – Richmond, **1999 – 2001**

Beauty therapist

Anita is an beauty therapist moving up in her chosen profession.

ANITA KELLER
1 Any Street, Anytown AX0 0AA
020 8123 4567 • akeller@123.net

PROFILE
An experienced beauty therapist seeking a rewarding career opportunity in a service-driven, team centred spa/resort setting.
Consistently exceed client expectations; recognized for a gentle, soothing touch with a pleasant attitude, while demonstrating capability in areas of:

• skin care/facials • body treatments/wraps • waxing • lymphatic drainage • chemical peels • masks • aromatherapy • multivitamin treatments • make-up • acupressure and Oriental massage treatments

Familiar with a wide product range including:

• Dermalogica • Murad • Obagi • Trucco • Jan Marini • Epicuren • Bio Elements • Biomedics • Skinceuticals • MD Forte • Neo Clean • Magica

Membership
• Beauty Therapists Association • Complementary Therapists Association

Experience
ABC Day Spa, 3/03 – 7/06   Brighton
XYZ, 4/03 – 7/06   Hove
Beauty Therapist
Working by appointment, provided comprehensive aesthetology services, from oxygen facials and anti-ageing skin treatments, to waxing, body wraps and aromatherapy for these upmarket spas.

• Noted for customer service excellence to build a loyal customer base.

OTHER
DEF Agency, 7/06 – Present   Brighton
Personal Assistant
Provide production support for advertising agency, monitoring media placement, preparing and analysing invoices and coordinating/scheduling talent for ads.

• Additionally serve as **make-up artist/stylist** on location/photo shots to maximize visual impact.

EDUCATION
ITEC
Diploma for Beauty Specialists 2005
Classroom and hands-on training in:

• European Skin Care Techniques • Vitamin Therapy for Skin Health • Aromatherapy • Body Therapy • Wellness Therapies for Body, Mind and Spirit • Results-oriented Tips for Maximum Prescriptive Retailing

ITEC
Diploma in Body Treatments 2003
Course work encompassed:
• Microdermabrasion • Salt Glow Body Scrub • Advanced Skin Care • Make-up Techniques • Colour Theory • Contouring and Corrections • European Skin Care Techniques • Vitamin Therapy for Skin Health • Aromatherapy • Body Therapy • Wellness Therapies for Body, Mind and Spirit • Results-oriented Tips for Maximum Prescriptive Retailing

Property management

Jane Swift
127 Anystreet, Anytown AT1 0BB
Tel: 020 8123 4567   jane@anyaddress.co.uk

OBJECTIVE
Position in Property Management

QUALIFICATION HIGHLIGHTS

- More than six years of experience assisting in the management of multiple rental properties.
- Thoroughly familiar with both tenant and landlord laws and guidelines; experienced in collections and county court procedures.
- Extensive business background in general management, customer service and support, and subcontractor supervision.
- Advanced computer skills and demonstrated proficiency in streamlining administrative tasks through the application of technology.
- Resourceful and innovative in problem solving; adapt quickly to a challenge. Strong prioritization, delegation and planning skills.
- Relate warmly to diverse individuals at all levels; respectful yet assertive communication style.

KEY SKILLS AND ABILITIES

- Perform background, reference and credit checks; select quality tenants and maintain high occupancy rates.
- Show available properties to prospective tenants; negotiate lease and rental agreements.
- Handle tenant communications; respond to requests for maintenance and answer questions.
- Troubleshoot and resolve disputes, including evictions and cleaning/demand deposits.
- Research legal issues using Infolaw, file court documents and represent property owner in court.
- Schedule and supervise subcontractors; oversee upgrades, maintenance and renovations.
- Plan and manage budgets; execute general accounting functions.
- Set up and maintain computerized property management systems.
- Coordinate and track rent collection, maintenance and repairs. Proactively address security issues.

CAREER HISTORY

Assistant Property Manager (2001–Present)
Owen & Gains, Portmere
Assist in the management and oversight of multiple residential rental properties. Set up efficient administrative systems, coordinate rent collection, handle tenant disputes and resolve legal issues.

Owner-Manager (1990–2001)
Computer Works, Danesford
Founded and managed this micro/mini-computer sales and systems integration company. Achieved status as a South East Bell Master Vendor.

EDUCATION

City Technical Community College (1988–1989)
OND in Business Administration

The new executive CV

Traditional thinking has it that as CVs only get a cursory first-time reading (about 45 seconds, and 90 per cent of that time spent on the first page), rarely get thoroughly examined, and that consequently all CVs must be as brief as possible. The standard chant for professionals who think constantly about these matters says this: 'One page for every ten years experience and never more than two pages.' This still holds true for the majority of professionals, but not for all.

In certain quarters I may be regarded as a CV heretic, because I believe that for some professionals in some situations such as senior technologists, scientists, and certain medical professionals – as well as many at director level, most CEOs, and just about all boardroom executives – this rule no longer holds true; in fact, adhering to it can be a detriment to a successful job search.

The practical issues creating the need for this change are really quite simple: the increasingly complex requirements for more senior jobs creates the need for adequate reflection of these multi-faceted competencies in a written document.

Such competency must be shown through ever-deepening experience supported by steadily increasing responsibility and illustrated by achievement. Management expertise and its achievements separate from professional and market sector skills also need clear illustration; additionally there are the necessities of professional visibility through publishing, speaking, and other leadership roles that are relevant in many senior level jobs. For example, I recently advised a CEO with a half-page history of board appointments alone, all of which had utmost relevance given his target job. Science is one of the 'publish or perish' professions, and you'll see a CV example in the next few pages that contains almost a full page addressing publications, presentations, and professional affiliations.

Let's take a moment to recall the roles your CV plays in a successful job search: it gives you an achievable focus (without which you cannot be successful); it opens doors; it acts as a road map for interviewers; and it is your spokesperson long after the last interview is over. In short, the thinking that goes into the focus and execution of your CV has a significant impact on every facet of your successful job search. Not surprisingly for professionals in the higher ranks of some professions, an adequate story cannot be caught on two pages, and cramming it in with 9- and 10-point fonts is certainly not the answer – the people in a position to hire such candidates are simply not going to struggle with the fine print.

At the same time the internet has changed the face of recruitment advertising in at least two dramatic ways:

1. Space is no longer an issue, so recruitment advertising has changed from a few terse lines to hundreds and sometimes thousands of words.

2. The descriptors used in the recruitment advertising and job descriptions increase the need for a data-dense CV – one that is going to be retrieved from the CV databases because it uses the right keywords in adequate frequency to catch the attention of the database spiders.

Putting these considerations together: the complexity of some professional and most executive work, along with the need to communicate effectively by using the traditional device of the CV in the new electronic media, has birthed knowledge-era executive CVs of considerable length and density.

My thinking has changed to such a degree on this issue that in my private counselling practice, where I counsel senior professionals on the national and international stage, I am suggesting, encouraging, supporting, and approving data-dense CVs in the three-to-eight-page range, because these CVs are clearly necessary. Executive CVs will still get a cursory first-time review, whether they come directly to human eyes or are dragged up by keywords from a database. This means that, just as much as ever, a CV needs to be clearly focused on a specific job with that first page screaming understanding, capability, and achievement in the target area of expertise.

When the first CV page communicates clearly and contains a compelling message, the subsequent pages will get read with serious attention. The established standards of clarity and brevity (wherever possible) still hold; it's just the complexity of work at the higher levels that has increased and requires explanation. So CV length for today's executive becomes a clear-cut issue of form following function.

Senior-level company executive

DONALD T THOMAS

1 Any Street
Anytown AX0 0AA
donaldthomas@gmail.com

Home: 020 8123 4567   Mobile: 07850 551536

SENIOR-LEVEL EXECUTIVE
FINANCE, CORPORATE STRATEGY AND DEVELOPMENT
Expert in Leading and Partnering Corporate Finance with Enterprise Strategies, Initiatives, Transactions and Goals

PROFILE & VALUE

Strategic Finance Expert – Dynamic CFO with extensive experience and exceptional success in conceiving, planning, developing and executing strategic and tactical finance initiatives that drive top-line performance and bottom-line results. Technically proficient in all aspects of the finance and accounting functions, and expert in partnering corporate finance with enterprise strategies, initiatives and objectives.

Corporate Strategy & Development Specialist – Characterized as a rare visionary, strategist and tactician. Consistent originator of bold, innovative business strategies that have extraordinary results on growth, revenue, operational performance, profitability and shareholder value. Heavy transactions background including startup financing, industry rollup, merger of equals, acquisition and sale.

Consummate Management Executive – Top-performer and valuable contributor to corporate teams. Extremely versatile with high-calibre cross functional management qualifications, experience-backed judgement and excellent timing. Outstanding role model. Talented team builder, mentor and leader.

Diverse Industry & Situational Experience – Public and private; small and FTSE 100 startup, rapid growth, turnaround, post-IPO, post, acquisition integration, bankruptcy – consulting services, real estate, hospitality, resort/vacation property, travel companies doing business in highly regulated industries in UK, European and global arenas.

Extraordinary Personal Characteristics – Articulate, intelligent, ambitious, self-driven and creative. Outstanding corporate ambassador to customers, industry groups, regulatory bodies, private investors, analysts, board members, and other internal and external stakeholders. Speak conversational French and German.

QUALIFICATIONS & EXPERTISE

Vision, Strategy, Execution & Leadership

Strategic Corporate Finance

P/L & Performance Improvement

Financial Forecasting, Analysis & Reporting

Cost Analysis, Reduction & Control

Treasury, Tax, Internal Audit

Corporate Development & Strategic Alternatives

Due Diligence, Deal Structuring & Negotiation

Financial & Legal Transactions

Growth Management & Business Development

Organizational Design & Transformation

Turnaround & Restructure

Crisis & Change Management

Internet Strategies & IT Projects

Team Building & Leadership

Investor, Analyst & Board Relations

Executive Advisory & Decision Support

PROFESSIONAL EXPERIENCE

ABC Management Consulting, London   2000 to Present
Successful Management Consulting Firm – Significant Repeat Business and Value-Added Partner to Leading Consulting Firms (e.g. XYZ Partners, PQR Consulting) – Retained by Startup, Small-Cap and Fortune 500 in US, UK, and Asia.

PRINCIPAL

Operate an independent firm specializing in the delivery of a full-range of consulting services – strategic business planning; strategic finance; corporate strategy, development and financing; organizational design; operational and financial turnaround; marketing; and market research and strategy. Identify and acquire new business, and manage all aspects of the project lifecycle – from scope of work through provision of deliverables, follow-up and relationship management – for large-scale, long-term projects. Engaged by corporate clients representing a broad-range of industry sectors – travel and tourism; hospitality; property development; marketing services; and technology and Internet.

Management Successes
- Leveraged professional reputation contacts worldwide to build and grow a successful management consulting firm.
- Acquired significant repeat business and positioned the firm as a value-added partner to high-profile management consulting firms in the US and UK (e.g., ABC Partners, DEF Consulting).

Key Engagements
- **Turnaround & Change Management** – Retained (by principal consultancy group) to evaluate a key strategic business unit of a £500 million sales company in receivership. Performed in-depth analyses of operations, identified deficiencies and risks, and presented recommendations for restructure and turnaround of call centre operations, programme management, inventory control and member services functions. Engagement contract was extended to serve as Chief Business Architect during execution and post-transition/recovery phases.
- **Operational Startup & Financing** – Retained by US-based clients of a £10 million marketing services business to advise and participate in creating a business plan, raising capital, and executing a startup in the global event management and incentives sector.
- **Corporate Strategy & Finance** – Retained by independent US resort developer to determine the viability and ROI of expanding into international markets. Analysed business, financial, marketing, competitive intelligence, and geopolitical issues impacting the world tourism and hospitality sectors. Pinpointed key target markets, and authored business strategy and financial plan for launch of a luxury boutique hospitality brand.
- **Corporate Strategy** – Engaged in joint consultancy project with ABC Consulting in developing a full-scale corporate strategy plan for £500 million public hospitality company. Researched and analysed internal and external organizations, market opportunities, competitive differentiators, business models and challenges.

CDE Group, Ltd., London   1999 to 2000
Venture Capital-Backed Dot-Com Startup Operating in a Niche Sector – Fine Arts and Antiques Online Sales/Auction

MANAGING DIRECTOR

Held full P&L accountability – recruited by and reported to the investor group and Chairman of the Board – for early-stage Internet company. Developed and executed strategy, managed finance and operations, directed sales and marketing, steered technology development, and managed relationships with internal and external stakeholders. Led a core team of three executives – Director of Sales, Director of Operations, Manager of Finance & Administration – and provided indirect oversight to team of 18 In sales operations, IT, finance and administrative roles.

Strategy & Leadership Successes
- Revised corporate strategy to leverage core competencies – a well-established network of dealerships and virtually unlimited source of product – and position the firm as inventory and distribution solution to another company.
- Conceived and executed viable exit strategy – vs. minimum requirement of additional 2+ years' investment to achieve break-even – by identifying a buyer and negotiating sale of the company to a US-based business. Provided investors with ROI on their original investment/commitment of 660%+.

STUV Corporation, Inc., London   1997 to 1999
£500 Million Company – One of Largest Resort Development/Sales Companies in UK – in Rapid Growth Through International Expansion.

DIRECTOR – BUSINESS DEVELOPMENT

Key member of the executive committee – retained in company's buyout of UK-based LSI Group   in charge of the strategic and tactical business development activities during period of dynamic growth and change. Crossed-over functional lines to address product development, marketing, branding, sales, corporate communications, legal and regulatory matters. Administered £40 million business development budget. Reported directly to the CEO, led a team of five Director-level executives, and interfaced with Board of Directors, Wall Street analysts and strategic alliance partners.

Strategy & Leadership Successes
- Led the company's single most significant post-IPO strategic initiative – conceptualization, development and execution of transformation of the company's infrastructure, business model, product offering and marketing strategy – without negative impact on sales, operational performance or customer service during execution.
- Shifted the business model and organizational structure – from a disconnected collection of resort properties – to a membership-based holiday sales company with an exclusive, points-based holiday product, and strong value proposition with single marketing message.

Business Development Results
- Credited with personal contributions to explosive growth – from £330 million in 1997 to £500 million in 1999 – by spearheading the development and rollout of an innovative vacation ownership product and complementary offerings.
- Expanded market reach and brand recognition by initiating and leveraging relationships with high-profile strategic business partners – ABC Airlines, DEF Communications, GHI, JKL Works and others in the travel, hospitality and marketing services industries.

DONALD T THOMAS

XYZ, Ltd., Lancashire   1994 to 1997
£65 Million, Privately Held Enterprise – One of Largest Vertically Integrated Holiday Ownership
Companies in Europe – Specializing in Development and Management of Resorts, and
Marketing and Sales of Timeshares and Travel Services.

DIRECTOR – BUSINESS DEVELOPMENT (1995 TO 1997)
CHIEF FINANCIAL OFFICER (1994 TO 1995)

Held two key executive positions on the management team – both reporting to CEO (one of two principal shareholders) – following a major debt restructure, physical relocation and preparation for sale. As CFO, managed all aspects of the corporate finance and administration functions (including treasury, tax and internal audit) for headquarters and 10+ overseas branches. Directed the preparation and analysis of financial statements, budgets, forecasts, desktop 'dashboards' and other essential management reports. Hired, trained, mentored and managed a team of 28 including three senior financial and accounting professionals.

As Director of Business Development, identified, created and capitalized upon both innovative and traditional business opportunities. Conceived, developed and managed strategic and tactical messaging, branding, marketing, sales, and relationship building initiatives. Directed product development, positioning and go-to-market strategies, and launched a series of breakthrough concepts and techniques – trial membership, incentive-driven referral programme, customer/prospect profiling, direct-to-consumer sales, interactive multimedia presentations.

Strategy & Business Development Successes
- Key contributor to providing deep due diligence to ABC in its purchase of LMN Group – activities and relationships that led to recruitment to executive position with the acquiring company.
- Credited with personal contributions (strategy, finance, operations, business development) – to growth – from £40 million to £65 million – profitability – from 5% pre-tax margin in 1994 to 11% in 1997 – and shareholder value – from £15 million to £55 million at sale of the company in mid-1997.

Financial & Operations Results
- Built and managed a best-in-class finance and accounting function. Managed the complete turnaround of the corporate finance organization to include new systems, technologies, processes and personnel.
- Provided the executive team and stakeholders with comprehensive, meaningful decision support by restructuring virtually all financial reporting systems.

WXY Group, London   1987 to 1994
One of London's Largest Public Accounting and Business Consulting Practices – Professional
Services for Entrepreneurial Public and Private Companies in Property, VC Funding, Hospitality
and Leisure Travel Sectors.

Rapidly Advancing Levels of Seniority to:

MANAGER – CORPORATE FINANCE & INVESTIGATIONS DEPARTMENT (1992 TO 1994)

Managed client engagements involving deep due diligence for numerous acquisition and funding transactions. Provided a full range of advisory services and functions including creating/opining on corporate development strategies, authoring business plans, preparing projection models, and performing operational and financial assessments. Developed expertise in fraud and litigation support, debt workout and internal audit. Interfaced with firm's Partners, investment bankers, private investors, senior-level corporate executives, board members, industry specialists, and regulatory officials.

Key Engagements
- **Debt Restructure** – Contributed to restructure of £100+ million debt with complex asset security position.
- **Fraud Investigation & Litigation** – Provided support on several high-profile engagements including collapse of a private financial services firm (represented WXY as the client) and a Formula One motor racing team.
- **Corporate Recovery** – Contributed to financial and operational turnaround of several hospitality and leisure firms.

EDUCATION & CREDENTIALS

British Chartered Accountant – ACA – (CPA equivalent), Institute of Chartered Accountants in England and Wales
G Mus (Hons) – Four year degree in Music (with honours), Royal Northern College of Music, Manchester
Training in Corporate Finance and Treasury, Association of Corporate Treasurers

PROFESSIONAL AFFILIATIONS

Institute of Chartered Accountants in England and Wales (ICAEW); Resort Development Association (regular speaker and panellist at conventions); Marketing Association (MA); Chamber of Commerce; Association of Chartered Accountants (ACA); American Real Estate Society (ARES); and Financial Management Association (FMA).

Senior-level company executive (addendum)

DONALD T THOMAS
donaldthomas@gmail.com

HIGHLIGHTS OF A CAREER IN EXCELLENCE
Addendum to CV

EXCELLENCE IN CORPORATE STRATEGY & TURNAROUND
Managing Director – early-stage Internet startup

Challenge   Revise corporate strategy and turnaround operational and financial performance of a venture capital-backed, early-stage startup – fine arts and antiques dot-com.

Actions   Evaluated the original business plan against actual conditions and projected outcomes based on multiple scenarios. Created and executed a decisive strategy for 'repackaging' the company's value proposition as an inventory and distribution solution to larger companies. Halted overspending, implemented strict financial controls, restructured operations and reengineered business processes.

Results   Provided investors with viable business strategies and alternatives, and at their direction, executed an exit strategy through the successful sale of the company for £10 million in stock. Provided investors with 660% ROI on their original investment/commitment.

Strengths   I am a turnaround specialist – I can rapidly assess a complex business situation, formulate a solution that meets overall commercial objectives (even if the solutions are a radical departure from initial direction), and inspiring and gaining buy-in for dynamic change.

EXCELLENCE IN STRATEGY & BUSINESS DEVELOPMENT
Director – Business Development, large resort development and sales company

Challenge   Lead high-profile, mission-critical strategic business initiative – characterized by CEO as 'betting the ranch' – to restructure and transform a £500 million resort development and sales company.

Actions   Developed and executed strategies, and planned and managed on virtually all cross-functional aspects of the business. Steered development of an appealing customer value proposition in an innovative product offering – 'Club Main Attraction' a points-based holiday club – communicated through a clear, strong brand and marketing message. Partnered with legal counsel in structuring products that met state/federal regulatory guidelines. Built and led a team of top-performing strategic marketing professionals to execute rollout to 1,000+ person sales force.

Results   Exceeded expectations of founder/executive management and analysts – rewarded in 1999 for exceptional corporate contributions by receipt of a specially created Award for Vision – in conceiving and driving innovation in corporate strategy, infrastructure and product marketing.

Strengths   I am a true visionary and talented business leader who is always originating new concepts, innovating bold strategies, creating opportunities, and applying highly developed finance, marketing, business management and people skills to take on huge challenges and overcome daunting challenges.

EXCELLENCE IN COST REDUCTION & PERFORMANCE IMPROVEMENT
CFO – large European, vertically integrated vacation ownership company

Challenge   Resolve serious financial and operational performance issues – increasingly high costs and productivity bottlenecks in the travel and reservations division.

DONALD T THOMAS   Page 2 of 3

Actions   Streamlined divisional operating processes, realigned key personnel, and updated and improved the payment processing and banking functions by establishing a relationship with a high-tech banking institution.

Results   Improved customer service while slashing invoicing and collection costs – from 10% to <5% and £5 million; and as volume grew to £25+ million, reduced the ratio even further – and created seamless connectivity in processes, communications and culture between the division and the rest of the organization.

Strengths   I am an expert in leveraging best practices, technologies and relationships to enable and maintain inter-organizational cohesiveness, and operational performance excellence.

EXCELLENCE IN DECISION SUPPORT

CFO – leading European resort developer

Challenge   Provide comprehensive, meaningful and accurate decision support to the Principals of a privately held, multi-site resort development and sales enterprise.

Actions   Led complete restructure of the corporate finance and accounting organization, and all related systems, controls, processes and technologies. Introduced sophisticated forecasting, analysis and reporting tools, restructured the financial reports, refined the budgeting/variance analysis process, and implemented open-architecture accounting IT solutions/applications. Rebuilt, retrained and mentored the 28-person finance and accounting team, and advised senior-level management in optimal use of new financial information.

Results   Created and led a top-notch finance and accounting organization that produced timely, precise, meaningful financial and operational data – executive decision support and departmental financial accountability credited with the company's realization of 65% improvement in profitability (despite zero revenue growth) within one year of implementing new corporate finance regime, and delivery of significant ROI in successful sale of the company two years later.

Strengths   I am valuable to any corporate executive team through my ability to provide mission-critical decision support, and I am proficient in building and leading best-in-class finance and accounting organizations.

EXCELLENCE IN STRATEGIC & TACTICAL BUSINESS DEVELOPMENT

Director of Business Development – European resort ownership company

Challenge   Continue to grow revenue and market share despite dramatic changes in the European holiday ownership sector – new legislation impacting multiple areas of the business model (ban on down-payment at point of sale, expanded disclosure requirement, statutory cancellation period).

Actions   Went to senior sales executives with a new sales model – multimedia technology, new sales showroom environment, upgraded sales presentation and collaterals and gained approval from shareholders for investing in the strategic and tactical innovations.

Results   Distinguished the company as an industry leader – first holiday ownership company (in both US and UK) to use new technology-enabled sales/communication tools – a significant feature in sale of company. Maintained corporate revenue performance while reducing cancellation rates by 5%+.

Strengths   I am continuously devising ways to drive growth, operational performance and profitability – despite any internal or external challenge. With acute understanding of the marketplace, I am able to create and execute business development strategies and tactics that put my company in front of the competition.

DONALD T THOMAS

EXCELLENCE IN TURNAROUND & CHANGE
Consultant – international resort and holiday timeshare company

Challenge   Restore financial and operational health to a key strategic business unit – an SBU critical to the survival of the company – for an enterprise in receivership.

Actions   Contributed industry and business unit expertise (personally created, developed and exceeded performance objectives during period of 1997 through 1999) to a joint venture consulting engagement with ABC Partners (turnaround specialists). Evaluated existing operations and mapped-out a new strategy, organizational structure, business model (personal property vs. deeded property and culture.

Results   Delivered the plan for putting in placing a robust organizational structure with best-practices for risk management, inventory use, call centre operations, programme management, financial reporting and member communications/satisfaction. Retained on extended contract to serve as Chief Architect (reporting to Interim CEO) to contribute cross-functional leadership to ongoing project phases. Received second extension (reported to permanent executive committee) to manage integration of the US and European programmes. Combined annual cost savings of turnaround initiatives exceeded £5 million annually.

Strengths   In addition to industry expertise – resort and holiday timeshare – I bring the full complement of business and finance management qualifications. I am quick to identify and create solutions to complex business issues, and am proficient in managing large-scale, long-term, mission-critical projects.

Senior executive–scientist

SAMUEL HARRINGTON, PhD

Office Address
1 Any Street
Anytown AX0 0AA
Office: 020 8123 4568
harringtons@dhhs.state.va.us

1 Any Street
Anytown AX0 0AA
Home: 020 8123 4567
Mobile: 07850 515536
harringtonsam@aol.com

SENIOR EXECUTIVE – SCIENTIST

Chief Science Officer – Executive Director – Programme Manager – Senior Scientist/Researcher

Biotechnology Enterprises – Molecular Research & Diagnostics Organizations

CAREER PROFILE AND DISTINCTIONS

- Dynamic, entrepreneurial business professional with high-calibre general management qualifications … strong orientations in finance and technology … proven leadership talents. Led the startup of three biotechnology R&D organizations and turned-around an existing test/surveillance laboratory.
- Accomplished senior-level scientist and recognized innovator in modern technical and managerial strategies, principles, methodologies and processes for the biotech industry. Designed and developed numerous scientifically/commercially significant diagnostic reagents and assays.
- Professional experience spanning diverse clinical and technical settings, private biotech firms … large R&D operations … public health organizations … hospitals … academic facilities … national security projects.
- Accustomed to, and effective in high-profile scientist executive roles … managing large organizations … overcoming complex business/technical challenges … gaining respect from competitors and peers … communicating complex concepts to technical and non-technical audiences … maintaining impartiality in politically charged environments … fostering consensus and generating cooperation from multicultural, multidisciplinary teams.
- Confident, assertive, diplomatic and outgoing with exceptional communication, public speaking and interpersonal relations skills. Multicultural, bilingual professional – speak fluent Arabic and English.

MANAGEMENT QUALIFICATIONS

Entrepreneurial Vision, Strategy & Leadership
Financial Planning & Management
Programme & Project Management
Staff Training, Development & Supervision
Team Building, Mentoring & Leadership
Marketing, Communications & Public Relations

P&L and Operations Management
Budget Planning, Analysis & Control
Process Design/Improvement – Business
 & Technical
Technology Investments & Solutions

AREAS OF EXPERTISE

Molecular Diagnostics R&D
Disease Investigation & Management –
 Infectious & Genetic
Laboratory Management Quality Improvement
 & Assurance
Advanced Laboratory Procedures & Technologies

Molecular-Based Surveillance
DNA Fingerprinting & Gene Banking
Regulatory Affairs & Compliance
Crisis/Emergency Preparedness &
 Response
National Security Strategies, Policies &
 Programmes

PROFESSIONAL EXPERIENCE

1999 to Present

MOLECULAR BIOLOGIST
Department of Health

Hold full P&L accountability for only public health reference laboratory – infectious disease testing and surveillance services, bio-terrorism detection, prevention and response. Manage all aspects of business operations (e.g., strategic planning, budgeting, financial reporting, staffing, workflow, administrative affairs, internal/external customer service, quality, regulatory reporting/affairs). Provide technical and managerial oversight to six primary areas of laboratory operations: test development, disease surveillance, disease outbreak investigations (including emerging infections, air-water-food-borne infections) and testing for bio-threat organisms/bio-terrorism. Manage £600K capital budget and £250K annual budget for operations. Lead a three-person management team and provide indirect supervision to seven technical and non-technical support employees.

DIRECTOR OF MOLECULAR DIAGNOSTICS
Management & Leadership Successes:

- Distinguished the facility as one of the best labs in the UK, and one of the first public health organizations to receive government funding for bio-terrorism testing and preparedness.
- Evolved a very basic laboratory operation into a dynamic scientific organization staffed with talented, highly trained professionals using state-of-the-art technologies and contemporary methodologies to perform sophisticated testing/surveillance of emerging infections.
- Led an ambitious campaign to secure £600K+ investment in technology (government sources). Achieved financial accountability and discipline throughout the organization in order to maximize ROI.
- Equipped the organization and prepared the staff to handle both routine and emerging infections (including potential bio-terrorism organisms) despite the challenges of operating under serious financial and staff constraints.
- Designed and led intensive training and career development programmes – trained/qualified four professionals in advanced molecular testing – and provided team coaching and one-to-one mentoring.
- Served as an effective representative/spokesperson for the organization to internal and external parties – scientific community, government agencies, regulatory officials, media, and the public – and continue to advocate on behalf of the laboratory and its activities, budgets, personnel and projects.

Clinical Projects & Achievements
- Distinguished and top-ranking science officer providing consulting, advisory and leadership services on matters related to molecular diagnostics.
- Led the entire development cycle – design, validation, application, training, troubleshooting – of molecular diagnostics-based assays for rapid investigation, diagnosis and surveillance of emerging/reemerging infectious diseases including E. coli, Salmonella, West Nile Virus and Noro Virus.
- Participated in validation of new rapid tests developed by CDC for BT organisms including anthrax, smallpox and the emerging virus responsible for SARS.

SAMUEL HARRINGTON, PhD   Page Three

City University Medical Centre (CUMC)   1992 to 1998

PROGRAMME COORDINATOR – DEVELOPMENT
Division of Molecular Diagnostics

Key member of a seven person management team for a key division within this large, diverse healthcare organisation – 2nd largest medical centre in the UK and largest in North Eastern area – comprised of several regional hospitals and speciality institutions (including the Cancer Institute and the Transplant Institute). Managed the business, clinical and technology aspects of test development. Led a team of 13 full-time techologists.

Management Achievements:
- Established the ABC developmental laboratories from the ground up – lab was a model followed by other laboratories throughout the UK – and provided the vision and operational framework for accommodating emerging technologies and future expansion.
- Contributed to planning, development and control of annual budgets of nearly £1 million for operations – including £200K for capital equipment.
- Developed/presented formal training programmes – one-month courses in lecture and web lab formats – to physicians on topics related to emerging/advanced molecular diagnostics methodologies, technologies and applications.

Clinical Projects & Achievements:
- Developed DNA fingerprinting method to distinguish between closely related isolates of Legionella pneumophila – causative pathogen for Legionnaire's Disease. Existence of this technique thwarted potential litigation (six-figure damage claim) by a former patient against the hospital.
- Developed test for identifying four most common gene mutations of Gaucher Disease among Ashkenazi Jewish populations. Delivered £110K+ per year in revenue from laboratory test fees.

The City Transplant Institute (CTI)   1995 to 1998

SCIENTIST/CONSULTANT

Contributed expertise in molecular diagnostics to a multidisciplinary team of professionals – immunology, molecular biology, genetics, cell biology, other disciplines – working clinical R&D activities for the oldest/largest comprehensive international organ transplant programmes in the world. Developed customized, speciality reagents used in research at the Institute.

Clinical Projects & Key Accomplishments:
- Developed 2-hour assay – vs. existing test requiring 24+ hours – for detecting presence of low-level HCF in donated livers to be used in transplantation.
- Established custom oligonucleotide design and synthesis service. Generated £150K+ in annual revenue (commercial value exceeded £300K).

Applied Genetics Laboratories Ltd (AGL), Melbourne   1991 to 1992

PROJECT LEAD/STAFF SCIENTIST

Managed a five-year, £2.5 million project funded by the National Institute of Environmental Health Sciences (NIEHS) for R&D of early cancer detection/treatment methods. Provided tech nical and managerial oversight to all aspects of the project lifecycle. Tracked and controlled project budgets. Supervised four laboratory technologists.

SAMUEL HARRINGTON, PhD   Page Four

Clinical Projects & Key Accomplishments:
- Designed and executed protocols for searching for TSGs in mice genome and detecting mutations enabling early diagnosis of cancer in humans.
- Participated in presenting annual project report to National Institute of Environmental Health Sciences.

Kuwait Institute for Scientific Research, Shwaikh, Kuwait   1985 to 1987

RESEARCH SPECIALIST
Department of Biotechnology

Established and managed Kuwait's first molecular genetics laboratory. Developed research strategies and managed projects. Provided consulting/advisory services on business and scientific issues. Built and led a team of 10 scientists, and hired/managed administrative support staff.

Research Projects & Key Accomplishments:
- Distinguished as the only molecular biologist in Kuwait, and independently started and managed mission statement, business/clinical strategy, business/laboratory operations, policy/procedure formation, budget, staff, equipment for this, the first molecular genetics laboratory in the country.
- Co-Principal Investigator on three-year £480K+ project involving establishment of basic tools and methodologies for subsequent production of high-value compounds – single cell proteins – for use as animal feed supplements.

TEACHING EXPERIENCE
University of the South   2000 to Present

ASSOCIATE PROFESSOR
Department of Microbiology

Served in a consulting role as a biotechnology subject-matter expert. Led presentations to faculty and graduate students on topics related to molecular diagnostics, public health and bio-terrorism. Provided advice on technical issues and made recommendations for academic/scientific programming.

Metropolitan University   1987 to 1991

RESEARCH ASSOCIATE

Supervised graduate students and taught undergraduate coursework in chemistry. Worked with senior scientists on projects.

Kuwait University Faculty of Medicine, Jabriya, Kuwait   1985 to 1987

LECTURER

Provided classroom and laboratory instruction in biochemistry and molecular biology to undergraduate students. Led/participated in scientific research with focus on rheumatic fever.

EDUCATION

Ph.D. – Medical Biochemistry, Metropolitan University, 1983
M.Sc – Biochemistry, London University
BSc – Biochemistry, Kuwait University, Khaldiya, Kuwait, 1977

SAMUEL HARRINGTON, PhD   Page Five

PUBLICATIONS – *a partial list*

Samuel Harrington. Molecular Diagnostics of Infectious Diseases: State of the Technology. Biotechnology Annual Review, Elsevier Publishing Company (2000).

Samuel Harrington, Robert Lanning, David Cooper. Rapid detection of hepatitis C virus in plasma & liver biopsies by capillary electrophoresis. Nucleic Acid Electrophoresis Springer Lab Manual, Dietmar Tietz (ed), Springer-Verlag, Heidelberg (1998).

Samuel Harrington, William Pasculle, Robert Lanning, David McDevitt, David Cooper. Typing of Legionella pneumophila isolates by degenerate (D-RAPD) fingerprinting. Molecular and Cellular Probes, 9 405-414 (1995).

John A. Barranger, Erin Rice, **Samuel Harrington**, Carol Sansieri, Theodore Mifflin, and David Cooper. Enzymatic and Molecular Diagnosis of Gaucher Disease. Clinics in Laboratory Medicine, 15 (4) 899-913 (1995).

Samuel Harrington, Robert W. Lanning and David L. Cooper. DNA Fingerprinting of Crude Bacterial Lysates using Degenerate RAPD Primers (D-RAPD). PCR Methods and Applications. 4 265-268 (1995).

Samuel Harrington, Carol S. Sansieri, David W. Kopp, David L. Cooper and John A. Barranger. A new diagnostic test for Gaucher Disease suitable for mass screening. PCR Methods and Applications, 4 (1) 1-5 (1994).

David L. Cooper, **Samuel Harrington**. Molecular Diagnosis: a primer and specific application to Gaucher Clinical Perspectives, 1 (3) 1-6 (1993).

PRESENTATIONS – *a partial list*

Samuel Harrington and Krista Marschner. 'A new, two-hour test for Bordetella pertussis using the SmartCycler', 103rd General Meeting of the Society for Microbiology (SM), London, May 2003.

Samuel Harrington. 'Methods & Applications of DNA Fingerprinting Techniques', Five 1- and/or 2-week-long workshops presented at the University of Puerto Rico, 1997 through 2003.

Samuel Harrington and Denise Bolton. 'Development of a duplex real time RT-PCR test for surveillance of West Nile and Eastern Equine Encephalitis viruses using the SmartCycler', 102nd General Meeting of the Society for Microbiology (SM), London, May 2002.

D.K. Voloshin, A.W. Pasculle, S.P. Krystoflak, **S. Harrington** and E.J. Wing. 'Nosocomial Legionnaire's disease: an explosive outbreak following interruption of hyperchlorination', Interscience Conference on Antimicrobial Agents and Chemotherapy, San Francisco, CA, October 1995.

S. Harrington. 'Genetic identification technologies: PCR and DNA fingerprinting', Second UN-sponsored Conference on the Perspectives of Biotechnology in Arab Countries, Amman, Jordan, March 1993.

S. Harrington, G. L. Rosner, D. L. Cooper and J. A. Barranger. 'A new PCR-based diagnostic test for Gaucher Disease (GD)', Amer. J. Hum. Genet, 53 (supplement) 1775, 1993.

Bahr, G., **Harrington, S.**, Yiusof, A., Jarrar, I., Rotta, J., Majeed, H. and Behbehani, K. 'Depressed lymphoprolypherative responses in vitro to different streptococcal epitopes in patients with chronic rheumatoid heart disease', Conference on Infectious Diseases in Developing Countries, Kuwait City, Kuwait, March 1987.

PROFESSIONAL AFFILIATIONS

Member, Society for Microbiology – SM

Consultant, INTOTA Corporation

Member, Association for Molecular Pathology – AMP

Member, Council of Healthcare Advisers, Gerson Lehrman Group

Senior executive–scientist (addendum)

SAMUEL HARRINGTON, PhD

Office Address
1 Any Street
Anytown AX0 0AA
Office: 020 8123 4568
harringtons@dhhs.state.va.uk

1 Any Street
Anytown AX0 0AA
Home: 020 8123 4567
Mobile: 07850 515536
harringtonsam@aol.com

Leadership Addendum – Science & Management

Dr. Samuel Harrington brings exceptional value through the combination of his core management qualifications, leadership talents and scientific knowledge, proficiency and experience. He continues to develop his cross-functional general management skills and remains on the cutting-edge of scientific advancements and contemporary topics in biotechnology.

BUSINESS MANAGEMENT & ORGANIZATIONAL LEADERSHIP
– Strategies, Initiatives, Contributions & Successes –

Much more than a scientist, Dr. Harrington is a management professional who is experienced and successful in directing organizations, programmes, projects and teams. He brings strategic perspective, business acumen, sound judgement and financial discipline to private and public organizations involved in the life sciences/biotechnology fields.

'His work ethic is exemplary and his professional demeanour a model for others to emulate.'
David L. Cooper, Director, Division of Molecular Diagnostics,
University of London Medical Centre
'The quality of Samuel's work is exceptional … and he excels in this area (communications).'
Director, Public Health Laboratories

Organizational Development & Leadership

Dr. Harrington has provided both technical and managerial leadership to scientific organizations, and over the course of this 20+-year career, he has:

- Established the Public Health Laboratory as an important participant/contributor to the national biotech industry.
- Led the complete organizational startup of the ABC development laboratory for the Division of Molecular Diagnostics at the University of London Medical Centre.
- Contributed the vision, technical expertise and business management capabilities to create and direct Kuwait's first molecular genetics laboratory.

Business & Finance Management

Dr. Harrington's ability to achieve operational and financial performance objectives within the departments he leads has made significant contributions to the ROI, profitability and value of the larger organizations. As demonstrated by his track record, Dr. Harrington takes personal responsibility for all general business, daily operations and budgeting/cost control initiatives. For example, he has:

- Authored and executed the business plan for the molecular development laboratory for the University of London Medical Centre, and integrated it into the main organizational structure.
- Participated in planning, administering and controlling £1 million operating budget for the Division of Molecular Diagnostics.
- Achieved all budgetary performance objectives and gained financial discipline within the laboratory.

Laboratory Operations Management

With more than 20 years' of academic, research and management work in science, Dr. Harrington is well-qualified in establishing, staffing, managing and improving the performance of laboratory operations/organizations. For example:

- Manage all aspects of operations – including disease surveillance, disease outbreak investigations, test development and testing for bio-threat (BT) organisms – in a 'best in class' public health laboratory.
- Established UK's first Microbial Gene (DNA) Bank.
- Modernized and improved performance in key operational areas – productivity, efficiency, personnel qualifications, quality, compliance – for the laboratory.

BIOTECHNOLOGY/BIOMEDICAL RESEARCH, DEVELOPMENT & DIAGNOSTICS
Projects, Activities, Contributions & Achievements –

'[Samuel Harrington's] strengths [include] ... scientific knowledge and technical expertise, quality of work, initiative, sense of humour and ability to get along with people.'

'[Dr. Harrington] set up an RT-PCR procedure for West Nile Virus which brought much praise to the PHL, for its ability to quickly deal with a developing public health problem.'

'[Dr. Harrington] has shown a great deal of initiative in learning about infectious disease needs and developing molecular procedures for their detection and identification.'

Director, Public Health Laboratories

Dr. Harrington's career is focused on Infectious Disease, Molecular Diagnostics and Genetic Disorders.

Molecular Diagnostics of Infectious Diseases

Dr. Harrington's work in molecular diagnostics of infectious diseases has involved extensive research, surveillance, testing, assay development and publication. He is proficient in the use of sophisticated laboratory methodologies, techniques and technologies including, but not limited to: DNA fingerprinting (PFGE, Ribo Printing, PCR-based fingerprinting – RAPD/AFLP), DNA/RNA sequencing; PCR (including Real Time, RT-PCR, multiplex); oligonucleotide printer/probe design and synthesis, Southern hybridization; molecular cloning; and recombinant DNA technologies.

- Developed a two-hour RT-PCR test for the detection of B. pertussis directly from crude clinical specimens, thereby eliminating the need for traditional labour-intensive, time-consuming specimen processing (DNA extraction) step. Laboratories across the UK and Europe (Germany and Spain) have requested permission to use this test in their laboratories, and a Canadian diagnostics company has expressed interest in participating with validation studies. Presented this work at the 103rd General Meeting of the Society for Microbiology in London, May 2003.
- Developed and presented (at the 102nd General Meeting of the Society for Microbiology, May 2002) a duplex RT-PCR test for surveillance of West Nile and Eastern Equine Encephalitis viruses using SmartCycler®.
- Developed and managed the design, validation, application, test and troubleshooting of molecular diagnostics-based assays for rapid identification and surveillance of emerging diseases.

- Distinguished the centre as one of the first labs in the UK to participate in proficiency testing (RT-PCR) for SARS using a RT-PCR test developed by the CDC – validated test is being performed routinely at the laboratory.
- Developed a RT-PCR test for the rapid detection of the food-borne pathogen Noro (Norwalk) virus from human stools using melt-curve analysis of the amplified product – several PHLs have requested permission to use this test in their facilities.
- RNA isolated from mosquito pools inhibits West Nile virus real-time RT-PCR. Presented findings at the 3rd International Conference on Emerging Infectious Diseases in March 2002.
- Investigation of simultaneous outbreaks of S pneumoniae and H. influenzae in major medical centre. Presented abstract at the 6th Annual PulseNet Update Meeting in April 2002.
- Molecular Diagnostics of Infectious Diseases: State of the Technology. Invited article summarizing emerging technologies and applications in the rapid diagnosis of disease. Published in Biotechnology Annual Review, Elsevier Publishing Company, 2000.
- Rapid detection of hepatitis C virus in plasma and liver biopsies by capillary electrophoresis. In: Nucleic Acid Electrophosesis Lab Manual, 1998.
- Developed and co-presented an abstract entitled 'Nosocomial Legionnaire's disease. An explosive outbreak following interruption of hyperchlorination', presented at the Interscience Conference on Antimicrobial Agents and Chemotherapy in October 1995.
- Co-developed 'Depressed Lymphoprolypherative Responses in vitro to Different Streptococcal Epitopes in Patients With Chronic Rheumatoid Heart Disease', presented at the Conference on Infectious Diseases in Developing Countries held in Kuwait in March 1987.

Molecular Diagnostics of General Diseases

Either independently or as a member of a team of multidisciplinary professionals, Dr. Harrington has conducted a wide-range of scientific research/experimentation, developed mutation screening assays, written/published numerous articles and delivered presentations covering a vast spectrum of areas related to genetic diseases.

- Developed mutation screening and detection assays for a number of genetic diseases such as breast cancer (BRCA-1 mutation screening). Fanconi's anaemia, Canavan's disease, Factor V Leiden, Fragile X syndrome and Huntington's disease.
- Molecular Diagnosis: a primer and specific application to Gaucher disease. Gaucher Clinical Perspectives 1 (3) 1-6, 1993.
- Phenotype, Genotype, and the treatment of Gaucher Disease. Clinical Genetics. 49 111-118, 1996.
- Enzymatic and Molecular Diagnosis of Gaucher Disease. Clinics in Laboratory Medicine. 15 (4) 899-913, 1995.
- A review of the molecular biology of glucocerebrosidase and the treatment of Gaucher disease, published in Cytokines and Molecular Therapy, 1995. 1 149-163, 1995.
- A new diagnostic test for Gaucher Disease suitable for mass screening. PCR Methods and Applications 4 (1) 1-5, 1994.

BioSecurity

Dr. Harrington champions interest and involvement in the conduct of scientific research and development, especially diagnostic test development and validation, of organisms and pathogens potentially used in biological terrorism/warfare. His work makes him of significant

---

SAMUEL HARRINGTON, PhD   Page Four

---

value to organizations and programmes involved in related medical practice and public health programmes, actions, projects and policies – to ultimately bridge the gap between public health specialists/organizations, the public, government agencies/intelligence community and primary care providers.

- Distinguished the Public Health Laboratory (PHL) as one of the first in the UK to be awarded funding for bio-terrorism testing and preparedness.
- Established the ABC laboratory as the first PHL in the UK to use SmartCycler® for the development and routine testing of emerging infections including BT organisms – enabling the laboratory to participate in validation studies with NHS and the National Laboratory in developing assays for BT organisms.
- Implemented and supervised internal proficiency testing – within NHS protocols – and personnel cross-training programmes at the PHL.
- Initiated PHL's participation in PulseNet (National Molecular Sub-Typing Network for Food-Borne Disease Surveillance), a network of laboratories adhering to standardized microbial surveillance procedures using Pulsed Field Gel Electrophoresis (PFGE) in performing gene sub-typing – a membership of particular importance to being equipped to respond to potential bio-terrorism threats/incidents.
- Adopted Anthrax testing procedures, facilitating PHL's selection as a testing beta site by the National Laboratory.
- Led participation in strategy for immunizing public health workers and first responders against Smallpox – including ensuring the capacity for testing for the vaccine strain of Smallpox and other related viruses.

DNA Fingerprinting & Gene Banking

- Establishing UK's first microbial DNA bank with 1,000+ DNA and RNA samples from various pathogens – food-borne pathogens, West Nile virus, Hepatitis C virus, Noro virus isolates – each containing nucleic acids in one or more formats: highly purified genomic DNA or RNA, immobilized (aerosol-resistant) purified DNA, agarose DNA plugs (ready for PFGE analysis) and viable organism (whenever possible).
- Developed and presented several one- to two-week long workshops on methods and applications of DNA fingerprinting techniques at the University of Puerto Rico during the years 1997 through 2003.
- Developed a DNA fingerprinting method to distinguish between closely related isolates of Legionella pneumophila, the causative pathogen for Legionnaire's Disease – providing the only way to track the transmission of this pathogen from patients to hospital rooms/hospital rooms to patients. A six-figure liability suit against the University of London Medical Centre (University Hospital) was thwarted as a result of the availability of this technique.
- Co-authored an abstract on tDNA-PCR amplifiction of species-specific polymorphic bands in plasmodium faciparum, plasmodium berghei and plasmodium yoelii at the University of Puerto Rico in San Juan, 2001.
- Authored 'Typing of Legionella pneumophila isolates by degenerate (D)-RAPD fingerprinting,' published in Molecular and Cellular Probes, 1995.
- Co-authored and presented 'Microsatellite Analysis (MSA) Using the Polymerase Chain Reaction (PCR) of Paraffin Embedded Material for Distinction of Tissues From Different Individuals', at the United States and Canadian Academy of Pathology (USCAP) Speciality Conference in Toronto, Canada in March 1995.
- Authored 'DNA Fingerprinting of Crude Bacterial Lysates using Degenerate RAPD Primers (D-RAPD)', published in PCR Methods and Applications, 1995.

- Authored and presented 'Genetic identificational technologies: PCR and DNA fingerprinting' at 2nd UN-sponsored Conference on the Perspectives of Biotechnology in Arab Countries, held in Amman, Jordan in March 1993.

Other Biomedical Research

- Authored, 'Prediction of biologic aggressiveness in colorectal cancer by p53/K-ras-2 topographic genotyping', published in Molecular Diagnosis, 1996.
- Authored, 'Distribution and evolution of CTG repeats at the myotonin protein kinase gene in human populations', published in Genome Research, 1996.
- Authored, 'Loss of heterozygosity in spontaneous and chemically induced tumours of the B6C3F1 mouse', published in Carcinogenesis, 1994.
- Authored, 'Identification of allelic loss in liver tumours from the B6C3HF1 mouse', published in Cell Biology Supplement, 1992.
- Authored, 'Antibody levels and in vitro lymphoproliferative responses to streptococcus pyogenes erythrogenic toxin A mitogen of patients with rheumatic fever', published in Clinical Microbiology, 1991.
- Authored, 'Isolation and characterization of developmentally regulated sea urchin U2 snRNA genes', published in Developmental Biology, 1991.
- Authored, 'The U1 snRNA gene repeat from the sea urchin (Strongylocentrotus purpuratus): The 70 kilobase tandem repeat ends directly 3 to the U1 gene', published in Nuclear Acids Research, 1991.
- Authored, 'A developmental switch in the sea urchin U1 RNA', published in Developmental Biology, 1989, and presented at the American Society for Biochemistry and Molecular Biology meeting held in San Francisco in January 1989.
- Authored, 'Isolation and characterization of tandem repeated U6 genes from the sea urchin Strongylocentrotus purpuratus', published in Biochemistry Biophysics, 1994, and presented at the Developmental Biology of the Sea Urchin meeting in Woods Hole, MA (August 1988) and at the Annual Meeting of Florida Biochemists in Miami in February 1988.
- Authored, 'Modified nucleosides and the chromatographic and aminoacylation behaviour of tRNA[ile] from Escherichia coli C6', published in Biochemistry Biophysics Acta, 1988.

Special reports

Once in a very long while a new idea comes along in the world of job hunting. The Special Report is one of those ideas. It presents you as an expert in your field without overtly saying you are job-hunting, and as such gets the reader to create an initial impression of you that is very different from that of a typical job seeker. A special report is not for everyone, but if you really know your business and you like to write, this can be a very helpful tool to add to your job-hunting arsenal.

A Special Report has the appearance of a newspaper, newsletter or trade magazine article that focuses on a commonly recognized challenge in your profession; but rather than mass publication it is created by you to send directly to end users. You create it by using your professional knowledge and packaging it in a written document. Just about anyone in your field who receives one will read a well-written and properly edited special report, and at the end they'll get to read the CV of the person who created it. While a CV gets very little initial time investment, your report can have the reader building a respectful relationship with you even before they know you are available and looking. Special reports have titles like:

Computer Conversion: Plan it, Move on it, and Roll It out!

Three simple things you can do that double the effectiveness of your school resource centre

Research reveals little used sales technique that dramatically improves product sales in financial investment market

Ten simple actions any company can take to head off trouble at the pass

Seven Secrets of the Successful Waiter

Special reports all aim to help the reader solve problems, make money, save money, or save time. Think of them as departmental reports, position papers, or articles (whichever works best for you), where the goal is to give the reader some useful information they can actually use. This is why a special report is not for everyone. You have to know your stuff and enjoy the writing process, but as I always say, anyone can write so long as they don't have a so-called life! If this is you (at least the part about having an affinity for writing) read on, you will not only learn a new job hunting technique you'll be contributing to your professional credibility and visibility in ways that reach well beyond this job hunt.

In the space available here, I can't show you how to write short, job-hunting-oriented, non-fiction articles – a.k.a. Special Reports. Instead, I'll explain the basic structure and packaging and then refer you to a couple of additional resources.

What goes into a special report?

- a benefit-oriented title;
- an introduction;
- the body copy usually in the form of 'tips' or 'mistakes to avoid';
- author info (usually, your CV);
- a binding.

The key to this Trojan horse approach is to include your CV with contact information in the author information section. If your CV isn't right for the job, you can use a biography that highlights information you feel is more relevant to the reader; in this instance you'll be able to cut and paste one of your broadcast letters without the salutation.

The proper length is up to you, and opinions differ. Some will tell you that special reports can be as long as you like, and I have seen some that run to 6,000 words (about ten pages). Personally, I think you should keep your report to between 600 and 1,000 words – in other words about the length of a regular newspaper column (or the length of this section on what goes into special reports, which runs to about 1,000 words). I say this for two reasons:

- Writing takes time away from the main thrust of your job-hunting activities, and you cannot allow this great secondary approach to affect your focus.
- You don't want to share everything you know about a particular subject on paper; you want to be able to continue the conversation in person with yet more information to share.

There is another benefit to this approach. Job offers usually go to the person who turns a one-sided examination of skills into a two-way conversation between professional colleagues. The nature of the special report goes a long way toward defining you as someone quite different to almost every other candidate.

If you look at the examples below and think that this might be a useful approach for your needs, but you feel you need more help, go to *www.salarynegotiations.com*, the website of long-time career consultant Jack Chapman, who developed the whole Special Report idea.

If you do try this as an additional approach for your job hunt, you will be able to re-use the fruits of your efforts. You can submit your article for publication to professional newsletters and magazines, and you can turn it into a presentation. In fact, your notes for the special report simultaneously form the outline of a business presentation. So even outside of the context of your job hunt, this approach of putting your professional expertise into a different delivery medium can have a significant impact on your professional visibility and credibility.

Now look at these samples.

Special report example 1: Waitress

Background:
With NO experience directly as a waitress, Christine, an undergraduate, got hired. She had been a hostess at ABC Restaurant near the University of London. She had observed waiters and waitresses, and she had definite ideas about what differentiated the satisfactory from the excellent. She wanted to 'jump over' the menial waitress positions and get hired by an upmarket, four-star restaurant (read: big tips!). This way, she positioned herself as an exceptional waitress who had the boss's viewpoint of the job.

Title: Christine's Four Keys to an Excellent Waitress
Excerpt from introduction:

> Excellent waiter, waitress? It's not all that complicated to be just satisfactory. Practically anyone can write down an order and bring food to the table. Surprisingly, it's not all that hard to be outstanding – but not everyone does it. I've put down my thoughts, here, on the 4 keys to excellence on the job as I see it. It will help you get an idea of my philosophy.

Excerpt from rules section:

> Key 3 There's always a way to get people what they want.
> When you know that customers want more than just food, that they want a pleasant time as well, possibilities arise. As hostess at ABC, waiters would often complain to me about customers ordering things not on the menu, or prepared a certain way. When, out of curiosity, I checked it out with the cooks, they almost always said, 'No problem.' So it was the waiter creating a problem for a customer – that problem didn't exist! I find that if you put your mind to it, there's always a way to keep the customer satisfied.

Outline of the rest of the report:

Key 1): Remember that your job is not 'things to do' but people to take care of.
Key 2) The friendlier you are, the friendlier the customers will be.
Key 3) There's always a way to get people what they want.
Key 4) It's a job for you, but it's a business for your boss.

Summary

RESULT: Christine leapfrogged into a fine-dining (and fine-tipping) job.

Special report example 2: Salesman

Mike's success at sales came from meticulous attention to detail (read: boring!), but he turns that dull skill into a reason to be hired! His report shows how astoundingly elementary your report 'rules' can be and still make an indelible impression. (His first rule is, 'Answer the Phone.') He focused on software sales to financial investors, but this type of report could be applied to almost any type of sales. Mike also got the Hiring Decision Makers' attention in the cover letter by mentioning that theirs was one of the firms he called in his 'secret shopper' research.

Title: Research Reveals Little Used Sales Technique that Can Dramatically Improve Sales [to the Financial Investment Market.]
Excerpt from introduction:

> Recently I undertook a research project to determine how companies might improve their sales. I called several companies and said, 'I would like to buy your software.'
> It was astonishing to me that from over twenty companies, I reached someone knowledgeable about the product only 14% of the time. Equally surprising was that only 28% of the organizations had someone return my call. Almost 40% didn't bother to send me any information. And even when they did, only 4% followed up with a phone call.
> This confirmed my hunch. Just by applying a sales principle I've used for 18 years, namely follow-up consistency, any one of these firms could experience a dramatic increase in sales. Here is how consistent follow-up can be easily applied in five areas to increase sales. I'm embarrassed at how basic these actions are, but remember – only 14% of my calls reached a salesperson!

Excerpt from rules section:

> *Follow-up Consistency Rule 1: ANSWER THE PHONE.*
> Having a dedicated line that is answered by a knowledgeable, helpful, friendly, live human being is essential in sales. No voice mail allowed! Not every line needs to be answered this way (although that's nice if you can afford it), but each and every call from potential customers must receive this follow-up consistency.
>
> On one of my calls an operator informed me she could not take my name and address for information – that would have to be handled by a salesperson. She then informed me that she could not transfer me to a salesperson because they were all gone for the rest of the day. It was 11am!
>
> *QUESTION:* Have you called your own sales line recently? What happened next?

Outline of the rest of the report:

Rule 2) Return messages;
Rule 3) Send the materials;
Rule 4) Don't just call the prospect, get through;
Rule 5) Never discard the names of prospects.

Summary

RESULT: Mike got interviews with EVERY ONE of the 20 firms he had called as a 'secret shopper.' He got job offers from two of them.

Special report example 3: Financial investment services CFO

Background:
Scott was seeking a high six-figure CFO job in the investment field. Billion dollar scandals at Enron, MCI WorldCom, and Tyco had just occurred so his report caught people's attention. His simple techniques to prevent these catastrophes were powerfully linked up with the war-stories attached to each rule.

Title: How to Uncover Financial and Operational Trouble Before Your P&L Blows Up... Ten simple actions any CFO, BD, Bank, Prop Trading and/or Financial Manager or Director can take to head off trouble at the pass.

Excerpt from introduction:

When a company is in, or about to be in trouble, there are <u>always</u> flashing yellow warning lights. The good news is that <u>problems rarely travel alone</u>. Usually they create a pattern of circumstances that aren't individually recognized as problems, but when the puzzle pieces are assembled – wham! It's an open invitation to red ink. It may be up to you to recognize enough of those pieces in time to stop the entire puzzle from being completed.

For the past 20 years, as a trouble-shooter CFO at financial services firms, I've learned to read the signs. And what are some of those signs?

Excerpt from rules section:

Rule 2: Pay attention to your cheques after they're cashed and cleared.

How are they endorsed?

Your employees? The ones who can't trade because you won't let them, why is one or more of their cheques endorsed over to a third party or brokerage firm – hidden trading account in their own name?

Your customer? Why are multiple cheques for identical amounts drawn on a single customer's account and endorsed over to multiple third parties? Unregistered pool? What if one of those third parties is your employee in a position to allocate trades or initiate commission rate or brokerage rate changes in your computer system?

Your vendor? Why are checks always endorsed to the name of a company you don't recognize? Is it an innocent d/b/a or are you dealing with a middleman who is marking up goods or services you could get for less by going direct?

Outline of the rest of the report [four samples of the ten rules]:

Rule 1) Periodically, sort your name and address file. Look for dual-identity payments.

Rule 3) Review a month of original trade tickets, blotters, out-trade sheets... Slowly. It's worth it.

Rule 6) Use simple line graphs to compare periods. It's easy to be caught up in the day-to-day.

Rule 9) Regularly review IB/RR/AP/Broker/Trader Payouts. Without exception, the most consistent source of hidden losses is linked in some way to Payouts.

RESULT: Scott's report opened doors to networking interviews with 'heavy hitters' in his field, which led to his new job.

Special report example 4: Shipping terminal manager

Background:
Keith worked for Yellow Freight. Besides getting all the lorries loaded, unloaded, and on the road on time, he also loved to catch cheaters – people taking sick days who weren't really sick. His title is very intriguing.

Title: A Simple Way to Put a Couple of Hundred Thousand Pounds Right to the Bottom Line: Watch People Who Aren't There, Make Sure Nothing Happens.
Excerpt from introduction:

> This report's title says how 'watching people who aren't there' and 'making sure nothing happens' can save you money. I have found that a few simple techniques to watch people who are out because of sickness, and a few principles of safety to make sure that nothing (bad) happens, will put £200,000 or more to the bottom line each year.

Excerpt from rules section:

> *Rule 1: Call at Odd Times*
>   I'll put in calls every once in a while ostensibly to get some information. 'Where is that bill of lading?' 'Truck 3 seems to be acting up, how did it run for you?' At 2:30 in the afternoon, or home at night. They soon learn they will be caught if they aren't there.
>   This cuts costs because besides clipping the wings of the ones who are playing hooky, having time off, sickness payments, it also alerts the 80% with real illness that if they ever want to fake it, they'll have a hard time.

Outline of the rest of the report [four samples of the rules]:

Rule 2) [Watch people...] Make them come in to the facility.
Rule 3) [Watch people...] Call the bluff of 'Regular Offenders.'
Rule 4) [Nothing happens...] Have safety meetings led by peers, not supervisors.

Rule 7) [Nothing happens...] Reward safety in teams to create peer pressure for safety.

RESULT: The report was the focus of several telephone networking conversations, which led to interviews and a great job.

Further reading from Kogan Page

Other titles in the *Ultimate* series

Ultimate Aptitude Tests, Jim Barrett, 2008
Ultimate Cover Letters, 2nd edn, Martin Yate, 2008
Ultimate Interview, 2nd edn, Lynn Williams, 2008
Ultimate IQ Tests, Phillp Carter and Ken Russell, 2008
Ultimate Job Search, 2nd edn, Lynn Williams, 2008
Ultimate Psychometric Tests, Mike Bryon, 2008

Interview and career guidance

A–Z of Careers and Jobs, 15th edn, Susan Hodgson, 2008
Changing Your Career, Sally Longson, 2003
Choosing Your Career, 2nd edn, Sally Longson, 2004
Graduate Job-Hunting Guide, Mark Parkinson, 2001
Great Answers to Tough Interview Questions, 7th edn, Martin John Yate, 2008
Odd Jobs, 2nd edn, Simon Kent, 2002
Online Job-Hunting: Great Answers to Tough Interview Questions, Martin John Yate and Terra Dourlain, 2002
Preparing the Perfect CV, 4th edn, Rebecca Corfield, 2004
Preparing the Perfect Job Application, 4th edn, Rebecca Corfield, 2007
Readymade CVs, 3rd edn, Lynn Williams, 2004
Readymade Job Search Letters, 3rd edn, Lynn Williams, 2004
Successful Interview Skills, 4th edn, Rebecca Corfield, 2006
Your Job Search Made Easy, 3rd edn, Mark Parkinson, 2002

Titles in the *Testing* series

Career, Aptitude and Selection Tests, rev edn, Jim Barrett, 2006
How to Master Personality Questionnaires, 2nd edn, Mark Parkinson, 2000
How to Master Psychometric Tests, 4th edn, Mark Parkinson, 2008
How to Pass Advanced Aptitude Tests, rev edn, Jim Barrett, 2008
How to Pass Advanced Numeracy Tests, rev edn, Mike Bryon, 2008
How to Pass Advanced Verbal Reasoning Tests, Mike Bryon, 2008
How to Pass the Civil Service Qualifying Tests, 3rd edn, Mike Bryon, 2007
How to Pass Graduate Psychometric Tests, 3rd edn, Mike Bryon, 2007
How to Pass the New Police Selection System, rev 2nd edn, Harry Tolley, Billy Hodge and Catherine Tolley, 2007
How to Pass Numeracy Tests, 3rd edn, Harry Tolley and Ken Thomas, 2006
How to Pass Numerical Reasoning Tests, rev edn, Heidi Smith, 2006
How to Pass Professional Level Psychometric Tests, 2nd edn, Sam Al-Jajjoka, 2004
How to Pass Selection Tests, 3rd edn, Mike Bryon and Sanjay Modha, 2005
How to Pass Technical Selection Tests, 2nd edn, Mike Bryon and Sanjay Modha, 2005
How to Pass the UK's National Firefighter Selection Process, 2nd edn, Mike Bryon, 2008
How to Pass Verbal Reasoning Tests, 3rd edn, Harry Tolley and Ken Thomas, 2006
How to Succeed at an Assessment Centre, 2nd edn, Harry Tolley and Bob Wood, 2005
IQ and Psychometric Tests, 2nd edn, Philip Carter, 2007
Succeed at IQ Tests, Ken Russell and Philip Carter, 2008
Test And Assess Your IQ, Ken Russell and Philip Carter, 2008
Test Your Own Aptitude, 3rd edn, Jim Barrett and Geoff Williams, 2003
The Advanced Numeracy Test Workbook, Mike Bryon, 2003
The Aptitude Test Workbook, rev edn, Jim Barrett, 2008
The Times Book of IQ Tests – Book Five, Ken Russell and Philip Carter, 2005
The Times Book of IQ Tests – Book Four, Ken Russell and Philip Carter, 2004
The Times Book of IQ Tests – Book Three, Ken Russell and Philip Carter, 2003
The Times Book of IQ Tests – Book Two, Ken Russell and Philip Carter, 2002
The Times Book of IQ Tests – Book One, Ken Russell and Philip Carter, 2001

Also available on CD ROM in association with The Times

Published by Kogan Page Interactive, The Times Testing Series is an exciting new range of interactive CD ROMs that will provide invaluable practice tests for both job applicants and for those seeking a brainstretching challenge.

Each CD ROM features:

- over 1000 unique interactive questions;
- instant scoring with feedback and analysis;
- hours of practice with randomly generated tests;
- questions devised by top UK MENSA puzzles editors and test experts;
- against-the-clock, real test conditions.

Current titles available:

Psychometric Tests, 2002
Test Your IQ, 2002
Test Your Aptitude Volume 1, 2002

Please visit the website at the address below for more details.

The above titles are available from all good bookshops. For further information, please contact the publisher at the following address:

Kogan Page Limited
120 Pentonville Road
London N1 9JN
Tel: 020 7278 0433
Fax: 020 7837 6348
www.koganpage.com

Index